WHAT PEOPLE ARE SAYING ABOUT THIS BOOK

Retire to an RV: The Roadmap to Affordable Retirement is by far the most comprehensive guide to full-time RVing I have ever seen. It is easy to read. In addition to getting the authors' knowledgeable information on all these topics, the opinions and comments from numerous other full-time RVers covers all of the bases. For anybody planning, or just considering full-time RVing this is a must, must read. Great book!

Mark Polk - *(RVEducation101.com)*

In an easy to read and understandable format, *Retire to an RV: The Roadmap to Affordable Retirement*, is an excellent introduction to the RV lifestyle that I wish had been available when we started our own full-timing RV adventure 11 years ago! Jaimie Hall Bruzenak and Alice Zyetz have put together a wealth of excellent information that will help you decide if making the transition to the RV lifestyle is right for you, and then how to make it happen.

Nick Russell - (*GypsyJournal.net)*

Absolutely chock-full of excellent information and advice provided, with authority, by the authors and backed up with real-life experiences and stories from 41 other full-timers. Whether you're trying to decide if you can go full time or just looking for advice to save money in your travels, you're sure to benefit from this book. I highly recommend it!

Marianne Edwards - *(Frugal-RV-Travel.com)*

Retire to an RV: The Roadmap to Affordable Retirement by Jaimie Hall Bruzenak and Alice Zyetz is a must read for anyone who is considering the full-time RV lifestyle.

Alan Weiner - *(Everything-About-RVing.com)*

Jaimie and Alice provide a wealth of knowledge that will guide anyone who is considering the RV lifestyle. They provide information and education that will go far in saving you money and time as you consider, enter and live the lifestyle. Don't dream any longer about this lifestyle. Read this resource. It will provide you the foundational knowledge you need.

Steve Anderson - Workamper Agency Services & *(Workamper.com)*

Those amazing, knowledgeable, and prolific wonder women, Jaimie and Alice, have written an invaluable guide to retiring on the road. This one is first-class. Not only do they provide worksheets, lists, advice on money questions, tips on working on the road, insurance matters, and a multitude of valuable information but also with their expert advice, they offer personal stories. They utilize the many contributions from fellow RVers, who freely share their experiences. You will find yourself referring to and quoting from these stories from RVers actually living this life successfully. This is a definitive and comprehensive guide to retirement on the road from the experts: those of us who are doing it.

Marcella Gauthier - Excerpt, *Escapees* magazine review.

In *Retire to an RV*, authors Jaimie Hall Bruzenak and Alice Zyetz have produced an easy-to-understand, comprehensive guide on how to achieve an affordable retirement in turbulent economic times and still live a full, rich life. This book is packed with real-life experiences of 41 seasoned RVers, and loaded with practical information, helpful tools and hundreds of resources.

Julianne Crane - RV lifestyle writer (R*VWheelLife.com)*

The authors, with input from dozens of other veteran full-time RVers, cover everything a would-be full-timer needs to know about living year round in an RV. Reading this book is like sitting in a room full of full-timing experts as they share their advice and best kept secrets. Even RVers who only travel seasonally will learn a lot from reading this.

Chuck Woodbury - *(RVTravel.com)*

Retire to an RV

The Roadmap to Affordable Retirement

By Jaimie Hall Bruzenak

and Alice Zyetz

Pine Country Publishing

Retire to an RV:

The Roadmap to Affordable Retirement

by Jaimie Hall Bruzenak and Alice Zyetz

First printing, July, 2012

Grateful acknowledgment is made for the use of the following material:

- Excerpts from *RV Traveling Tales: Women's Journeys on the Open Road*, with permission from the publisher.
- Clipart by Denny Cox *(Clipart.com)*

Cover Design by Robert Aulicino
Cover Photograph by Betty Prange ©2012

Library of Congress Cataloging-in-Publication Data

Bruzenak, Jaimie Hall

Zyetz, Alice.

Retire to an RV: The Roadmap to Affordable Retirement

by Jaimie Hall Bruzenak and Alice Zyetz.

ISBN 978-0-9716777-5-3

1. Recreational vehicle living--United States.
2. Retirement--United States.

For all our contributors—and for those adventurous enough to follow their dreams—wherever they may lead.

and

To Alice Zyetz, who passed away before seeing this book in print.

Warning - Disclaimer

This book is designed to provide information on traveling in your RV full- or part-time. It is sold with the understanding that the publisher and author and contributors are not engaged in rendering legal, financial, mechanical, or other professional services. If legal or expert assistance is needed, the services of a competent professional should be sought.

It is not the purpose of this book to reprint all the information that is otherwise available, but to complement, amplify and supplement other books and resources. You are urged to read all the available material, print and Internet, and learn as much as possible about RVing and to tailor the information to your individual needs. For more resources, see Resources at the end of this book.

Every effort has been made to make this book as complete and accurate as possible. However, there *may be mistakes,* both typographical and in content. Therefore, this book should be used only as a general guide and not the ultimate source for making a major lifestyle change. Furthermore, this book only contains information up to the printing date.

The purpose of this book is to educate and entertain. The author and Pine Country Publishing shall have neither liability nor responsibility to any person or entity with respect to loss or damage caused, or alleged to be caused, directly or indirectly by the information contained in this book.

If you do not wish to be bound by the above, you may return this book to the publisher for a full refund.

Table of Contents

Introduction

Join us (Jaimie Hall Bruzenak, Alice Zyetz and 41 other RVers) as we take you on a journey down the road in an RV towards an affordable way to retire and live a rich life at the same time. Jaimie and Alice are RV lifestyle experts, each starting out more than 16 years ago. When we began, fuel prices were lower and savings were more secure, but we still didn't have a lot of money, yet we fell in love with the lifestyle.

Today, cost is even more of a concern. So many people are finding their retirement funds are worth less, plus fuel expenses keep rising. In this book, you will learn about all of the aspects of the lifestyle, but especially, how you can make it happen in these trying times.

Cost is a key factor for many when considering the RV lifestyle. Not only is there an investment in the RV itself to figure, but also what will it cost on a day-to-day basis? We devote a chapter to answering this question. Chapter 15: "What if I can't afford it?" and Chapter 16: "How do I Volunteer?" address working and volunteering on the road if you need to add to your income or significantly reduce your expenses. Other chapters discuss additional areas where RVers can be flexible in their spending. In the Resources section at the end of the book, you will find a summary of more than 50 money-saving tips.

In almost every chapter, we have the experiences of 41 RVers in their own words, to give you a realistic view of life on the road and choices they made. We also went back and asked our contributors specifically if they found the RV lifestyle to be less expensive than living in a regular house or apartment. While there are no clear-cut answers, many pointed out how it is easier to economize by boondocking, volunteering, staying in less expensive parks, etc., according to the choices you make. Here are their comments.

Flexibility

Joan Pomeroy notes the budget can be more flexible when RVing and that costs vary from state to state.

> "After discussing this with Jerry, my husband, we decided that full-time RVing was about the same price as living in a house. The big difference is we had a choice whether to stay at Resort Walmart and save money, for a one-night stay, or go to an RV Park. In other words, our budget could fluctuate more than after we bought our house.
>
> "Many people we have talked to spend their nights on the road, traveling between two destinations in any free RV parking space they can find. This of course was a lot less expensive on the budget, but we felt it would be more expensive on our health.
>
> "We also found that the price of food varies from state to state and area to area, and some groceries are not available in every state. This had a direct effect on our budget. In Kroger's, for example, grapes in one state were cllose to $3.00 a pound, but when we crossed the state line the same day we found the same grapes at Kroger's for less than $2.00 a pound."

Frugal

Bill Chatham has found the RV lifestyle to be frugal.

> "I live a frugal existence on my Social Security ($1,300 month). This is only possible because I don't move around much, usually from one National Wildlife Refuge to another every two or three months, which saves me campground rent and fuel. You can't live my lifestyle without an all consuming hobby, pastime or avocation. Mine is writing. It doesn't cost

much to bang away at a laptop. I don't have any female distractions, taxing my wallet or mind.

"I haven't seen much published on the volunteering aspect of full-timing and have been toying with that idea. I'll write something about my experiences and the little-known benefits of volunteering in the near future."

Lower cost way of life

Larry Brauer says:

"We can't really compare the cost of retirement in an RV as a money-saving alternative to other forms of retirement. We have been full-time RVers since we retired. However, our opinion is that it is certainly a relatively low cost way of life. Even the high fuel prices simply mean that we sit in one spot for a longer period of time."

Initial costs are more

George Stoltz has found they have spent more than planned during their first few months on the road.

"We are a little over budget, but only because we have made some optional but not necessary comfort improvements to our RV. This is often the case with people like us who are new to the RV lifestyle. So far we have been on the road for four months. Within the next few months we will be back under budget and again begin to save money. We do live on a fixed income."

Save even more when Workamping

Karin Callander says they spend less than $1000 a month and even less than that when Workamping.

"Well, SOME months, it's more—like when we buy a new computer or tires. Luckily, we don't have to do that often. It helps that I'm a decent cook and hubby will eat just about anything. But, some of our favorite meals can be had in 20 minutes and for less than $5. We eat lots of pasta & salad!"

Adrienne Kristine agrees:

"Oh, absolutely it is a cheaper way to live, especially if you're Workamping or volunteering for your site. Your groceries, activities and hobbies are much more economical too. "

Sharon Van der Zyl and her husband also find they can live frugally by combining the RV lifestyle with Workamping.

"Taxes are much less and so are 'utilities,' especially when you volunteer some time in exchange for a FHU (full hookup) pad. Since we volunteer at National Wildlife Refuges, our pad, full-hookup RV site and propane are covered by the Refuge in return for helping three days per week. That cuts our expenses down a lot."

Costs down from career days

Betty Prange explains how her costs are less than her career days and probably less than she would have living in a house or apartment in retirement.

"I know costs went down significantly from the days I had a career. No commuting, no pantyhose, nor the continual cycle of work parties for birthdays, new babies, go away, retirement etc. Clothing, hair care, etc., also dropped ten-fold or more.

"It is harder for me to compare to what costs would have been had I had retirement time in a stick house. I am sure it would be less. Since I have solar (now 16 years old so paid in savings a long, long time ago), and I boondock a lot, just energy costs are a fraction. We had a small house but a huge garden. Our shopping at the local nursery was a major item. I have far less 'stuff' now which is also a savings, in terms of electrical use, in buying and replacing. Thrift stores are great for the casual clothes I wear. Last week, I bought three 'new'

> pairs of pants. And I only bought those because I am going to Yellowstone for eight days in March and needed wool pants and ski pants for warmth. The three pairs cost me all of $5.00. My biggest expense is medical insurance. It just went up again—$466 per month. But that cost would be the same in a stick house or as a full-time RVer."

Long-time full-time RVer **Bernie Fuller** agrees, though they are off the road now.

> "Looking back at expenses, I would estimate that we spent somewhere in the $2000 to $2500 range (more or less). At the time, this was a bargain compared to the home expenses we dealt with anchored in one house, etc. I can't say for sure if it is a money-saving alternative to our retirement lifestyle NOW."

Costs less, especially taxes

Patty Lonsbary has these comments about costs:

> "As to the cost of RVing, Ed and I spend about $2,000 a month on our lifestyle. I never really thought of myself as retired—just a full-time RVer. We started our RV lifestyle when I was 52 and now I am 54, back to work. We have found that living in the coach was definitely less expensive than a house. The biggest noted savings were in taxes—I loved writing my last check for property taxes back in 2007."

Annise too cites lack of taxes:

> "I do think RVing is a more economical way to live. I'd cite the lack of taxes tied to home ownership: city tax, county tax, school tax. Also there are no association fees (for condos), water bills, trash pickup bills. The caveat however is that the RV depreciates in value over years while real estate typically has appreciated."

No more consumerism

Barbara Bowers, while not retired, finds they do save:

> While we are not retired, we do find that living full-time in an RV is more cost-efficient for us. We are able to control our housing and utility costs through choices in location. Because the RV does not allow for extra 'stuff,' we also save money because we do not participate as much in consumerism as many people who live in a 'traditional' sticks-and-bricks home.

Not full-time RVers

A few of our authors are not full-time RVers. **Carol Weishampel** keeps her expenses down when traveling in her RV.

> "With my daughter and grandsons living in my home and paying the bills, I live cheaper when traveling by motorhome. I volunteer for months at a time, hookups etc. go with the 'job' so my cost is gas and upkeep. I cook for youth camps, so food is included. Clothing cost? Who needs all those shoes and dress clothes, anyway?
>
> "The benefits of seeing America and meeting new people, writing and stretching myself, far outweigh any financial costs."

Lynne Benjamin and her husband say they are most-of-the-timers. They still have a condo, however.

> "There is such a difference between full-timing and most-of-the-timing that it is difficult to determine our actual costs, and we don't really bother keeping track. We do consider it to be the best way for us to spend our retirement dollars. So as long as we can afford it and can actually travel, it will be our chosen lifestyle."

JJ Dippell still has a house. A financial type, she shares these thoughts about costs:

> "Costs merely get 'exchanged' for other costs. If you already owned the RV before retiring to it, then your insurance will double. Full-timers insurance is double, maybe two and one-half times 'part-timers' insurance.
>
> "On the other hand, if you didn't own the RV and bought it to use instead of a house, then it can be cheaper, but only if you owned a house and sold it. Utilities would be cheaper. On the other hand, if you lived in an apartment, the monthly cost of an RV slot is cheaper than an apartment. However, if you don't use the monthly rates then 30 nights at different RV parks can be as much as apartment rent! Utilities would be about the same.
>
> "For Internet, the cost of an Air Card (if you go that route) is more expensive than having DSL at home. WiFi is pretty easy to get without carrying a satellite (or an air card), but you take your chances.
>
> "For television, I don't know about cable costs, as I tend to take a 'just the basics' on cable at home, but I'm thinking if you get a satellite TV dish, it would be more expensive than cable at home. I rely on parks to have cable already. If not, I take what I can get over the air or I do without.
>
> "You may ditch the landline when you retire to an RV, but your cell phone costs will go up, as you will need to change to a plan that has more minutes. Although I chose a less expensive route. I carried a regular telephone with me (in addition to my cell), and a cheap Costco phone card (the Verizon ones that are 3 cents a minute and no funky fees), and sometimes I would sneak into the exercise room at the

> RV park, plug my phone in (if there was a live phone hookup), and use my phone card.
>
> "Also, you have to figure in the gas costs. If you travel a lot, your fuel costs will go up. If you park it for a month or two, you are okay.
>
> "Bottom line? Maybe it is cheaper, maybe it isn't. Depends on whether you can live with 'just the basics' or you must have satellite TV and Air Cards."

All about choices

Jill and Jose Ferrer sum it up the best:

> "As far as your question about this being an economical way to retire—we vote a qualified yes—it can be. It all boils down to the choices one makes. The flexibility to move to or stay in a given location where you can afford the living expenses is a plus. The fact that you can take advantage of the many Workamping opportunities is a big plus. The lifestyle lends itself to avoiding the unnecessary accumulation of stuff and 'keeping up with the Joneses.' The travel, diverse destinations, campground activities, etc. make for interesting and active days—often at little cost. It can be a frugal lifestyle—but it really depends on the choices an individual or couple makes. If one chooses the more expensive parks, and buys a new RV every two years and eats out a lot, plays golf often, etc., well, that may not be so frugal a lifestyle. So, a qualified yes."

It does boil down to the choices you make. You can spend a lot or a little. People make it work on limited income; they have decided the benefits of RVing are worth living frugally. It's also possible they may be better off financially than had they stayed in a house or apartment. Certainly they are living a more interesting life.

With that in mind, let's answer some of the other questions that come up about the RV lifestyle. If you decide the RV lifestyle is for you, these chapters will help you plan how to move forward and decide if you want to live the RV lifestyle on a full-time basis or a part-time basis. You'll have some ideas of how to deal with the inevitable challenges that come up.

> Whether you have some experience, are new to RVing, or are looking for new ideas for living in an RV or making a little extra money to enhance your retirement in an RV, the chapters ahead will position you to make informed decisions. You'll find more information on retiring in an RV and a whole world of possibilities.

NOTES

Section I. RV LIFESTYLE

Chapter 1

Is the RV lifestyle for me?

The RV lifestyle encompasses many ways of living this life. There is no one "right" way. If you are living in an RV (recreational vehicle) even part of the time, you are living the RV lifestyle.

RETIREMENT LIFE IN AN RV COMES IN MANY FORMS

- Some people sell their house and live in their RVs full-time 365 days a year.
- Others sell their house and live in their RV in a campground in the north during the summer months and in a campground in the south during the winter.
- Some retain their houses (particularly if they're paid for) and travel part-time.
- Some people downsize and live the RV lifestyle most of the year.
- Some people pride themselves on NEVER staying in commercial campgrounds but boondock (with no water, sewer, or power hookups) on national forest lands or Bureau of Land Management (BLM) lands.
- Some people alternate boondocking and staying in commercial campgrounds.

The RV lifestyle encompasses many ways of living.

WHAT ATTRACTS PEOPLE TO THE LIFESTYLE?

- **Freedom:** Living on the road is the ultimate freedom from the stresses of jobs, household tasks, and unpleasant neighbors. If you don't like your job, you can travel somewhere else to get a new job. Household tasks are greatly reduced by living in a smaller house on wheels. If you don't like your neighbors, you don't have to wait until they move; you move instead. If you don't like the weather, leave.
- **Saving Money:** Most costs are reduced and some are eliminated altogether. Considering the high cost of real estate, the price of an RV is much less (unless you opt for the million-dollar bus). You need less electricity and gas so you have control of your energy costs. Your desire for extra clothing and "things" is limited by the space available.
- **Scenery:** One day you are drinking your morning coffee next to a beautiful lake. Another day you are surrounded by a pine forest, or sitting by the ocean, or admiring the Snoopy-type desert cactus in bloom.
- **Change in Lifestyle:** After all those years of seriously doing what you had to do to make a living and raise a family, now you can be a clown, work at Disneyland helping Mickey Mouse, build new homes for Habitat for Humanity, or just be lazy in scenic surroundings.

Living the RV lifestyle gives you a passport to the American Dream.

- **Living the American Dream:** The essential American experience, from the immigrants who landed on our shores to the pioneers who expanded our frontiers to the Pacific, has been to explore the unknown and travel the "open road." Living the RV lifestyle gives you a passport to the American Dream.

The choices are endless. The common denominator in RV travel is that all of these people (more than nine million households) travel to places other than their homes to see beautiful sights, learn more about their country, fish, hunt, or just relax in a beautiful environment.

What would propel you to get out of your comfortable space to live the RV lifestyle?

WHAT IS THE DEFINING MOMENT?

What propels people out of their comfortable space and sends them into an RV for life on the road? Here are the stories of eleven RVers who share their beginning experiences.

Patty Lonsbary traces her moment to Dolly, the character in a little 29-cent book her parents bought to teach her how to read:

> "Some people ask me, *'What is inspiring such a bold move to give up a Texas home, secure surroundings and hit the road in your RV?'* My desire to do this can be traced to a 29-cent book my parents taught me to read back in 1961. I read the book so often that I memorized *Dolly Goes Around the World* and recited it to Sister Joel's first grade class at St. Benedict's School in Johnstown, PA. I was only six years old, but even then I wanted to be like the blinky-eyed doll featured in the book traveling to the forests of Peru, on the pampas of Argentina, ashore in Hawaii and fishing in Alaska. Over the years, the book disappeared, either given to a cousin or tattered and tossed out. But the rhyming phases always reminded me that traveling means new experiences and fun. Last spring, I found an antique bookstore with a copy of this beloved

book. I ordered it online for the inflated cost of $32.99 plus shipping. This little literary treasure will go with Ed and me as we travel. We've already been to Alaska and Mexico. Thanks, Dolly. Here are her original rhymes:

Alaska

Dolly lives in igloos,
Wears a parka made of fur.
Going fishing through the ice
is lots of fun for her.

Mexico

Here Dolly is in Mexico
Dressed for a pleasant stay
Perhaps she'll buy a big straw hat
To keep the sun away."

In this situation, **Betty Prange's** boss was the catalyst.

"*'Betty, you ought to send the jerk a thank-you note.'*

"Several of us were sitting in the desert sharing stories of how we decided to hit the road. I had just finished mine. She was right. A couple years earlier I arrived home from work fuming. My fairly new boss was a jerk, and I knew I could no longer work in that environment. My husband Lin and I discussed the alternatives; I was still focused on my profession and debating between moving to another agency or altering the direction of my career.

> **"A few months later... we became full-time RVers."**

"Lin suggested another idea. A few months later we sold the house, purchased a motorhome, gave notice at work, established a mail-forwarding address, and held farewell parties. We became full-time RVers.

"I never sent the jerk (I used a stronger epithet) a thank-you note. He didn't last long in that job or the succeeding one. I wasn't sure where to send the letter."

For **Bernie Fuller and wife Ruth**, snow was the definite influence.

> "The snow was well over 100 inches for the season; we had paid the plow guy three times in the past couple of days to clear the driveway, and our Brittanies were feeling the stress of being cooped-up.
>
> "I turned to Ruth saying, *'I don't think that this is our idea of the perfect retirement!'*
>
> "We re-read Kay Peterson's book *Home is Where You Park It* (the original edition). A light came on that showed the way to a more carefree lifestyle. Shortly after we joined Kay's new organization, Escapees (we are Escapees members #32), we started shopping for a trailer and tow vehicle; put the house on the market; held a garage sale, and began planning for full-timing. Within a month, the house was sold for a fair price and we headed SOUTH for warmer climes.

Do you need a change?

> "Was it too quick a decision? Without a doubt it was the best decision we had made in years, if for no other reason than to be able to truly understand what retirement was all about. Sure, we could have stayed in place mowing a couple of acres of lawn, shoveling several feet of snow, and falling prey to the rat race of community life. But ... we took the freedom route instead."

The Fullers started in the late '70s. The Escapees membership number is now more than 100,000!

Kimberly and Jerry Petersen's decision was a matter of life or death to them.

> "Our decision came during a very sad time in our lives. My brother passed away at the very young age of 40. A little more than a year later, my mother passed away. They had both been in hospice before passing so we had time to share

thoughts with one another. Most of the conversations were of their regrets of not having the time and courage to follow their dreams. They made us promise to follow ours.

"During our soul searching we recalled a moment in our lives shortly after we married when we were sitting on our patio, sipping some wine and sharing our dreams with one another. Surprisingly, they were identical; we both wanted to travel around the United States in an RV, take photos, write our stories, attend all the NASCAR races and visit each state together as a team. But, as life would have it, our lives took us in an entirely different direction. Our daughter announced she was pregnant with our first grandchild and our business began to flourish, so we put our dream lifestyle on hold. The folder of gathered information went back into the drawer, and we began living the life we thought we wanted—until the deaths woke us up to our heart's desire once again. We began our planning in earnest."

Would you like the fun of RVing?

For **Sharon Whitaker** and her husband, it was simply a case of Fun.

"*'This is fun—we should do it all the time!'* That statement from my husband triggered one of the most important decisions of our lives.

"We had retired in 2000 and made several short trips in our 21-foot Spirit on a Toyota chassis. In 2002, we took our first long trip and had been traveling two months when Bill made his fateful statement. What he didn't know was that I had been thinking the same thing for several days. He was totally shocked when I agreed.

"That was 5 ½ years ago and we haven't looked back once. We still love the lifestyle and would do it again in a heartbeat."

Lynne and Fred Benjamin decided it was Time.

"A big grin came across Fred's face when I told him *'I'm not having fun, anymore. Maybe it's time.'* Time meant giving up my work; time meant doing something else. He'd been after me for years. For Fred, it meant going on the road. For me, it meant escaping a very disturbing and unhappy work situation. Three big clients cancelled or postponed projects—projects I was depending on to take us through the year. I'd always worked, and suddenly I was saying that I was ready to give up a thriving consulting practice that it had taken years to build.

"Now what?

"If it were up to Fred, we would jump in the fifth wheel and go! I was excited at the prospect of traveling but I wasn't sure I could just get up and go.

"*'I can't do that! We have the house and everything that's in it; we can't just take off. We haven't got enough money—how are we going to live?!'*

"*'Easy enough,'* he says. *'We'll just get rid of everything and sell the house. That should do it.'*

"*'You mean, no home—just the trailer? We can't do that!'*

"*'Why can't we do that?'* he retaliated.

Maybe it's Time.

"*'A million reasons! To start—we'll never fit everything into the trailer: I'm not willing to give up everything; I can tolerate camping for a couple of weeks, but camping for months is not my idea of fun; I'm not sure I'm ready to retire. I want to leave my options open; we need to have a residence in the Province to keep our health insurance, besides which, I need a place to come home to. I need to be grounded, and I'll get bored without a project to work on!'*

"Our relationship is and always has been based on what he thinks he wants, what she thinks she wants, and what we can both live with. In this case, the compromise became to upsize our fifth wheel, downsize our belongings and living space, purchase a small secure condo (primarily an expensive storage unit), and I agreed to take a major sabbatical for two years.

"This all happened six months before 9-11. By mid-October the adventure began. We were off to find a place where they didn't sell snow shovels. From that time to this, we have downsized to a Class C motorhome and traveled in three countries, eight provinces and more than 33 states. We have conducted workshops at the Okanogan RV Lifestyle Seminars in BC, seen sights and had adventures we never dreamed of, and each of us has found our new passions—Fred works with fellow RVers to iron out their computer challenges and I'm writing and loving it.

Ask yourself the simple question: a 10-day cruise or a lifetime on vacation?

"Was it time? You betcha!"

George and Sandy Stoltz answered a simple question: A 10-day cruise or a lifetime on vacation?

"*'Let's talk,'* she said.

"*'O.K,'* I replied.

"*'I don't think we should spend all that money on a cruise,'* Sandy said. *'I've been thinking about how nice it would be to retire in a motorhome, see the country, and not have our lives controlled by the calendar and the clock. Let's save that cruise money and use it toward a motorhome.'*

"We did and that is exactly how we began our 36-month journey to become full-timers."

Larry and Adrienne Brauer extended their love of camping into the full-time experience.

"When we married in 1993, we were pushing 50. Together we had three girls, three boys, and three dogs. We called ourselves the 'Brauer Bunch.' We both had experience with camping and six months after we were married, we bought a 26-foot, 1977 Winnebago Chieftain. It wasn't expensive but it would give us an idea about how we liked the lifestyle. As it turned out, we didn't like the lifestyle, we loved it. Although retirement was eight years away, we started developing plans for becoming full-time RVers.

"In 2001 we put the house on the market. We told our kids we would be selling everything and to come and get what they wanted. Fortunately, they did. Sure, there was plenty of 'stuff' left, but most of that was donated to various charities. A few keepsakes went into a rented storage shed.

What would you like about the RV lifestyle?

"People often ask how we like our lifestyle. Well, we love it. Sometimes people ask how long we plan on maintaining our lifestyle. Our answer is always, when we get tired of it and, after seven years, that hasn't happened yet.

Joan and Jerry Pomeroy thought they would travel for two years, but it's Year Seven and they're still counting.

"Early in our courtship days, Jerry and I agreed that when we retired, we would travel full-time and see the United States. We set our goal to go to Alaska first, and the lower 48 in the years after. It must have been a surprise to our family members that we did just as we had planned.

"In March 2002, we planned to RV for two years and then settle down and get a house. When the two years ended we thought we would travel one more year. We liked it so much that we are now coming close to our seventh year of RVing."

Bess McBride couldn't help it. After all, she was raised to be a gypsy.

"Perhaps I inherited the gene. I was born and raised overseas to American parents. We lived a life of comfort and returned to the United States every year for a month where we traveled throughout the country, spending time in the glamour and glitz of Miami, Las Vegas and Arizona in the 1960s.

"My midlife crisis came rolling around right on schedule, and I thought I was prepared. I'd seen my one and only child off to college five hours away, had a brand new college degree in hand with subsequent well-paying job in a city another five hours away … and I'd just bought my first house. What could be more perfect than that?

> **"We are now coming close to our seventh year of RVing."**

"A year into the new career, I had itchy feet. Six more months and the responsibilities of home ownership weighed heavily on my shoulders. Another six months passed and I could scarcely bear to drag myself in to work at 8 a.m. sharp one more day.

"I longed for the open road. I wanted to be one of those folks flying down the highways in my rig. I was 52; my mother had died at 56. The probable law of genetics convinced me there was no time to waste. The gypsy could no longer stay still.

> "I came home one day and told my significant other, *'I'm selling the house and buying an RV. You should come with me.'* (I really didn't want to go alone). Naturally, he refused. Some nonsense about how he would pay bills and such. Who cared? I had the luxury (and the comfort) of receiving a monthly stipend from the federal government for my 21 years of service in the military. I knew that if I sold the house and bought an RV with the proceeds, my military retirement could help cover space rent and insurance, if nothing else. *'Hah!'* I laughed. *'Who needs to work?'*
>
> "I sold the house out from under him and bought an RV. He quit his job and said, *'Why, yes! I can get a job working as a carpenter wherever we go.'* That was, of course, once I promised to work full-time during the summer to supplement our adventure.
>
> "Two years later and we travel biannually like geese, heading north for cool summers and south for warm winters. I don't know how I could live any other way. Why wait until the aches and pains are too severe to climb into the RV? Start young!"

Finally as **Jane Kenny** sums up the experience, the draw is both travel and freedom—the American Dream!

> "Retirement dreams! We look forward to that time of life when we won't have to report to work every day, when we can kick back, relax and enjoy 'the good life.' The good life means something different from person to person and from couple to couple. Things people dream of doing during retirement are as varied as the people themselves. But, for many of us, travel is high on the list of retirement dreams. We want to be adventurous, travel to places we've always wanted to see, return to places where we

The RV lifestyle experience is both travel and freedom—the American Dream!

vacationed in the past and visit friends and relatives in far off places. A recreational vehicle helped fulfill my dream of traveling in retirement. As a matter of fact, I've been to more places in this country than I ever thought possible. I've seen hundreds of sites that, in the past, I'd only read about! All this travel has been achievable and affordable because of the RV.

"When my husband first brought up the idea of selling our traditional 'stick-built' home and moving into a 'motorhome,' I was flabbergasted. This being the second marriage for each of us, our backgrounds were somewhat different. My idea of camping was a resort hotel, while he was more familiar with RVs, trailers, camping and traveling in a recreational vehicle. So, we researched options and discussed the RV retirement idea thoroughly before arriving at a decision.

"We're sure the bathroom is clean."

"Not knowing whether I would successfully adjust to living in a motorhome full-time, I agreed to try it for a year. It was so much fun, we stayed on the road full-time for the first nine years of our retirement, and we are still enjoying extended RV traveling.

"I have wanderlust, so it was easy for me to go RVing. I like the convenience of setting our own travel schedule, not having to pack/unpack and schlep suitcases in and out of hotels. Our clothes are with us all the time and we don't need to worry about forgetting a toothbrush or hair spray. We're sure the bathroom is clean. We have our favorite pillows with us.

"Traveling in a motorhome, we are able to see our children and grandchildren more frequently, sometimes for short stays, sometimes longer. When we go for a family visit we hook-up at a nearby campground, so we're their neighbors for a couple of days, weeks or a month or so. There's a difference between being a houseguest and being a neighbor. Our visits are not intrusive and they are so much more enjoyable.

"The RV lifestyle is perfect for retirees who love to travel and who want to be free to go where they want when they want."

RESOURCES

- **Visit our website for free information and a variety of resources for the new RVer:** ***(RVLifestyleExperts.com)***
- **Check out the Escapees RV Club for some of the best support in the RV community:** ***(Escapees.com)***
- **Visit the Resources section at the end of the book for a list of helpful RV books, websites and RV groups.**

NOTES

"Nothing at all will be attempted if all possible objections must first be overcome."
Samuel Johnson

Chapter 2

How do I make THE DECISION?

Generally prospective RVers read a number of books, go online for more information, and interview various people to hear about their experiences. Finally, they must make THE DECISION: To go or not to go.

Sharon Vander Zyl and her husband applied an engineering decision-making tool to their quandary. You may like to try it if you have any lingering doubts.

> "We struggled with our decision for a couple of years as our retirements approached. We had considered several retirement scenarios but the one that called to us most was full-time RVing.

THE DECISION: to go or not to go?

> "All of our marriage we had loved camping—first in a tent and then in small trailers. But would we like it full-time? As we tried to decide, we talked with several couples who were full-timers, including a former high school classmate of ours who told us about the Escapees RV Club. We joined immediately and read their monthly magazine from cover to cover. Early in 2006, we took a two-month trial trip south. We toured the Escapees' home park, learned more about it and talked to more full-timers. We were impressed, but still unsure.

"Something was holding us back. In my former life as a Life Coach, I worked with many people who were stuck in one decision-making process or another. So I asked myself, *'What assignment would I give to a client in a situation like this?'* It came to me immediately. I would have my client (in this case, me) do a Force Field Analysis.

Using a tool to weigh pros and cons may help you make THE DECISION.

Force Field Analysis

A Force Field Analysis is a decision-making tool that comes from the field of energy engineering. As its name implies, it is an analysis of all of the forces in play on a given field, both the propelling forces and the opposing forces.

Force Field theory holds that if the propelling forces are stronger than the opposing forces, forward movement occurs. Conversely, if they are not, forward movement is prevented.

A Force Field Analysis has five steps. Rollie, my husband, and I did all of the five steps separately and without conferring. This is the recommended way to do a Force Field when a joint decision is being made. The steps:

1. Divide a sheet of paper in half with a line drawn lengthwise.
2. On one side of the page, list all of the forces that are pushing toward a decision (in this case toward full-time RVing).
3. On the other side of the page, list all of the forces that are pushing against a decision (in this case against full-time RVing).

Coach's note: With steps 2 and 3 it is important to be completely honest and to take time, coming back to add to the lists over a period of hours or days. Steps 2 and 3 result in a traditional pro and con list. The next step (4) moves the lists into new territory.

4. Go back to the pro and con lists and with each item ask, *'On a scale of 1-10 (10 being highest) how much do I value this particular item?'* That is, *'How important is to me?'*
5. Add the numerical values of each item in the two columns and compare the totals.

"This lifestyle would fit our values at this time in our life."

Coach's note: For example, on the pro-side of my list was the item 'simplifies life.' The value I gave it was 8, near the top. On the con-side was the item 'decreased opportunity to entertain.' The value I gave that item was a 2, near the bottom. On my lists I had 27 pro items and 24 con items. At first glance I thought, *'No wonder I am stuck.'* But when I added the values the totals were 192 pro and 107 con.

"After separately completing our Force Field Analyses, my husband and I compared our findings. His analysis was similar to mine with a nearly equal number of items and when the values were assigned and added he had 84 pro and 49 con.

"We were no longer stuck! We could proceed with confidence that this lifestyle would fit our values at this time in our life. In March of 2006 we put our house on the market and began the process of divesting. By mid-July we moved into our 29.5-foot Hitchhiker fifth wheel and hit the road. Although we are relative 'newbies' at full-timing, we are so glad that we got 'unstuck' and took the leap. We love our new life."

COMMITMENT

Using the above tool will help you make the first decision. Now how big a commitment do you want to make? Do you want to be a full-timer with no home base? Do you want to travel part of the time and keep your stick house or condo? Are you planning to work but will live in the RV? There is no "right" way—only what is right for you and your partner if you travel with another person.

A test trip can help you make THE DECISION.

Many of us make a test trip before we commit to selling the house. In Alice's case, she and her husband wanted to see what it was like living in such a small space and whether they could afford the lifestyle on their retirement income. They decided in the affirmative after three months. Here is **Sharon and Bill Whitaker's** story.

> "During our test trip we discussed our options and decided to rent our home for at least one year, just in case we found we didn't really like it. We stopped in Joplin, Missouri, and traded for a 34-foot Winnebago Itasca with one slide. Wow. It was huge!
>
> "When we got back to San Diego in September, we began to get our home ready to rent. This took five months and a lot of elbow grease. In April, we sorted through our belongings, gave some to the kids and put the rest in storage. There were three huge wooden shipping containers of stuff!
>
> "Our tenants moved in May 1 and we took off. That summer we went to our first rally in Wichita Falls, Texas, where dealers had new RVs on display. Of course, we had to check them out. When we walked into a 39-foot 2003 Discovery with three slides we were smitten. By the end of the week, it was ours and we headed to Sioux Falls, South Dakota to change our legal residence."

George and Sandy Stolz used the Internet to learn about their new lifestyle.

"We knew nothing. We had been in half a dozen motorhomes a few years earlier when we visited an RV show in Rosemont, Illinois. We soon began to learn in earnest. The World Wide Web became our friend, our encyclopedia and our gateway to new friendships. In chronological order we discovered RV-Dreams, the Escapees website (I'm SKP 99899), Life on Wheels, Nick Russell who is the *Gypsy Journal* editor, and many more invaluable resources. We also began most conversations with: *'When we are on the road…'*

"Within two days of that evening conversation we visited a local dealer, drove a 36-foot diesel pusher (heart thumping and knuckles turning white) and began looking for an RV show within 300 miles. We had to wait until the winter show near O'Hare in 2007. It seemed as though our departure date of September of 2009 would never arrive. Now we barely have enough time to get everything done.

The RV community is a remarkable collection of like-minded people who are willing to lend a hand.

"We soon began to get rid of stuff we weren't using, didn't need or would not take with us. CraigsList *(CraigsList.org)* and eBay *(eBay.com)* became partners in our goal. All the money from these sales went into our RV savings accounts. We held one big garage sale with one more scheduled for this October and a final one next year.

"Now with less than a year to go, the most important thing we have learned is that the RV community is truly a remarkable collection of like-minded people who are willing to lend a hand either over the Internet or in the campground. When we jump on the bus we will have good company in George and Sandy's Great Adventure."

Arline Chandler's experience with her first RV was a bit daunting, but she persevered.

"When I looked at the 26-foot fifth wheel my first husband proposed to buy, an old country song, *I'm Going to Hire a Wino to Decorate Our Home,* played through my head. The trailer had been lodging at a duck hunting camp. A dozen folks had eaten meals fried on the tiny stove. Muddy boots had ground a layer of black delta dirt into the yellow plaid carpet. Stained red and green block-patterned upholstery covered two bench seats—the only furniture. Pale green satin drapes with shiny tassels covered the windows, downstairs, that is. Green paisley cotton with black fringe hung in the bedroom over the fifth wheel. A king-sized mattress with one corner turned up covered the floor.

A used unit may be an economical way to acquire your charming RV cottage.

"*'At $6,000, we can sell the trailer if we don't like it,'* James reasoned. We had never been in an RV; never even camped in a tent. Yet, we bought the unit.

"We stripped the old carpeting and upholstery—and hauled out the curling mattress. I scrubbed the dark wood cabinets and polished the stove and yellow plastic bathroom. We laid neutral carpeting and covered the cushions in beige tweed. I hung fresh white curtains. The dingy old trailer turned into a charming cottage.

"On our first outing to a fishing lake, the hot water heater malfunctioned, but did not discourage us. RVing totally hooked us on the second weekend. We loved sleeping in moonlight peeking through crisp white curtains. We liked having a house that could go to the woods, a lake, or a town. We decided to shop for a new fifth-wheel that we could make into our very own home. The dealer gave us exactly $6,000 on a trade. Twenty-six years, a second fifth-wheel and two motorhomes later, I would take up the lifestyle again in a heartbeat."

RESOURCES

- **Visit our website for free information and a variety of resources for the new RVer: *(RVLifestyleExperts.com)***
- **Check out the Escapees RV Club for some of the best support in the RV community: *(Escapees.com)***
- **Visit the Resources section at the end of the book for a list of helpful RV books, websites and RV groups.**

NOTES

"Nothing is particularly hard if you divide it into small jobs." Henry Ford

Chapter 3

How do I get started?

You have made the decision to go on the road. What do you do next?

DO SOMETHING WITH YOUR STUFF

GET RID OF IT! This may sound harsh and uncaring, but, in truth, how many can openers and vegetable peelers do you really, really need? And what about that waffle iron you've used three times since you received it as a wedding present thirty-five years ago? The same principle applies to your clothing and shoes. How many satin bridesmaid pumps will you ever wear again?

Here is an excerpt from **Terry King's** story about giving up her things, "Grandma's Lace Tablecloth," published in *RV Traveling Tales: Women's Journeys on the Open Road*, reprinted with permission. Terry and her husband had rented out their house during their first few years of travel. But when it came time to sell, she had to make the decision about her things.

How many satin bridesmaid pumps will you ever wear again?

> "I'm a sentimentalist at heart. I love nostalgia, mementos, and keepsakes from the past. I amassed quite a few closet and cupboard fillers, heirlooms to me that I just knew I could never part with, including my grandmother's lace tablecloth. As we began traveling more and more, it became clear our home was a bottleneck for us. It was time to sell. And then I

> really panicked. That was the scary thing, the 'getting rid of' part. What was important to me, really important? Before I made any decision about the things in my home, I took some time out and thought about the trips we had made in the past few years.
>
> "I remembered watching gorgeous sunsets reflecting soft pastel pinks, lavenders, and oranges splashed with fiery reds and purples; climbing spiraling staircases to the tops of lighthouses for incredible ocean views; driving through drippy, dark and moody rain forests; going around curvy mountainous, heart-stopping roads that gave way to spectacular scenery; driving through areas of unusual and seldom seen wildlife; and getting immersed in new lifestyles and cultures in various cities.

Decide what's really important.

> "But what touched my heart the most were the people experiences. We met such wonderful, friendly and caring people on the road, willing to help, no matter what the situation. It became very clear what was really important to me. We packed up our house quickly, gave our furniture to our children, had a huge garage sale, and donated the rest. And those mementos and keepsakes that were so important to me? Well—some still are, packed away in boxes at my daughter's house. When we finally hang up the keys, Grandma's lace tablecloth is coming out again."

Jill and Jose Ferrer made that decision while still planning to work at their corporate jobs while living in their motorhome. They had no problems until it came to their furniture.

> "We did a lot of research and thinking before we embarked on our full-time lifestyle. Certainly our hearts were ready to go for it. On the practical side, we had planned thoroughly

for the logistics and financial considerations. Nevertheless, we started in a rather unconventional manner by selling our three-bedroom townhouse to move full-time into a 40-foot motorhome in the cold of winter in New Jersey, while still working in our corporate careers. We planned to stay in those corporate careers for at least another two to three years and then take an early retirement while still in our fifties.

"First, we decided what we would take with us into the motorhome."

"Perhaps because of these somewhat risky circumstances, we were a bit wary about totally disconnecting from all our household furnishings. So here is what we did:

"First, we decided what we would take with us into the motorhome. This meant scaling back our wardrobes, pots and pans, dishware, tools and so on to just those essentials we could take with us. This was particularly challenging since we would be living in a four-season climate requiring a business wardrobe and cold-weather gear.

"We gave away many things to family and friends if they had use and space for them—some of our furniture, household furnishings, clothes, knickknacks, etc. We packed up all our photo albums to be stored indefinitely with a relative. We had a garage sale. We donated excess clothing and belongings to charity. After much deliberation, we decided to pay for storage of a major part of our good furniture. It was of good quality, but not antiques. We checked around and soon concluded that there was not really a decent market for used furniture, so we would have to sell it at a loss or give it away.

"On the other hand, if our corporate RV living turned out to be unworkable, it would cost us a bundle to replace the furniture. We shopped around for the best storage rate and found that we could get a better price if we paid upfront for long-term storage. We did the math (storage costs vs. potential cost to replace the furniture) and decided it would be a good safety net to pay for storage for a few years, 'just in case.'

"Well, we made it through three snowy and cold winters. We managed to hold down our corporate jobs while living in our unconventional home and were able to retire early as planned. As for the furniture, we had long since realized we didn't have any need for it and didn't miss it in the least.

Try to limit your household items to one of each.

"Thankfully, soon after we retired and hit the road, family circumstances had changed. A sister now had a place where we shipped the furniture, so it could be parceled out to family and friends as they needed it. We were glad to know that it would be put to good use. It was a huge relief to finally be rid of 'the stuff.'"

Joanne and Nick Alexakis said it most concisely.

"Whittle down all of your household items to just one of each thing. And everything should serve at least two purposes. A knife can butter bread and open a letter. A big book can be read and press fresh flowers to make dried ones. A bike can bring you exercise and save gas money if you are not peddling far."

Juanita Ruth One says that moving into an RV is like moving into a dollhouse.

"It calls for a MAJOR release (to kids, Goodwill or into storage) of most of life's accumulations. The keyword is 'simplify' and the measure is 'lightweight and multi-use.'

"For example, downsizing the large modern kitchen into a compact galley means returning to basics. Instead of many specific-function gourmet 'gadgets,' keep only those with multiple uses, favoring plastic over wood or metal (less weight). Example: an adjustable plastic measuring spoon instead of a set of spoons.

"Find smaller versions of many conveniences: coffeemaker, Foreman-style grill, toaster oven, blender, electric skillet, crock-pot and hot plate. I rarely use my propane stove and have never used my oven (except for dry storage) because I often cook outside placing the electric appliances on a folding table and plugging them into my external outlets ... Keeps the RV kitchen cool!

"I used a self-imposed numeric system (only 1, 3, 5, 7, 9, or at the most 11) to limit the number of items in any single category. Example: 1 set of guest linens, 3 coffee mugs, 5 pairs of slacks, 7 pairs of shoes, 9 T-shirts and 11 pairs of sox.

"Instead of matching sets, have multi-colored plates, cups, towels and washcloths. Each guest chooses a color to use throughout the duration of his or her visit. Saves washing.

"**TIP:** The adjustable device (found in automotive stores) used by mechanics to loosen oil filters is THE BEST jar opener—offering great leverage for any-size stubborn lid!"

"When you travel you don't need to change clothes because you are changing people."

Juanita Ruth One also has great suggestions for downsizing clothing. She discusses women's wardrobes but the same concepts apply to men's clothing as well.

"Most of us women LOVE our wardrobes and find downsizing a challenge. Mom's guiding principle was, *'When you travel, you don't need to change clothes, because you are changing people!'*

"Just keep them clean! As we traveled, a bucket of soapy water riding in the shower provided 'washing-machine' action for delicates and lightweight drip-dries, then we hung them to dry. An occasional visit to campground laundries (or friends/family) took care of the rest.

"When Mom and I went on the road for 19 months, we each had three drawers for our clothes and shared a two-foot-wide hanging closet! Specialty hangers that put 4 – 6 items in one space were a must. We each were allowed one multi-skirts, one multi-slacks, and one multi-shirts hanger. Otherwise we were limited by our drawers' space. (Rolling clothes takes less room than folding. Cut-to-size shoeboxes categorize drawer sections for underwear, socks, etc.)

"We chose three favorite colors to build inter-changeable wardrobes around."

"We each chose three favorite colors to build inter-changeable wardrobes around. We favored knits for winter, crinkled cottons for summer and avoided anything requiring dry cleaning or ironing. Layering was essential to span all four seasons. Every wardrobe piece could mix-and-match and/or served multiple functions. For example, front-buttoning long-sleeve shirts became transitional-season 'jackets' over T-shirts or turtlenecks.

"Our casual sporty (not 'sloppy') wardrobe carried us almost anywhere. We each had one dressy outfit for the rare special occasion. Because shoes take up a lot of room, we chose two comfortable all-round walking shoes, a casual loafer, a dressier flat, a beach/bathhouse shoe and a black dressy heel."

Jerry and Kimberly Peterson did all the right steps, but life does interfere sometimes. They found an alternative solution until they were able to get the RV of their choice.

"The diligent research began. Jerry was a bit apprehensive and less enthused than I was, but nevertheless he came on board once he began to see that we could really do this. The plan was to sell everything, get a rig and go full-time, and as we all know things don't always go according to the plan. After months of research, planning, selling, donating and putting our life in order, we thought we had it all set in motion, but then, just weeks before we were to get out here, everything began to take a terrible turn for the worse.

You can adapt your plans for the RV lifestyle to your changing needs.

"Our plans went haywire and things began to fall apart quickly but by this time it was too late to turn back so we went forward on the craziest roller coaster ride we had ever been on. But we did go and don't regret it. We worked at jobs that provided housing until we were able to afford to buy an RV.

"We did keep a small storage unit for about 18 months before disposing of that as well. It was our intention to keep this unit for only a year, but it was a bit harder to let go than we had anticipated. Now whatever we have travels with us."

Arline Chandler and her husband bought a used motorhome and decided to refurbish it before they got started.

"With our first very-used fifth wheel, we jumped in with hands and feet as though we were refurbishing a traditional home. After pulling up the dirty carpet, we shopped at a regular store for a neutral, basic rug. Regular installers laid the new carpeting, covering the living area, the steps over the fifth-wheel, and the bedroom.

"Our local upholsterer recovered the cushions in the benches that served as furniture. I ordered white cotton cottage curtains from a catalog. We replaced the oversized king mattress with a queen-sized bed.

"As we became more experienced in RVing, we discovered that furniture and furnishings produced specifically for the RV market come at a higher price. Some items, such as a refrigerator or toilet, need to be purchased through a reputable RV dealer. There are also companies that major in RV makeovers. However, with careful shopping, an RV owner can replace many components with standard household furnishings.

"As we progressed over the years to two new fifth wheel rigs, we purchased regular recliners that were more comfortable and less costly than the ones designed for a slide-out space. We also purchased made-to-order mini-blinds from a department store that were cheaper than those offered by an RV manufacturer.

Learn how to smile sweetly as you say "No, thank you."

"With some planning and extra shopping, refurbishing an RV can come with a reasonable price tag."

LEARN HOW TO SAY NO

Many of us have had to grapple with some emotional leave-taking from well-meaning friends and family who don't understand our new path. You will find you own way to deal with the various situations that arise. Know that we've all gone through some variation on the theme. Learn how to smile sweetly as you say "No, thank you." Here are two typical examples.

Once we make the decision to go on the road, we realize how hard it is for family and old friends to understand our lifestyle. No matter how much you try to tell them, they still offer you a "real bed," which is usually a pullout couch, when you have your comfortable queen-size bed in your rig. Then they say, "I bet you haven't had a home-cooked meal in a while," not realizing you have your own refrigerator, range, microwave, and probably a convection oven.

Adrienne Kristine tries to explain the facts of life to her sister.

> "I told my sister I was living in a 27-foot motorhome, and I was planning to visit her and her family at Thanksgiving. The RV parks near where she lives in Orange County cater to the Disneyland/Knott's Berry Farm visitors and nightly site rents were out of my budget. So I asked her if there was someplace safe near where she lived where I could blacktop boondock. She recommended the bank parking lot across the street. I quickly eliminated that possibility since the bank was open. A closed business parking lot would not be as obvious.

The RV lifestyle allows you to visit family while staying in your own home.

> "Then she said I could park in the alley behind her apartment building. Her husband is a long-haul trucker and would park the truck there occasionally when he was home waiting for a load. I thought sure: if he can park a semi there, I can park the RV. She said I could run an electric cable through their garage and I would have power. Even better.

> "I knew she had a two-bedroom apartment with two adults and two children, 14 and 6. She said, *'And you can park your mobile home behind the garage and sleep in a real bed. Leanne* (the oldest) *can sleep on the couch.'*

> "Great. Sharing a room with a 6 year-old.

"'*Uh honey? It's a motorhome and I have a real bed in it.*'

"'*Oh.*'

"'*If it's all right, I'd like to use your shower. Do you have a schedule of who uses it so I don't interfere?*'

"'*Sure. The kids take their baths and showers at night so you could use it in the morning.*'

"'*Fine. If I can't, I'll just clean up in my place.*'

"'*How do you do that?*'

"'*I have a shower.*'

"'*How do you get the water?*'

"'*The RV has a water pump and sends the water from the fresh water tank.*'

"'*But it's cold!*'

"'*No, I have a water heater.*'

"I could tell her processor was working overtime.

"'*Honey, I've got everything I need inside the RV. All I have to do is find someplace to dump the black and gray tanks. You have RV parks all around you so I could always dump there.*'

"'*Black and gray tanks?*'

"I explained the difference and received, '*Ewww!*'

"'*OK silly. Where do you think the toilet flushes and your bath water and dishwater goes?*'

"'*Into the sewer.*'

"'*So does mine. Eventually.*'

"I let that percolate.

"'*OK. When are you bringing your mobile home here?*'

"I explained the difference, although a 'mobile' home that never moves again after its been set up is a little strange.

"*'OK. I think I understand.'*

"*'Good.'*

"*'So you have to do everything by yourself? Filling the water tank and dumping and driving?'*

The RV lifestyle lends a life of independent self-reliance.

"*'Yep.'*

"*'Can I ride in it with you?'*

"*'Sure.'*

"*'That would be fun.'*

"She turned from the phone as her husband came into the room. *'Hey babe! Adrienne is going to visit and bring her mobile home!'*

"<sigh>"

Patty Lonsbary faced another issue when a relative accused her of being inconsiderate of her adult children by giving up her house to go on the road.

"*'I thought you would be more responsible than that. How can you not have a home for your children to go to especially at the holidays?'* That was stinging commentary I received when I shared with a relative details on Ed's and my plans to live in our bus conversion motorhome. Ouch! No support here! And, I suppose that others who have elected this lifestyle heard similar criticism.

"My grandmother experienced the same commentary in 1975 as relatives whispered disapproval among themselves when she sold her Pennsylvania home, let go of the Indiana County farm, and packed up for an RV retirement community in

Bradenton, Florida. There was no stopping her and likewise no stopping me. My children live dispersed across the United States (Greensburg and Lake City, Pennsylvania; and Fulton, Missouri)—none of which were close to my former Whitehouse, Texas, home. For years when we gathered as a family, we'd meet at my mother's Greensburg home—a house that she has been tethered to since 1963. We exchanged presents, ate too much, and played competitive games of Canasta; then we'd all go our separate ways drawn by careers or school.

"Advancing toward new dreams keeps me stimulated and excited about what each new day will bring."

"From my perspective, I have done my duty raising the children and providing for their needs. They were a part of my dream, as was my career with one of the most highly regarded consulting firms in the country and several years in broadcasting. Advancing toward new dreams keeps me stimulated and excited about what each new day will bring. That is why I won't be made to feel my entrenched Catholic guilt to keep a home with the expectation of the kids coming once a year for the forced holiday visit. Let them come to me on the beach of Mexico, the rain forest of Costa Rica, or the mountains of Chile—all more enchanting than a three-bedroom ranch in a suburban neighborhood."

RESOURCES

- **Visit our website for free information and a variety of resources for the new RVer: *(RVLifestyleExperts.com)***
- **Check out the Escapees RV Club for some of the best support in the RV community: *(Escapees.com)***
- **Visit the Resources section at the end of the book for a list of helpful RV books, websites and RV groups.**
- ***RVers: How do they live like that?* Judy Farrow and Lou Stoetzer: *(RVLifestyleExperts.com/RV-Books/Life-on-the-Road)***

NOTES

"I look to the future because that's where I'm going to spend the rest of my life."
George Burns

Chapter 4

How do I get my mail?

The first question non-RVers always ask is "But how do you get your mail?" Apparently they visualize a mail carrier dashing down a narrow country road yelling at the RV in front, holding the mail satchel with one hand and extending the other hand, barely able to hang on to the jumble of envelopes as they fall and litter the road behind him. Now they also ask how to get email and an Internet connection on the road and which is the best cell phone plan for RVers.

In truth, getting your mail is simple nowadays.

MAIL SERVICE

In truth, getting your mail is simple nowadays. Large RV organizations supply mail delivery services. Your mail is sent to them. When you know you will be in a specific place for a few days, find out the post office zip code, call your mail service, have them send your mail in a priority mail envelope in care of General Delivery, and then pick it up. One big advantage is that the mail service gets rid of your junk mail for you. Most RVers learn to pick small towns for delivery. It's easy to find the post office and there is only one. Large cities have multiple locations and you'll need to know which one accepts general delivery mail.

Some people rely on friends or family to collect their mail and send it. The advantage is that it's cheaper. If you are just taking short trips and you can return the favor, go for it. But if you are on extended or full-time travel, it's a big burden to ask others to do it for free.

These clubs provide mail-forwarding to their members for a fee:

- ➤ Escapees RV Club *(Escapees.com)*
- ➤ Family Motor Coaching Association *(FMCA.org)*
- ➤ Good Sam Club (*GoodSamClub.com)*

Jaimie has used the Escapees mail service for years. After she married George, she switched her domicile to South Dakota where George got his mail. They use Alternative Resources *(AlternativeResources.com).* There are other mailbox services available, especially in the states where many RVers establish their domicile. (See Chapter 17: "How do I choose my domicile?")

Cell phones make it easy to stay in touch.

Our Canadian friend and author, **Lynne Benjamin**, provides insight into Canadian mail service:

> "It's tougher and more expensive for RVers from Canada. Cross-border mailing is exorbitant. We do most of our important business online or by telephone and the rest of the mail waits six months until we get home. It's fun to open Christmas cards in April."

CELL PHONES AND TELEPHONES

With the advent of cell phones and special plans that include no roaming and no long distance charges, it's easy to stay in touch. For backup, have a telephone card available if you are in an area without cell phone coverage.

Lynne Benjamin continues with this cross-border cell phone tip:

> "Canadian cell phone plans that cover calls from the USA to Canada are very expensive. When we come into the USA for an extended period of time, we put our Canadian phone on vacation and buy a disposable phone and phone cards when we cross the border."

The main companies that provide cellular service in the U.S. are:

- Verizon Wireless *(VerizonWireless.com)* The most popular since it covers more areas than the others, particularly more rural areas.
- AT&T *(ATT.com)*
- Sprint *(Sprint.com)*

RVers on a budget can purchase cell service on a prepaid basis as well. Family plans can also save money. With Verizon, you can call another Verizon cell phone without using your minutes. Weekends may be free, or some AT&T plans have unlimited calling anytime to any other mobile phone.

You can use Skype for affordable calling between the US and Canada.

Two other methods for making phone calls are Skype and MagicJack. Both require a decent Internet connection. With Skype you can talk to anyone at no charge who also has a Skype account. For $8/quarter you can call telephone numbers in the U.S. and Canada. Other plans allow international calls. MagicJack has a set-up fee and a monthly fee. Long distance is included in the monthly fee. Other Voice Over Internet Protocol (VOIP) methods are also available and include service offered by companies like Vonage and AT&T plus Viber (free international) and FaceTime on i-devices.

EMAIL AND INTERNET

Email is an inexpensive way to keep in touch. Web-based email addresses such as Gmail, Yahoo and Hotmail allow you to check your email on any computer. You can set up Gmail to come to your Outlook Inbox so when you are online with your own computer, you can download your emails to your computer rather than have them online. You can then compose or answer other emails offline and send them when you have your next connection.

Email is an inexpensive way to keep in contact.

Many RVers now have Blogs (short for Web logs) to chronicle their journeys. Free services such as *(WordPress.com)* and Google's Blogger allow you to post accounts and photos of your travels. Friends and relatives can check your blog for your latest news.

For an Internet connection, RVers often have a device that allows them to connect to the Internet or they rely on finding an Internet connection as they travel—or both.

DEVICES

Devices used by RVers include:

- **Aircard or modem:** A small device you plug into a USB port. It acts as a cell phone device to transmit data. You must be near a tower belonging to your service provider to receive a signal. A Wilson antenna can be used to boost the signal in areas where it is weak. The monthly fee for Verizon's Aircard is $39.95 per month at this writing. Often you can get the device free when Verizon offers a rebate. Other wireless modems, which look like a flash drive, operate in a similar fashion. Virgin Mobile offers pay-as-you-go mobile broadband service with several levels of service.

- **Satellite Internet:** A dish mounted either on a tripod or your roof captures the signal from a satellite and brings that to your computer. Motostat is the roof-mounted system that automatically finds the signal. This system is $5,500 with a monthly service fee of around $80. The other option is to mount the dish on a tripod. You set that up each time you stop and locate the signal. George and Jaimie used this method for two years and George could get the whole system set up and receive a signal in about 15 minutes. The Hughes system costs $1000-2000 and is $59.95 per month at this writing.
- **Two or more computers:** Whichever method you use to get your signal, you can set up a router to transmit the signal to more than one computer. Verizon sells the MiFi, a small device that acts as a modem plus WiFi. Some Tablets can act as a mobile hotspot for up to five computers.

> **If your business requires the Internet you'll probably need your own wireless device and plan.**

Finding WiFi: RVers may find a Wireless Fidelity (WiFi) signal at RV parks, coffee shops, libraries, other public buildings, hotels, or signals from other RVers. If that signal is unsecured, you can take advantage of free WiFi. In some places, you'll have to pay a fee to use the Internet for a specified period of time. While most RV parks now provide free WiFi, some still charge. See (*WiFiFreeSpot.com)* for listings of free hot spots including those in RV parks and campgrounds. **Note:** Do not conduct financial matters over an unsecured network.

Realities: If you are conducting a business using the Internet, you'll probably want your own device. Even then, you may find it necessary to find a WiFi signal elsewhere when you do not have service. Signals in RV parks are not always reliable and may not reach all sites. Ask the person checking you in to put you in a site where there is a good signal.

Patty Lonsbary explains how they stay in touch:

> "As new full-time RVers, Ed and I explored communications technology during our first 60 days on the road through the U.S. and Canada.
>
> "Ed has a Blackberry; my cell phone is in the Verizon network. Both work great in the U.S., but the roaming charges in Canada, we were warned, would feel like highway robbery. It was true. Calls from my family to wish me happy birthday topped out at $20 a call when we were in Quebec. More sensibly, we managed by using a calling card for eight cents a minute for calls to the U.S. and five cents a minute for calls within Canada. Skype is an affordable option when we have access to the Internet (if you can manage the voice intermittent delay in transmission). We had access to the Internet in the U.S. through Verizon's Broadband Network. In Canada, we found Internet access through the customer lounges at Prevost and Trans Arctic where our coach had repairs.
>
> "Once, we used the coin-operated Internet in a Youth Hostel at the rate of 20 minutes for $2. This became costly due to the slow dial-up connection in the remote Gaspè Peninsula. Email has been the best way to connect with family and friends who are interested in knowing our whereabouts. And, I created a blog (*Glotours.Blogspot.com*) that is the detailed chronology of our experiences.

"I send postcards weekly to my four-year-old granddaughter."

> "Connecting via the mail is one way to stay plugged in as well. I send postcards weekly to my four-year-old granddaughter Brianna and on occasion to my son and daughter, Chris and Suzie. When I find something like a special salmon fly for Chris and a Chinese good luck charm with a horse on it

for Suzie, I drop these in the mail. We have a contract with a mail-forwarding service through Escapees, an RV club for full-time RVers, but they do not ship mail outside the U.S. [NOTE: Urgent mail or mail out of the country can be sent via UPS or FedEx.] So our mail waited in Livingston, Texas, until we came back to the States.

"Some mail had gone to my Mom's house in Greensburg, Pennsylvania, where she opened the mail. Then every week she and I decided over the phone what needed attention and what could wait for our return or be tossed out. We have made some headway with bill paying online or by phone, but there are still a few things that require a physical mailing location. For example, I renewed my Texas driver's license online, but it had to be mailed to a specific location. Orders for books and RV products we made online, but the shipments had to be timed to arrive in RV parks where we knew we were headed.

Many campgrounds now have WiFi.

"As we traveled on this 'shake down' cruise, we got better at living aboard our coach. And we are building confidence in our abilities to adapt what we learn today as we advance to tomorrow's next part of our full-time RV lifestyle."

Larry and Adrienne Brauer explain how they have stayed connected:

"Communicating on the road isn't a problem. We use cell phones and email. On occasion, email and cell phone connections have been a little tricky. When we first started our full-time lifestyle, we had to use a computer modem to connect to get email and pay bills. Now, we usually use WiFi. Many campgrounds now have WiFi; sometimes there is a fee, and sometimes it's free. When we worked at a National Forest Service Campground in Colorado, there was no WiFi or cell phone service. We had to drive about 15 miles down the hill to get cell phone service. Fortunately, the local library had free WiFi. So we visited the library once or twice a week.

"When we're traveling we send out emails to all of our family. This started on our first trip as full-timer RVers. We learned that some of our grandchildren would ask their parents, *'Where are Grandma and Grandpa?'* That led us to start writing emails when we change locations. We title the emails *'Where are we?'* We start the email by describing something about the place we are located, but without telling exactly where we are. Then we describe our activities, what we've done and what we've seen. Then, in the last paragraph we finally tell exactly where we are. The idea behind this is to attempt to give history and geography lessons in the email. Although there are only eight related families we send our emails to, our email list includes about 50 people."

RESOURCES

- **In addition to the resources listed previously, see the articles at RVLifestyleExperts.com under: *(RVLifestyleExperts.com/Free-RV-Info/Full-Time-RVing)***
- **List of free blogging platforms: *(NewestOnTheNet.com/Ultimate-List-of-Free-Blogging-Platforms)***
- **Skype: *(Skype.com)***
- **MagicJack: *(MagicJack.com)***
- **Find the best cell phone rates: *(BillShrink.com)***
- **Virgin Mobile with pay-as-you-go mobile broadband options: *(VirginMobileUSA.com/Mobile-Broadband)***
- **Vonage- VOIP plans: *(Vonage.com)*. Do an Internet search on VOIP for additional services.**
- **Find free WiFi hotspots, including RV parks and campgrounds at: *(WiFiFreeSpot.com)***

"Since there is nothing so well worth having as friends, never lose a chance to make them."
Francesco Guicciardini

Chapter 5
How will I find friends?

Most RVers find the biggest problem on the road is having too MANY friends! People seem to have more time to socialize when no longer stressed by job responsibilities and other obligations. Because there are no longer the old roles in the community, everyone starts fresh and is open to meeting new people, exchanging ideas about the RV, discovering places to visit, traveling together, participating in activities together like golf, hiking, boating, fishing, tennis, shuffleboard, playing music, doing crafts, and so on.

And of course, there's always eating. It's almost as if the potluck was invented for the RVer, particularly since nobody can accommodate more than four to six people in their RV. Just pull the picnic tables together and dinner is ready.

Most RVers find the biggest problem on the road is having too many friends!

BUILDING YOUR COMMUNITY

Here are some other ways to meet people and build community:

Join organizations. There are organizations for everything: type of RV, brand of RV, special interest groups, volunteer organizations.

Suggests **Joanne Alexakis:**

> "Join Escapees RV Club and their Boomers BoF ('Birds-of-a-Feather' special interest group). You will need their camaraderie and companionship on the road."

The Boomer group, like many other RV groups, has a Yahoo Group bulletin board and a newsletter, allowing members to post travel plans and connect with other members. It is a large social and support community. Others find groups of RVers with a common interest such as metal detecting or geocaching, a certain brand of RV, members of a membership park, to name a few. Regional groups like the Escapees chapters are very helpful when you are thinking about getting started. You can meet people in your home area and learn about the lifestyle. Most groups do have some planned get-togethers, but the bulletin boards or discussion groups allow individuals to meet up throughout the year as they travel.

"I've met some fine future friends in the RV park laundry rooms."

Meet people in RV parks. Men, just raise the hood of your truck or motorhome and six new friends will appear to lend a hand, give advice, or just "chew the fat." Women, you already know what to do.

Here's another suggestion from **Joanne Alexakis.**

> "Through our travels, I've met some fine future friends in the RV park laundry rooms. I try to be friendly and chatty—not hide my head in a book or magazine. As I begin talking to folks, I make sure to mention that I like to walk around the park for exercise. I guess that idea overcomes shyness, so we start strolling around, checking out all the rigs in the park. Soon, we are sharing many thoughts and then heading out to shop or explore the rest of the area. After Nick and I move

> on, I keep in contact with my galfriends through email. Being able to email photos that reinforce our bond to each other is a great help. Some buddies I have lost track of and some I have been lucky enough to cross paths with again."

Give out personal "business" cards. Print them on your computer. Include your email address, cell phone number, mail service address. You can add "home" address if you still have one, RV park address and lot number. Add a photograph to help people remember you. You can also print on both sides, so get creative!

Keep in touch. As Joanne suggested, send emails and photographs. Let your new friends know where you are so you can meet up.

Jerry and Kimberly Peterson add their thoughts.

> "We have met many wonderful people out here and keep in contact by email, blogs, websites and the occasional phone call. Whenever we are in the same area, we try to get together with old friends or new acquaintances we meet on the Internet in the many different RV communities we associate with."

Participate in RV forums. RV forums are a great way to meet people plus exchange information on the RV lifestyle. Often forum members have meet-ups in an area where two or more are located. You can have your own meet-up by picking a time and place and getting the word out.

Keep in touch with new friends.

Find the local people. If you are in a community for any length of time, meeting the local people will enrich your experience. Attend religious services, bridge clubs, square or contra dances, etc. Remember, the locals want to know all about you. You are living the life they have been dreaming about. They will also share with you the special places to visit in their community.

Betty Prange shares her thoughts about meeting people:

> "Volunteering is a great way to meet other RVers and local members of a community. Habitat for Humanity has RV groups connected with it. Working at a seasonal job also makes friends. My summer jobs at Bodie State Park, Glacier and Yellowstone Parks have resulted in lasting friendships. I am typing this as I sit in the kitchen of a friend from Glacier who lives in Tucson. When we first started RVing, most of our new friendships were with other RVers as we were moving about a lot. Now, after 16 years and being widowed, I have worked out a pattern of working part of the year, usually summers, and rambling the rest. Those summer jobs give me time to make some new connections outside the strictly RV world. I get the best of both."

DON'T FORGET YOUR PARTNER

Kimberly and Jerry Peterson tell us,

> "Living on the road never gets lonely for us since we truly are each other's best friend. It is truly amazing just how compatible we are. We both love doing the same things, traveling, sightseeing, writing, taking photos, reading, gambling, and taking on new exciting adventures whenever they arrive. We have always worked well together and this new lifestyle fits us fabulously."

RESOURCES

- **See Chapter 31 for a list of RV clubs.**
- **Do a search at Google or Yahoo Groups for groups for your brand of RV.**
- **Start a blog using one of the free blogging sites. Here are two:**
  - ★ **Google's Blogger: (*Blogger.com/Start*)**
  - ★ **WordPress: (*WordPress.com*)**
- **Forums:**
  - ★**RVNet: *(RV.net*)**
  - ★**Workamper: *(Forums.Workamper.com)***
  - ★**Escapees: *(RVNetwork.com)***

NOTES

"For my part, I travel not to go anywhere, but to go. I travel for travel's sake. The great affair is to move." Robert Louis Stevenson

Chapter 6

What will I do all day?

What won't you do all day? People who have been retired for a while often say: "I don't know how I ever found the time to work." The beauty of this lifestyle is that you can continue to do all the activities you never had enough time for and then add the ones you've always dreamed about.

Everything is acceptable. For some people, this is the first time in their lives they've been able to be completely selfish and just do the things that feel good to them. For others, this is the time they can do the humanitarian work they never had time to do while they were earning a living and raising their families. And for some, they have permission to literally do nothing but watch the leaves fall from the trees.

You can try things you never had time for plus the ones you only dreamed about.

The following are only a few of the activities you might want to do while you are on the road. Take the time to think about your plans. But remember, a favorite expression of RVers is "Our plans are chiseled in Jello." You are free to change your mind. The operating principle is that you do what you love. The only person to consider is your traveling partner so that you both enjoy your life together.

MORE THAN BEAUTIFUL SCENERY

Visiting scenic areas is always a rich experience (see Chapter 9: "Where will I go?"), but it is only part of the equation. One of the great joys of the RV lifestyle is following your interests wherever they are located, as well as discovering interests you never thought you had. How do you find out what is available nationally? For every interest there is a website.

The RV lifestyle lets you follow your interests and discover new ones along the way.

Do a search by starting with a simple expression inside quotation marks—for example, "Square dancing" or "balloon fiestas." You'll find a wealth of information. If fuel prices limit your travels, look for festivals and activities within your own state or a neighboring state.

If you like to attend different types of festivals, go to a website featuring Festivals. See Resources at the end of this chapter for one example. Search by the state you are planning to visit next or by category—for example, culture, sports, kids, music, arts, or motor sports. If you have a specific hobby, see Resources at the end of this chapter for a comprehensive website. First find your hobby, then locate specific sites and festivals celebrating your hobby.

ALWAYS TALK TO PEOPLE

Some of our favorite festivals came to us that way. Who knew there was a festival for kite flying? **Alice** and her husband met friends in Long Beach, Washington, stayed together at an RV park, bought kites and learned to fly the two-stringed variety—not your childhood kite! They watched an expert controlling five individual but identical kites flying in perfect formation. They were awed by five-foot circular kites that lifted as if they were meant to be aloft. The sky was filled with unusual shapes and sizes.

As amateur musicians, **Alice** and her husband enjoyed music festivals. Friends introduced them to the annual Jew's harp gathering in Oregon. The Jew's harp is an ancient instrument shaped like a miniature harp that you hold in front of your mouth and pluck to produce the twanging sound.

THERE IS NO END TO THE VARIETY

Want to visit or volunteer in a lighthouse, go to *(USLHS.org)*. Want to soak in a hot spring, go to *(Soak.net)*. Need a place to play in a Bridge tournament, go to *(ACBL.org)*. To volunteer for Habitat for Humanity, visit *(Habitat.org)*. Recently we heard about Disc Golf. It uses discs, similar to Frisbees but smaller and heavier, and is played on the basis of the game of golf including etiquette, pars, tees, etc. Go to *(PDGA.com)* to find out how and where to play.

The RV lifestyle will easily adapt to your changing interests and needs.

Finally, **Alice's** very favorite unusual experience on the road was attending a Tuba Christmas in McAllen, Texas—more than 350 tuba players performing Christmas carols. One of her RV friends plays the tuba and every Christmas checks the website *(TubaChristmas.com)* to find out where tuba players are gathering so he can put on his Santa hat, schlep his tuba, and join the local tuba community. Yes, Virginia, there is something for everyone out there.

YOUR INTERESTS WILL CHANGE

As time goes on, you will be attracted to different interests. Your rate of travel will change. You'll come across opportunities that you never knew existed. Be open to the changes.

Betty Prange describes her experiences in the last fifteen years. Midway, she lost her husband to cancer. She continues to travel. The remainder of her story, by the way, is in Chapter 20: "How can I travel by myself?" for people who travel solo.

> "Life on the road changes, just as life anywhere changes. After fifteen years on the road I too have changed the way I travel.

> "Only weeks into our travels we (my husband Lin and I) boondocked with Betty and Jim in Alamagordo, New Mexico. They took us under their wings and taught us boondocking skills. But the most important lesson they shared was that what we were embarking on was a lifestyle, not a vacation.

"Relax. You don't have to see it all in a few days."

> "Each morning Lin and I rushed off, carrying handfuls of visitor guides and local maps, to see what the area had to offer. One evening, after a day that included both the Space History Museum and the White Sands National Monument, not to mention lunch out, we arrived home pleased but tired. Jim said, *'Just watching you wears me out. You aren't on a two-week vacation any more. Relax. You don't have to see it all in a few days.'*

> "Wow. What a concept. We were not returning to jobs or yard maintenance. Our time was our own. We continued to explore avidly because that was our passion. Nothing like a winding dirt road to capture Lin's curiosity. Nothing like an interpretive talk, wildlife refuge, or interesting restaurant to lure us in. But we did slow down and learn the art of relaxing.

> "We spent a summer in Alaska and the Yukon. Another year we did the Maritime Provinces and fell in love with Newfoundland. As fall came, we followed fall colors down the East Coast and along the Blue Ridge Parkway and Natchez Trace. We

wandered the Rockies, went to Indian Pow Wows, traversed Puget Sound on ferries, visited friends and relatives, historic cities, sites, and national parks. Winters we found new joys in the deserts of the Southwest.

"One summer we decided to spend time near my aging parents. We didn't want to be on their doorstep, but close enough to visit regularly. We applied for camp host positions but the first responses indicated they wanted five-month commitments. We looked at each other aghast. Stay in one place for so long? We couldn't do it. Then one park asked if we would fill in for six weeks for another volunteer who needed to leave mid-season. Five months, at that time, was unthinkable. Seven weeks at Patrick's Point State Park was ideal."

CURB YOUR ENTHUSIASM

Once you discover this lifestyle, you want to share your joy and persuade EVERYBODY to go on the road. Betty Prange's story echoes all of our stories. Besides, if everybody did go on the road, those roads, parks and free camping spots would be overrun with vehicles and people. **Betty** continues:

"As a new RVer I sounded like a religious convert. I was compelled to share the enthusiasm I felt for my new lifestyle with everyone I met.

"Stay in one place for so long? We couldn't do it."

"I caught myself sounding like a proselytizer as I shared the joys of simplifying life, getting rid of 'stuff,' exploring new places, meeting people and the joy of seeing them unexpectedly as I traveled, and embracing a relaxed and enriching lifestyle.

"After fifteen years on the road I'm still a confirmed full-time RVer. I've been through changes and my travel lifestyle has changed over time. My RV friends continue to be my chosen family, something that becomes more important as my own family decreases in size. But I am more relaxed now about my lifestyle. I live it for myself. I gladly answer questions people have, but I don't feel as strong a need to sell the idea."

RESOURCES

- **For a complete list of festivals, go to *(Festivals.com)*. Search by the state you are planning to visit next or by category—for example, culture, sports, kids, music, arts, or motor sports.**
- **For hobbies, go to *(Buzzle.com/Chapters/Hobbies-and-Special-Interest.asp)*. First find your hobby, then locate specific sites and festivals celebrating your hobby.**

"Life is just a series trying to make up your mind." Timothy Fuller

Chapter 7

Where will I stay at night?

Many people assume the only place to stay is in a private RV park. That is certainly a fine option, but it can get expensive paying by the night. On this page you will find a variety of options. To make the right choice, consider the following:

A private RV park is one of many places you can stay in your RV.

- Are you just passing through on your way to another destination?
- Do you have a generator or solar panels to provide your own electricity?
- Do you want to be in a natural setting or do you want to be in a campground with some amenities and contact with other people?
- Is money a concern for you?

Here is a partial list of resources to get you started.

PRIVATE CAMPGROUNDS

These vary from overnight parking in simple campgrounds with only hookups, a restroom and laundry to full resorts with amenities like pools, clubhouses, a Jacuzzi, tennis and bocce courts and more.

- **Costs:** vary depending on location and amenities. Often weekly and monthly rates are less expensive.

- **Locations:** Find campgrounds listed in directories from *Trailer Life* and *Woodall* (converting to Good Sam directory as of 2013) and automobile clubs. These are available from RV stores and dealers or online.

PUBLIC CAMPGROUNDS

National, state, and local public lands often have campgrounds. They are many times in more remote and scenic areas.

- **Costs:** Usually less expensive than nearby private parks. Many are half-price for seniors and disabled on national lands and some state lands. Public land passes are often available.
- **Locations:** Check with agencies for campgrounds and dispersed camping areas.
  - ★ Bureau of Land Management *(BLM.gov/nhp/index.htm)*
  - ★ National Forest Service *(FS.Fed.us)*
  - ★ National Park Service *(NPS.gov)*
  - ★ National Wildlife Refuges *(FWS.gov/Refuges)*
  - ★ US Army Corps of Engineers *(Spn.USACE.Army.mil)*
  - ★ Each state park system has a website. Do an Internet search.
  - ★ Check regular campground directories. Some public campgrounds are listed there.

ORGANIZATIONS

Some clubs and organizations offer camping. Their places to park range from dry camping areas to full hook-ups and amenities.

- **Costs:** Vary. Start as low as $5.00 for dry camping at Escapees parks, for example.
- **Locations:**
  - ★ Escapees RV Club has a number of parks for members. *(Escapees.com)*
  - ★ Elks Clubs and Moose organizations often have parking at urban lodges for members. Directories available.

MEMBERSHIP PARKS

You buy into the membership park and pay an annual maintenance fee. Each has its own system of parks for members only. Two camping clubs offer half-price camping at certain parks.

- **Costs:** Buy-in fee plus annual and/or nightly fees. Plans differ. Camping clubs have half-price camping; conditions must be met. Note: Before you buy, make sure it is a fit for your style of travel. Check to see if they have campgrounds in areas where you want to spend time regularly. Some are restrictive on reservation requirements, which won't work as well for people who like to meander without plans. The locations may also be off the beaten track so are not good for stopoffs when in the travel mode.
- **Locations:**
  - ★ Western Horizons (*WHResorts.com/aor*)
  - ★ Coast to Coast *(CoastResorts.com)*
  - ★ Resort Parks *(ResortParks.com)*
  - ★ Thousand Trails *(ThousandTrails.com)*
  - ★ Passport America– half-price club *(Passport-America.com)*
  - ★ Happy Campers– half-price club *(CampHalfPrice.com)*

BOONDOCKING OR DRY CAMPING

Boondocking is camping without hookups. There are different kinds of boondocking. Blacktop boondocking is the term used for parking overnight in Walmart and other parking lots, truck stops and rest areas. Usually those stays are for one night and the RVer chooses to stay there rather than an RV park because they don't need the amenities that an RV park has to offer when traveling from point A to point B.

RVers also boondock for longer periods of time by choice. Some government campgrounds don't have hookups so you have to rely on your battery power and conserve your water and propane, or make a trip to where you can dump and refill your tanks. Government land run by agencies other than the National Park Service may also allow dispersed camping. If you can find a spot to park where you don't damage plants or dump your tanks, you can stay. Most have a limit to any one stay—usually 14 days before you have to move at least 25 miles. More popular areas may restrict stays to shorter periods. The Bureau of Land Management (BLM) has Long Term Visitor Areas (LTVAs) where you can purchase a permit for two weeks or seven months. They provide locations for obtaining water, dumping your holding tanks and disposing of trash.

RVs can be used as they are for an overnight stay if your batteries are charged, your water and propane tanks full, and your gray and black tanks empty. Some RVs have a larger capacity and can last longer. However, it also depends on the occupants and if they are conservative with use of electricity and water. If you run all your lights, radio or TV and especially your heater, you could end up with no power.

On her first solo trip, **Jaimie** boondocked south of Ajo, Arizona in her Lance truck camper. She had a light on, her computer plugged in and the radio on. After an hour or so, the lights started blinking. It took a couple of minutes for her to realize her batteries were low. She tried to start the generator but the inside switch would not work. She went outside and tried to start it there. There wasn't enough battery power. Soon it was totally dark! Then she remembered that if she ran the truck's engine for a while, it would power the batteries enough to start the generator and finish charging them. Whew! After that she was more careful. She only had one house battery in the Lance and one small solar panel.

RVs can be used as they are for an overnight stay.

Serious boondockers set up their rigs for boondocking. They may add solar panels and additional house batteries, a catalytic or ceramic heater, and an inverter. These, as well as conservative use of electric and water, can extend your stay to days or even more than a week.

- **Costs:** Boondocking is usually free, with some exceptions. Solar panels, more batteries and an inverter are needed for extended boondocking.
- **Locations:**
  - ★ Contact public lands for information.
  - ★ Escapees RV Club has special interest group for boondockers, plus their parks have a boondocking section.
  - ★ See Don Wright's *Free Campgrounds West* with campgrounds that are free or with fees of $12 or less. *(CottagePub.com/index.html)*
  - ★ Free campgrounds at *(FreeCampgrounds.com)*
  - ★ The Frugal Shunpiker Guides to RV Boondocking (6) by Marianne Edwards (*RVLifestyleExperts.com/RV-Books/Other-ebooks)*

Serious boondockers set up their rigs for boondocking.

BOONDOCKING—IS IT SAFE?

Boondocking can be a bit scary or intimidating to some RVers. RVs are self-contained and are set up to operate when not plugged in, for at least a short period of time. Extending that time does take additional equipment as we noted above. Solo RVer **Betty Prange** looks at the safety issue and boondocking.

> "I boondock more than I stay in RV parks. I use truck stops, Walmart parking lots, and rest stops when traveling through. For longer stops, I stay in quiet desert and mountain BLM and Forest service dispersed camping areas.
>
> "Am I afraid? No. I feel safe in my home on wheels. I could turn the ignition and move away if I didn't. But it hasn't been an issue.

"I travel alone, don't carry a gun and don't have a dog. My life experiences tell me that strangers are not out to harm me. Statistics back me up. Most violence is perpetrated between family members and people who know each other. We live in a society that is afraid. Television news, gated communities, alarm systems all feed that fear. I don't choose to live my life that way. Better than fear is a friendly 'hello' or a smile to make a bond with a stranger.

"Years ago, when I was working and living in an inner city, someone told me that fear attracts danger. Think about dogs you have owned. If you were nervous, didn't your dog pick up on it? People do too. If you are walking in a strange neighborhood, or you see something questionable, the best defense is to walk boldly and decisively. Someone nervous and afraid is a more likely target.

"My life experiences tell me that strangers are not out to harm me."

"I use common sense. I lock my door and look out before opening it. If a place doesn't feel right, I keep going.

"In 15 years of full-time RVing, only once, and that was while my husband was still living, did we move during the night. At 3:00 a.m. a trucker pulled within 8 feet of us in a huge mall parking lot, where RVers were welcome but truckers were not. The noise, lights and his strange behavior drove us to the far side of the lot.

"People's imagination can run amok. I was boondocked in a desert area with friends. One night two of us went to town for a program. The person who stayed home was startled to see cars and trucks, bright lights and people running around my motorhome. Within minutes, a sheriff's deputy was at her door demanding to know if she knew anything about my motorhome and occupants. The sheriff's office had received a call about a possible hostage situation. They took it seriously and sent out a half dozen well-armed vehicles and flack-jacketed officers. It turns out, a woman driving by, imagined a hostage situation, an imagination I'm sure was fueled by too many TV and movie dramas and an overactive, perhaps paranoid, image of the world. People standing around outside, conversing in a relaxed manner was hardly an image to bring on her reaction.

"There is room in the RV lifestyle for different styles of camping."

"Some people feel comfortable in secured RV parks. I'm comfortable boondocking. There is room in the RV lifestyle for different styles. I can do without RV park owners who use safety as an argument for banning overnight parking in retail parking lots or on the street.

"I once heard someone say he didn't weigh his rig because he and his wife didn't want to know how overweight they might be. That person carried a gun and talked about possible attacks. I don't have statistics to back me up, but I am sure far more RVers have been injured by tire blowouts than by acts of violence by strangers."

BOONDOCKING GETS EASIER

Boondocking becomes more comfortable as RVers give it a try. **Jerry and Kimberly Peterson** share their experience.

"Boondocking has become more natural to us and we would love to be able to do more of it, but our rig is not set up to do it for more than seven to ten days at a time. During that time we have to ration certain things that become uncomfortable after a few days.

"Eventually, when we upgrade our rig, two major factors at the top of our lists will be miles per gallon and being more boondock friendly. For now when we boondock, the things we miss most are the showers. Instead of being a time of relaxation, they are more rushed and less enjoyable since our gray tank is what limits us the most while boondocking.

"Another factor at this time is keeping us supplied electrically. We do not like running our generator 24/7 and even though we do have a solar panel that works well recharging our battery, it does not always seem to be enough.

"Each time we boondock, we learn something new to extend our stays. When we first began we were only good for two to three days, now we are good for seven to ten days at a time by just adding a few items and finding different ways to do everyday things."

Be sure you are prepared for inclement weather.

MOUNTAIN BOONDOCKING

Here is a case of boondocking high in the mountains after the weather has turned. In September, the desert might still be 90 or 100 degrees during the day. High in the mountains, snow can fall from late August on. And, wouldn't you know it—Sharon and Rollie, along with their camp host, did get caught in the snow. Here's how they managed and their advice for being prepared.

This piece was contributed by **Sharon K. Vander Zyl.**

"On September 16 I looked out the window and my eyes widened. I had awakened during the night once and heard it rain. Now I saw huge snowflakes and a completely white landscape.

"*'It's snowing.'* I said to my sleeping husband, Rollie.

"He murmured sleepily, *'Yeah.'*

"*'No, I mean it's REALLY snowing. It looks like the picnic table has four inches on it already,'* I said.

"He opened his eyes and looked out the bedroom window on his side. *'You aren't kidding!'*

"We got up and dressed quickly in the chill. We had prepared for our mountain camping experience with lots of layers so we pulled on long johns, turtlenecks, sweats and our waterproof Gore-Tex® pants and jackets. Mittens, hats and boots were next. Nothing had prepared us for the beauty that greeted us as we stepped out of the trailer. It was truly a winter wonderland. The pines were laden with snow. The whole landscape was white and the snow was still coming down. The trout stream below our campground and the dark green of the pines under the snow were the only contrasts to all of the white that surrounded us. We walked in silence, taking in the beauty and snapping pictures. Fortunately, we were secure in the knowledge that we were prepared for this eventuality.

"The previous September we had camped in a lower campground of the Big Horn National Forest—at the North Tongue Campground. On September 14 it had snowed six inches; then the sun had appeared and melted it by 10 a.m. This year we were camped at Tie Flume, at 8000 feet in the same forest. The NOAA weather radio that we had brought with us had indicated that this storm would be similar to last year's so we were sure we would be fishing by the afternoon. Instead, it continued to snow all morning and off and on all afternoon. The sun did not come out at all that day. After our walk, we settled down in our snug four-season Hitchhiker 2LS 29.5 LKTG and enjoyed some in-

The beauty is you can move your RV to milder climates.

door activities—fly tying, writing, reading, cribbage, warm soup and later hot chocolate. Eight to ten inches of snow fell that day. The next day there were still thick clouds with another inch of snow forecast for the day. Aparently the front had stalled. Even more snow was forecast that night.

"Our campground host, Tom Smith, was also a member of Escapees RV Club. The two of us and Tom were the only ones left in the campground. He told us the Forest Service said (and confirmed by our NOAA weather radio) that there would be a brief clearing in the weather on the 18th and then another front would be moving in on the 19th so he was to close the campground on the 18th.

"We had prepared for our mountain experience with two full propane tanks, extra diesel fuel for our truck, and extra gasoline for our Honda 2000 generator. One thing we hadn't thought of was a ladder that would help us reach our slides to clear snow. Our trailer ladder held our bicycles and it didn't seem prudent to take them down with all of the snow. Fortunately, Tom had a ladder that would reach. We borrowed it and on the 17th Rollie used a telescoping brush/scraper to clear our slides, planning to leave on the 18th.

Listen to NOAA weather radio.

"Tom had a solar panel for recharging his battery. With no sun, his battery was running low. We offered him our generator in exchange for the use of his ladder and we were all grateful. Escapees helping each other!

"Besides clearing the slides, building a snowman, making snow angels and more walks in our winter wonderland, we continued to enjoy our indoor activities for a second day. I must confess, though, that we were beginning to get a bit of cabin fever.

"On the morning of the 18th we had more snow to clear from the slides. Before we did, we prepared the inside for travel. As we cleared each slide, we brought it in. When we returned the ladder to Tom he was preparing to leave as well. Rollie helped him load his motorcycle on the hitch mount on the back of his trailer and we wished each other safe travel.

"By 10 a.m. we were ready to roll. Still no sun. On the way up the Forest Service road toward Highway 14 we met a Forest Service truck. The man driving the truck told us that we would not make it to the highway because around the next curve was a 4-foot snowdrift. He told us that if we waited right where we were he would go and get the snowplow that we had just passed and clear the way for us. It took a half hour of plowing and we were on our way, giving thanks for the serendipitous arrival of our Forest Service 'angel.'

"After all, one of the reasons we chose our new Escapee lifestyle was to miss Wisconsin winters."

"We were grateful for the beauty and solitude of the experience and grateful to be on our way to lower elevations and warmer temperatures too. After all, one of the reasons we chose our new Escapee lifestyle was to miss Wisconsin winters!"

Sharon's husband, **Rollie**, provided us with preparations one should make if you decide to give mountain boondocking a try.

"Our experience illustrates the importance of being prepared for a mountain boondocking experience. Snow can come in most any month at higher elevations. For maximum safety and comfort, preparations should include the following:

- ➤a four-season rig
- ➤a good NOAA weather radio
- ➤at least two full propane tanks for heating and cooking

- a towing vehicle with four-wheel drive
- enough fuel to get your towing vehicle to the nearest station (diesel or gasoline)
- a generator with extra gasoline
- adequate food and provisions for at least 3-4 days in case of a snow-in
- a ladder that allows you to reach your slides and the top of your trailer
- a telescoping brush/scraper for snow and ice removal
- adequate warm clothing and foot gear to negotiate snow
- patience and lots of hobbies to do indoors
- slow driving on mountain roads to avoid getting stuck in the drift that may be just around the bend."

Other RVers have noted that you need a way to keep your black and gray water tanks from freezing as well. A light bulb in the tank compartment is one possible solution.

RESOURCES

- **Links for boondocking: (*RVNetLinx.com/DBA/DBA.php?ID=6626&Cat=Genl*)**
- **See articles at *(RVLifestyleExperts.com)* for more articles on camping, boondocking and solar.**
- **BLM Long Term Visitor Areas. See website for locations and current fees: *(BLM.gov/CA/ST/EN/FO/ElCentro/Recreation/LTVAs.html)***
- **Boondockers Welcome– membership site with boondocking spots all over the world: *(BoondockersWelcome.com)***

"The greatest mistake you can make in life is to continually be afraid you will make one."
Elbert Hubbards

Chapter 8

How will I stay in touch with my family?

When your children are grown, they often move away, taking your grandchildren with them. You may have done the same thing, so your aging parents live elsewhere. You may actually see more of them when you travel. You have the time to spend at their home and the ability to travel there; yet you can maintain your privacy and routines because you've brought your own "home" with you.

You may actually see more of them when you travel.

MAINTAINING RELATIONSHIPS WITH YOUR GRANDCHILDREN

Use the time to establish your own special relationships with each child, just as you would if you were living down the street from them. With one child, you may enjoy cooking together, another child may be a game player, a third child loves to talk about sports. When you leave to travel, you can maintain your contact using those topics as a starting point. Be prepared if you are gone for six months, they will have changed somewhat by the time you visit again.

Here are 25 ways to stay in contact with them while you are traveling:

1. Send picture postcards from different places you visit.
2. Send email messages.
3. Send small, inexpensive mementos from places you travel to.

4. When telephoning, be sure to make time to speak to each child separately.
5. Keep those photos coming so your face is never far away.
6. Use a tape recorder to record your messages.
7. Write short letters. For an older child, start a story, ask them to complete the story, and send it to them with an enclosed stamped, self-addressed envelope to encourage them to mail it back.
8. Put together a scrapbook of people, places and things you see.
9. Buy T-shirts from different places you visit.
10. Buy Christmas ornaments from different places.
11. Take children with you for special trips together.
12. Elderhostel has special trips designed for you and your grandchildren. See Resources at the end of this chapter.
13. Post your photos on Facebook or special online photo sites like Picasa.
14. Stay in touch on Twitter. Let them know what you are doing. Find out what they are doing.
15. Download Skype so you can stay in touch for free. Purchase a Web cam for yourself and their families so you can see each other as you talk and watch them grow. See Resources at the end of this chapter.
16. If you have a craft or hobby, share it with your grandchildren. When Alice visited, she took her granddaughter to a bead shop so she could pick out the beads she liked. Then Alice used those beads and made earrings for her and delivered them on her next visit.
17. If you're near an American Girl store, take the girls and their dolls for special treats and activities.
18. Take your sports lovers to one or more baseball stadiums.
19. Check out the Factory Tours site in Resources at the end of this chapter to find the special tour for your little ones. Do they love chocolate? Take them to Hershey's Factory to see how to make

chocolate bars. Who doesn't love their crayons? Take them to the Crayola Factory.

20. Go to a pottery store together to make your own.
21. Write your life story based on the questions your grandchildren want to know about you.
22. Take them to an historical site or reenactment that ties into what they've learned in school. Travel along the Oregon Trail, the Natchez Trace, or the mighty Columbia River. Visit Gettysburg, the Boston Harbor, gold rush towns.
23. Sit by a campfire and sing the old camp songs, tell ghost stories and tall tales, and don't forget the S'Mores.
24. Go Geocaching.
25. If you run out of ideas, there are a slew of grandparenting sites with lots more suggestions. See Resources at the end of this chapter.

Mostly have fun with them and their parents. Celebrate holidays and special events together when you can. One holiday season, Alice celebrated Passover together with her family, her 15-year-old granddaughter's birthday, and a visit to Suisun Bay where a ghost, or mothball, fleet of old U.S. Navy and merchant reserve ships are stored. The family accompanied her son-in-law Steve who had served on the Coast Guard cutter his father had captained in Antarctica 40 years earlier. What an exciting memory to share with him.

RVing provides many opportunities to have fun with family.

Myrna Courtney missed her grandchildren when she traveled and came up with creative ways to stay in touch.

> "This was a huge problem for me, especially at first. My little grandgirl and I 'lost' letters to each other. We wrote letters to one another, addressed and stamped them and left them lying around, as if they had been lost, in phone booths, grocery

stores, doctor's offices, park benches, libraries. Then we waited to see if someone would pick them up and mail them. They always did, until we tried it without a stamp! Kelsey would call me on the phone and say, *'Grandma, I just lost a letter for you!'*

There are creative ways to live the RV lifestyle at any age.

"We also had a hug jar. We hugged and hugged and she jumped up to catch them and put them in the hug jar. When she got lonesome for me, she opened the hug jar and caught one or two."

MAINTAINING RELATIONSHIPS WITH OTHER FAMILY MEMBERS

Many of the previous suggestions will work with relatives of any age. Blogs with photos are especially useful to stay in contact. If the parents don't have access to a computer, run hard copies and mail them home.

Elderly parents present additional problems. Some RVers will temporarily halt their travels and stay near the parents who need assistance. Others will share caretaking responsibilities with their siblings. Many have siblings who are the prime caregivers, but they will come for a month to give the sibling a well-earned vacation.

Here are two examples of another RV option: either taking the parent along or being present when the parent runs into problems. Alice recently met the Nasco family and blogged about her reactions to their choice:

"As people move into their 70s and 80s, they start thinking about hanging up their keys. Mike Nasco, 106 years old, just started RVing two years ago! In truth, he doesn't drive himself; he stopped driving at 104. But Mike and his son and daughter-in-law, Ron and Rose Marie, have resolved the issue of what to do with an elderly parent who is still independent. They travel together in a 40-foot converted toy hauler fifth wheel.

"Keystone, the manufacturer, redesigned the rear area to build a complete apartment for Mike. He has his own outside entrance, refrigerator, microwave, sink, storage areas, bathroom (including shower, toilet and sink), flat screen TV, and an inside door leading to the main section. No bed is necessary since Mike is more comfortable sleeping in a recliner. He prepares his own meals and is entirely self-sufficient—and yet connected to his family.

"The pattern of being together started a long time ago. When Ron was full-time military, Mike and his wife always visited wherever Ron was stationed. So it was natural for Mike to visit Ron and Rose Marie when they started RVing. When asked why he decided to begin RVing at age 104, he said *'I love to be with Ron and Rose Marie and the people they meet. All the RVers are happy. I love everybody and everybody loves me.'*

"What's not to love? I fell in love with him too. Although he can barely hear, he made a point of leaning forward so he could listen to my questions. He shared his early history easily and especially his love for his wife Clara, who died more than 20 years ago. He slowly got out of his recliner, moved the oxygen tank out of the way so he could pull out the large framed photograph of them on their wedding day in 1922. He came back to sit under the two photos on the wall that dominate his small space—he and Clara in later years and their marriage certificate. *'I still love her and dream about her to this day. There was never anyone else.'*

"I love everywhere I am."

"*'What places do you love best?'* I ask him.

"*'I love everywhere I am,'* he says with a slow impish smile lighting up his face. My face lights up as well when I think of this man loving life at 106 and greeting each new day for the joy it brings. I admire his son and daughter-in-law, who are clearly delighted to have him in their life for as long as they can.

In *RV Traveling Tales: Women's Journeys on the Open Road*, **Verna Baker** described seven years of adventures rescuing her elderly mother and the new husband. Here is an excerpt from "Caregiving-RV Style."

"Mom loved RVing, traveling far with her solo RV friends. Then at age seventy-five, she had a major stroke. She worked hard at recovery, learning to talk again and even walk, but she never regained use of her right arm, her main driving arm. She was forced to 'hang up her keys.' She figured her RVing days were over, and for quite a few years they were. But then along came Tom.

"Mom and Tom were married when she was 83."

"Mom and Tom were married when she was eighty-three. Mom had enough money to buy an old trailer and Tom had an old truck. Actually all four of them—Mom, Tom, the truck, and the trailer—were in poor physical condition, but they put the dog in the back and took off anyway. As Mom said, '*Just rattle your keys and I'll follow you anywhere.*' And she did. As it turned out, so did we. It was the beginning of our seven-year odyssey of rescuing Mom and Tom.

"Now Tom was an inventive and hard-core boondocker, traveling with ladder, generator, solar panels, ham radio antennas, blue tank, and just about anything else he could put in or tie onto the rig. Most of these and the rig itself were held together by baling wire and duct tape. Our rescue missions were often of the repair type.

"Once we received a phone message: '*This is Tom. The dog got into some cactus. I pulled most of it out with pliers. She'll probably be all right. Your mother seems to have had a stroke so we're headed to your sister's in Reno. But the truck motor blew up so we got hauled to a one-casino town north of Las Vegas. We're parked out back. I think we need help.'* CLICK! CLICK?

"We weren't lost. We were just exploring."

"We followed and fixed as needed. We worried and fussed. But they sallied forth unafraid into the unknown, with Mom in her wheelchair and Tom on oxygen with his pacemaker and defibrillator. They hardly ever used a map. Amazingly, they always got where they were going—or close enough—sometimes sooner, sometimes later. *'We weren't lost,'* they'd laugh after we found them. '*We were just exploring.*'"

RESOURCES

- **Elderhostel programs for grandparents and grand-children: *(Elderhostel.org/Programs/GrandparentTravel.asp)***
- **Factory Tours: *(FactoryToursUSA.com)***
- **Skype: *(Skype.com)***
- **Web cams: *(Shop.Skype.com/WebCams)***
- **More great ideas for grandparents: *(Grandparents.com)***
- **For information about Geocaching see: *(Geocaching.com)***
- **Online resource for caregivers includes information for navigating through Medicare, lists of caregiver organizations, and support from other caregivers.**
  - ★ **Medicare site on caregivers: *(Medicare.gov/Caregivers)***
  - ★ **How to find caregivers nationwide. The motto is "Don't give up your parents for adoption. Keep them at home." Here's a directory of caregivers: *(ChoiceElderCare.org)***
  - ★ **Free information on all aspects of elderly issues like living will, etc: *(Caring.com)***

"A good traveler has no fixed plans and is not intent on arriving." Lao Tse

Chapter 9

Where will I go?

This must be the easiest question to answer. Go where your heart takes you. There are no wrong answers. RV stores sell the outline maps of the United States to post on the outside of your RV's door. Many people, when they start out, want to visit every state in the union including, of course, Alaska. As you travel to each state, you attach the plastic insert for that state. You even make your own rules. You can't count the times you flew there. You must drive there. But, you can't just drive through; you must sleep there too. One couple's rule was that they couldn't affix the insert until they made love in that state. What will your rule be?

Go where your heart takes you.

Some RVers travel with a theme, like following the Oregon Trail, visiting all the national parks and monuments, or visiting every major league baseball stadium. Others have special interests they combine with their general travel plans. One of our friends, a very serious beader, has visited every bead store in the nation. Another couple loves to explore unusual regional eating places. Birders look for wildlife refuges to add new sightings to their lists.

HERE ARE SOME RESOURCES TO HELP YOU DECIDE WHERE TO GO

- Auto Club handbooks and maps.
- Guidebooks from Chambers of Commerce.

- Travel websites.
- State guides: Always stop at the Information Center when you cross into a new state. Or check online at the state's visitor website too.
- Travel magazines.
- Word of mouth- in person or on RV forums.
- Newspaper travel sections.
- Your camping organizations' magazines and newsletters.
- Federal guides from BLM, National Forest Service, etc.
- Travel books.

KEEP A FILE BOX FOR YOUR TRAVEL INFORMATION

Make folders for each section of the country you plan to visit. Clip articles of interest and place in the appropriate folder. Make notes when you hear other people share a favorite travel destination and place them in the folder. Myrna Courtney said that she kept a calendar with notes of events happening all over that she and her husband were interested in, which they found out about from magazine calendars, word of mouth, etc.

The RV lifestyle is not an extended vacation.

TAKE IT EASY

When people start out on the road, they usually think of the RV lifestyle as an extended two-week vacation that will last for the rest of their lives. They cherish the thought they don't have to restrict their trip to just one national park; now they can visit ALL the national parks. After that is done, they can see ALL the national monuments. Phew. I've met people who say that they couldn't wait to get off the road because it was exhausting—moving every few days, little contact with others, miles and miles and miles of driving.

Don't let this happen to you. Alternate your sightseeing with days of rest in one place, meeting people, volunteering, etc.

The **Brauers** spend time visiting their children, doing extensive sightseeing, and Workamping® (working in a campground for a period of time).

> "Our travel plans seem to vary considerably, depending on the decisions we make. However, we generally try to visit all our children and all of our grandchildren at least once a year and, if possible, twice a year. That means California, Arizona, Oregon, and now Wisconsin.

Avoid exhausting yourself—alternate sightseeing with days of relaxation in one place.

> "First we had two major trips: We spent the winter traveling from the Gulf of Mexico coast to Key West Florida and then had a summer trip through Canada to Alaska and back. After that we started Workamping, which has given us a new perspective on life and RVing. The good parts of Workamping include meeting people, staying in one place for several months, being able to explore a specific area for several months, forcing us to get some exercise, giving us more of a purpose, and saving a few dollars. The pay is not great but we typically have fun.

> "So far we have workamped in Crater Lake National Park in Oregon, El Centro, California, Manchester, California on the northern coast, Yuma, Arizona, and the Arapaho National Forest in Colorado. We still want to travel to more states as well as attend some rallies."

Part of the pleasure of traveling is letting things happen. Make reservations for the big holiday weekends so you have a place to stay at busy times, but try not to over-schedule yourself.

JJ Dippel has learned to stop and "smell the flowers."

"Sometimes the best part of RVing is stumbling on those wonderful hidden away places and RV parks that you find simply by happenstance. This works if you aren't on any particular schedule and don't have reservations anywhere. There have been times when I started out with the intent of heading to a certain city, but on the way to that place a sign for an RV park beckoned to me and it turned out to be a hidden gem. Even if it was a 'just the basics' park, sometimes it was just what I needed.

"One time I felt like I wanted to 'get out of town.' I threw a dart at a map of Washington State and landed on Omak. Why not? I started out for Omak. On the way there, between Winthrop and Twisp, I saw an RV park on a river, with plenty of available sites overlooking the river. I stopped and got a great river spot. The surprising thing was that it was middle of summer and a Friday night, yet this little gem was not full! This was just what I needed!

The RV lifestyle lets you discover wonderful hidden away places by happenstance.

"Another time, I had left Grants Pass, Oregon, and temperatures in the 90's with the intent of heading to the coast to cool off. Somewhere between Grants Pass and Roseburg, Oregon, I found a park just off an exit on Interstate 5, and again, right on a river. This park didn't have cable or WiFi, and I could barely get TV stations over the antenna. I decided that a media blackout period would do me some good, and I got in some reading and some 'time to smell the flowers.'"

Myrna and Gerry Courtney explored other eating options.

"Once on a long trip we decided not to eat in ANY chain restaurant. We went out of our way and were rewarded with meeting lots of locals and finding unexpected gems."

DECIDE WHAT KIND OF EXPERIENCES YOU ARE LOOKING FOR

One reader wrote asking for input about which is a better state for RVing—Nevada, New Mexico, or Colorado. There is no correct answer. If you love gambling casinos, Lake Tahoe, Red Rock Canyon, Valley of Fire State Park, historic mining towns, choose Nevada. If you prefer intense colors of sky and land formations, early native ruins, contemporary pueblo life, artistic cities like Santa Fe and Taos, mountains, international balloon fiesta in Albuquerque, freshly roasted chilies, Carlsbad Cavern, UFO museum in Roswell, and many others, visit New Mexico, appropriately named the "Land of Enchantment."

Travel to do and see things that you love.

But if you LOVE mountains, then you must go to Colorado, the home of the Rocky Mountains. While you're there, head to Pike's Peak, hot springs, historical locations and many more.

HOW DOES THE PRICE OF FUEL AFFECT SIGHTSEEING?

Recent studies show that when fuel prices go up, RVers still travel, but they tend to stay closer to home. Check out Resources at the end of this chapter for a website with a trip fuel calculator. How do you find out the specifics of your state and neighboring states? Traditionally, travelers used automobile club guides and maps. They are still a great resource. For RVing and camping, also ask for the camping guides in that area.

If you have chosen a specific state, be sure to stop at a Welcome Center at one of the main entrances to the state to get your visitor's guide. When you get to a location, stop at the local Information Center and the Forest Service or (in the West) the BLM (Bureau of Land Management) offices for more information.When you go

Use these resources to find interesting sites closer to home.

online, do a simple Internet search for Travel in (name of state) and you'll find a wealth of information. The following Internet sites provide information on interesting sites:

- RV Net Linx *(RVNetLinx.com)* is a great all round site.
  - ★The Tourism *(RVNetLinx.com/wpTourism.php)* site will take you to the tourism guides for each state.
  - ★The Shows and Events site *(RVNetLinx.com/wpShows.php)* will give you access to RV shows as well as different festivals throughout the country. Find one near you.
- Explore the website for factory tours *(FactoryTourUSA.com)* to find unusual places to include in your travels. In California, for example, you can visit Mrs. Grossman's Sticker factory and the Jelly Belly jellybean factory, two fun activities for little (and very big) kids to enjoy.
- National Scenic Byways Program *(Byways.org/Explore)* includes many of the most beautiful drives in the United States. Some of the routes are designated byways because of their cultural or archaeological qualities. On the website, check out the byways in your state of interest.
- United States Adventure Travel *(iExplore.com/Travel-Guides/North-America/United-States/Overview)* features a multitude of activities to do throughout the country.
- Finally, Road Trip America *(RoadTripAmerica.com)* has many free road trip articles and interesting locations to guide your choices.

VISIT NATIONAL MONUMENTS

Most RVers don't want to miss Yellowstone, Grand Canyon, the Everglades, to name a few of the most famous (and most crowded) national parks. The 74 national monuments are not as well known, but they possess historical, cultural, or scenic values. Many have camping facilities on the premises.

Visiting a national monument provides a variety of experiences from the pure beauty of Muir Woods, California, to the unusual rock formations of Chiricahua, Arizona, to the historical significance of the Statue of Liberty and Ellis Island in New York/New Jersey waters, or to the pre-Columbian remnants of the "big house" in Casa Grande, Arizona.

National monuments provide a variety of experiences and often have camping facilities.

For a complete list of national monuments by state, visit the GORP site listed at the end of this chapter. Then to find out more detailed information about any site that interests you, go to the government body that administers that monument. Many of the national monuments are administered by the National Park Service *(NPS.gov)*, some by other agencies.

For a list of monuments by their governing agencies, go to *(Answers.com/Topic/List-of-National-Monuments-of-the-United-States)*.

The other agencies are U.S. Bureau of Land Management *(BLM.gov)*, U.S. Fish and Wildlife Service *(FWS.gov)*, and U.S. Forest Service *(FS.Fed.US)*.

WHAT ARE THE OTHER NATIONAL SITES TO VISIT?

In addition to the national parks and national monuments, we are blessed with a multitude of recreation areas and historical sites:

National Preserves
National Seashores
Wilderness Areas
National Rivers
National Cemeteries
National Historic Sites
National Memorials
National Lakeshores
National Scenic Trails
National Battlefield Parks
Wild and Scenic Riverways

You'll have time to visit these special places.

For more information about these other sites, visit National Atlas *(NationalAtlas.gov/Articles/Government/a_NationalParks.html)* or the National Park Systems Units *(NPCA.org/Explore_the_Parks/Park_System/Units_Monuments.html)*.

SPECIAL PLACES

Carol Weishampel loooooves Alaska. She was there again recently and has also written an RV novel that takes place in Alaska.

> "Alaska! The Alaskan Highway was built in 1942, the year I was born. I fulfilled a lifelong dream by driving the Alcan, solo, to celebrate my 60th birthday. Two return trips have not yet satisfied my dream to go back again."

Bernie Fuller and his wife started traveling full-time in the 1970s. They had a series of jobs that took them to beautiful state and national parks. Here's his partial list of travels in those years:

- Assigned as U.S. Forest Service Campground Hosts in the Huachuca Mountains along the U.S.-Mexican border for 3 months. (Free site and basic hookups provided)
- Being asked to participate in an archaeological site survey of an ancient Hohokam site. (Arizona)
- Standing within five feet of our hummingbird feeders and clicking away with the camera as four species of hummingbirds accessed the nectar. (Davis Mt State Park in Texas)
- Photographing petroglyphs and pictographs all over the Southwest on a magazine assignment that culminated in a series of magazine articles.
- Spending a restful two weeks on a ranch in the Black Hills of South Dakota.

➤ Boondocking in the company of Kay and Joe Peterson (founders of the Escapees RV Club) at The Slabs near Niland, California, brainstorming the early years and future of the Escapees.

Bernie continues:

> **The RV lifestyle allows you to "move down the road" when the mood strikes.**

"Memories of our years as full-timers flood back as I write this. It is difficult to pick just a few highlights, since it was a total experience in terms of enjoying life. I think that the most important aspect was the freedom to be able to hook-up the RV and move down the road when the mood struck us (or budget allowed). ... Or ... When another magazine assignment came along we didn't have to endure the hassle of making elaborate travel plans."

Canadian author **Joei Carlton Hossack** travels based on her work schedule.

"I am still working so my travel patterns are dictated by where I choose to work, and I'm slowly but surely getting a routine down. December, January, February and part of March I spend in Southern California. I have discovered a luxury RV resort that is perfect for my needs in Hemet. I return to British Columbia late March and work at home writing and book signing in my local area.

"I'm back out on the road lecturing and signing May and June and return home for July and August because it is way too expensive in campgrounds and way too many kids out of school. September and part of October I'm back out on the road signing and then home until it's time to leave for California. Life doesn't get any better than that.

"I love attending camping rallies and that too is part of my work. I have achieved much in the 20 years that I've been on the road. I've motorhomed through Great Britain and most of Europe. I've traveled parts of Canada and most of the States including driving solo from Florida to Alaska."

A NOTE ABOUT FUEL COSTS

Betty Prange offers excellent advice about reducing fuel costs so you can enjoy all this great traveling.

"You can do a lot to help keep these in line with good driving practices. Practice smooth starts and stops, anticipate stops and slow downs, and drive at an optimum speed for your vehicle. My motorhome has a gauge showing my mpg either instant or average. Watching the instant for a while in the beginning helps you understand what circumstances impact mileage, but now I keep it on the average mode. I found that 58-60 mph gives me my best highway gas mileage. RVs should not be keeping up with passenger vehicles doing 75 and up anyway. But putting it on cruise control at a lower speed does make a gas consumption difference.

Drive at an optimum speed for your vehicle to get the best gas mileage.

"Obviously, you don't hold up traffic, so this is for multi-lane highways. When driving on secondary roads and going slower than average, plan to pull over often. Weight of vehicle also plays a role. In my car, I try to plan my errands to not back-track or make unnecessary trips."

RESOURCES

- **RV Net Linx:** ***(RVNetLinx.com)***
  - ★**RV Net Linx Tourism Guides:** ***(RVNetLinx.com/wpTourism.php)***
  - ★**RV Net Linx Shows and Events:** ***(RVNetLinx.com/wpShows.php)***
- **Factory Tours USA:** ***(FactoryToursUSA.com)***
- **National Scenic Byways Program:** ***(Byways.org/Explore)***
- **United States Adventure Travel:** ***(iExplore.com/Travel-Guides/North-America/United-States/Overview)***
- **Road Trip America:** ***(RoadTripAmerica.com)***
- **National Monuments by state:** ***(Gorp.com/Parks-Guide/Index-SP.html)***
- **Trip Fuel Calculator: Get a rough idea of what fuel costs will be at AAA's Fuel Cost Calculator. While you are asked to put in the make and model of the vehicle you are driving, the most telling characteristic is the miles per gallon you get on the road:** ***(FuelCostCalculator.com/TripGasPrice.aspx)***

NOTES

Section II. SELECTING THE RIGHT RV

Chapter 10

What type of RV do I want?

After you decide to retire to an RV, choosing the type of RV, or recreational vehicle, to buy is probably the next most difficult decision, particularly if you have had little prior experience with RVs. Take your time, examine the options, talk to people, rent if you can, or buy secondhand for the first one to give you time to travel in it and see how it fits your lifestyle.

Choosing the type of RV to buy is the next most difficult decision.

There are two basic types of RVs:

1. Motorized RVs that have the driving compartment within the vehicle.
2. Towable RVs that rely on a separate vehicle with a driving compartment.

MOTORIZED RVS

This is the rig most people think of when they hear the expression "RV." Generally it's called a motorhome, ranging in length from under twenty to more than forty feet. The price can vary from a few thousand dollars for an old well-worn rig to almost a million for a luxurious, customized vehicle.

Motorhomes are easier to drive and park, plus they afford greater safety since if there is an emergency or anything suspicious in the middle of the night, the owner just turns the key in the ignition and leaves. The trailer owner must go outside to get into the tow vehicle. Generally solo women travelers choose motorhomes for these reasons, although one solo who lives in her fifth wheel trailer (see following page for definition) says that she prefers to stay in RV parks so she always feels safe and doesn't worry about having to leave in the middle of the night.

Class A: The Class A motorhome is often rectangular in appearance. The driver and passenger seats can swivel around and become living room furniture when the rig is parked. The amenities are self-contained bathroom, kitchen, dining area, living room, and bedroom. Class As handle more like a car (a very large car for the 30- to 40-foot rigs) and when you remove the towed car, they back up like a car so the driver doesn't have to learn new skills.

RVers find the Class A motorhome more handicap accessible.

The larger motorhomes usually tow a car behind, affectionately referred to as the "toad." Although the mileage is poor on the motorhome, the toad can get excellent mileage and is used for local transportation and sightseeing. If you will tow a car or dinghy behind your motorhome, check at *(MotorhomeMagazine.com)* for its Dinghy Towing guide on what cars are towable with all four wheels on the ground. Another toad option is to tow on a trailer rather than on the ground.

Although the motorhome has steps to mount from the outside, once inside there are no further steps, making it easier for a handicapped person to get around. In addition, it is easier for the handicapped person to get in and out of a passenger car than a large truck. Many motorhome owners cite the advantage that the passenger can get up to prepare lunch or go to the bathroom while the vehicle is in motion. In fact, that is a great danger. While traveling in an RV going down the highway at speeds up to 60 mph, every passenger should be securely seated.

One disadvantage to the larger Class A is having two engines to pay for and maintain. Another concern is that despite the number of stuffed bears they use, people who live in their motorhomes cannot disguise the fact that they have a steering wheel in their living room. For those who are looking for luxurious accommodations on the road, it is generally more expensive to purchase a motorhome and toad than a large fifth wheel and truck.

With the Class A you can have two engines to maintain.

Class B: The Class B is built on a van chassis with a raised roof. Class Bs are smaller, compact, and very easy to drive. They contain the same lifestyle amenities, but usually on a smaller scale. New ones are expensive, particularly compared to a similar-sized Class C or Class A. The Class Bs have less sleeping space for a small family than other small rigs or trailers.

Class C: The Class C looks like (and drives like) a truck chassis with an RV unit built on it although most are also built on a van chassis. The cab is over the driver/passenger unit. Again, the rig contains all the lifestyle amenities but often on a more limited scale than the Class A. The Class C is often used to tow a boat or motorcycle, and can tow a car. This type is the least expensive of the motorhomes.

TOWABLE RVS

The advantage of the towable RV is that when you arrive at your site, you can unhitch the tow vehicle and use it as your mode of local transportation.

Fifth wheel: The fifth wheel is a trailer that hitches in the bed of the truck. Depending on the size and construction of the rig, it may be too heavy to tow with a big pick-up truck. Check the weight rating carefully. An overweight vehicle can cause great problems to the tow vehicle, the trailer, and ultimately to your personal safety. You might damage the transmission, axles, tires, and so on. (Check out *RVSafety.com)* People who live in a big fifth wheel the majority of the time should consideer purchasing a medium duty truck (MDT) to safely compensate for the heavy weight of their trailer.

Fifth wheels have the amenities of luxurious motorhomes but are less expensive.

The inside of the rig has all the amenities of the motorhome, including more varied living room layouts. Financially, a luxurious newer fifth wheel and MDT combined is still less expensive than a luxurious motorhome and toad. When it comes time to upgrade, you may only have to replace the fifth wheel or truck, again saving money.

The disadvantage is that it usually takes longer to park than the big motorhome. One motorhomer told us that after she parks, she sits down with her glass of wine and waits patiently while her friends in their fifth wheels are still getting it together. Another problem is that it is not as convenient and cost effective to sightsee or do errands in a truck or MDT. In a recent poll of full-timers, the results were evenly matched between owners of large motorhomes and large fifth wheels. The pros and cons seem to balance each other.

For the occasional RVer who would buy a smaller and probably an older fifth wheel, the price and inside space are very appealing IF the family already has a big truck or would use it in their daily work. A larger family would need a truck with an extended cab since it is not safe to have the children inside the trailer as they travel. A motorhome may be more effective.

Travel trailer: The travel trailer, more familiar to most people, hitches to the back of the tow vehicle, which can be a truck, van, or even a heavy car, depending on the weight and size of the trailer. The trailer length varies greatly. The longer trailers tend to sway and don't complete turns as easily as the fifth wheel. They are also more difficult to back in to a campsite. Less underneath storage is available than in a fifth wheel. Full amenities are in the longer trailers. For the family, there can be more space in the van or heavy car, which makes pulling a travel trailer a more attractive option than a fifth wheel. The travel trailer is generally less expensive than the fifth wheel.

Pop-Up Trailers When closed, it looks like a box. When opened, the front and back open and occasionally the sides open as well. The pop-up trailer is a great starter trailer for a family. Towed easily by a car or van, it is less expensive than other trailers and can accommodate a larger family. If you don't already use a truck, you won't have to go out and buy one. Set-up and tear-down time is longer and can be frustrating if you are traveling to a new location each day rather than going to a single destination and staying there for the whole vacation. Since the sides are usually canvas, the pop-up can be very uncomfortable in the rain and cold. There are also expandable trailers available that are half-height for towing and slide up to full height for camping.

A travel trailer is less expensive than a fifth wheel.

Camper: The slide-in camper is a camper shell that can be removed from the body of a pickup truck. A "slide-out" side provides more space, but overall space is limited compared to most travel and fifth wheel trailers. This is an excellent rig for one or two people or it can be used as the tow vehicle for a travel or pop-up trailer for a larger family. Be sure you have a truck that can carry the weight of the camper. You may need to beef up shocks to safely carry it.

SLIDE OUTS: PROS AND CONS

When the newer rig (motorhome or trailer) is parked, part of the room can "slide out" providing additional living space, a great advantage to counter the living-in-a-submarine feeling. The newest models have three and even four slide-outs. The disadvantages are threefold: 1) this is one more mechanical part that can be a problem, 2) older campgrounds may not be able to accommodate the additional space you need, and 3) you have added more weight to your axles, chassis, and tow vehicle. You may also give up some basement storage room plus payload. You should note that resale value of RVs without slide outs is not as high since most people prefer slide outs.

Lightweight RVs leave a smaller environmental footprint.

LIGHTWEIGHT RVS

Lightweight RVs have always been present, but in recent years as the fuel prices have risen and individual savings have deflated, consumers have been searching for lighter rigs that give greater gas mileage and are also less expensive. In addition, as our nation is concerned with leaving a smaller footprint on the environment, the lighter rigs approach this standard.

As always, there's a disadvantage. **Bill Chatham**, a part-time RVer, enjoys RVing in the Pennsylvania mountains during the winter. He describes his experiences with his light rig. Remember this is one person's frustrated reaction, but it will provide you with guidelines to explore if you decide to go this route.

> "Any RV product labeled as 'Lite' means they left something out, like screws or instead of a sturdy roof, 3/8 inch Chinese plywood is all that keeps the pinecones from crashing through. I tried to order a ladder to attach to the back so I could climb up there, and was told, '*...it's not made to hold you on the roof.*'

"Molding to cover seams keep popping off because they were held there by tiny little finishing nails. Didn't anybody tell these dopes that these things sometimes bounce along on unimproved roads? Fiberboard hides openings where the 'non-light' versions would have cabinet doors to get at the space behind for storing things.

"Once you've made the decision to tear into your lightweight palace by putting doors where once there was only 'lite,' you'll be amazed at the unprofessional, cluttered, haphazard mess called plumbing, electrical and heating ducts. It's a good thing you don't need a building inspector's 'Certificate of Occupancy' before moving in, because mine would've been condemned right on the assembly line. In one spot where plumbing and wiring come up through the floor, it looks like they shot the hole through with a shotgun load of buckshot, ran the plumbing and electric through the same hole and filled the voids with insulating foam—very unprofessional, and normally never seen by the uninformed buyer.

"In fairness the utilities and appliances are all top quality and working flawlessly through three winters. Since adding cabinet doors to three previously blank spaces, I've almost doubled storage. The added advantage is that they can all be left open when the outside temperature gets down to 5°, helping warm formerly hidden plumbing.

Be sure to thoroughly inspect any RV before you buy, keeping your specific needs in mind.

"Still, waterlines occasionally freeze if the temperature gets much lower. I did discover a simple solution. If you'll look at your furnace, you will discover that one of the ducts from it goes through the floor to warm the tanks underneath. With high winds and the unforgiving cold, the little heater strains to keep up. My trailer has three cabin heat vents and a fourth for the tanks. To force more hot air down there, you must close at least one of the cabin vents. Now, my 'light' delight doesn't have dampers to close on these vents, so you have to put something over it, which in my case is a soup bowl, backed up by a case of wine to hold it there. The 'light' vents will be replaced with dampered versions ASAP.

"Remember, anything labeled 'lite' is definitely lighter due to the lack of screws, wiring and plumbing running the shortest distances like cobwebs, and in my case, the road cover under the tanks is nothing more than tar impregnated, corrugated cardboard. I suggest that you look 'under the hood' thoroughly or you too will be taken in by the lure of 'lite.' Be sure to spend some time in the RV before purchasing it if you are looking at one of the small retro trailers like the T@B *(Tab-RV.com/Index.php)*. While very cute, space is quite limited. You may not be able to stand up. You may not have a full bathroom or the kitchen may be outside. When not traveling, there is limited place to sit. In the smallest ones, you lie down or sit outside. Make sure it will suit your needs, especially if you will be using it more than on weekends."

All RVs, whether lightweight or heavyweight, have pros and cons.

HEAVYWEIGHT RIGS

Larger rigs have disadvantages too. Places to park are more challenging to find; public and older campgrounds may have limited space at each site; narrow, winding roads limit long rigs; in various states owners might need a CDL (commercial driver's license) or a special non-commercial license.

RESOURCES

- **Information about RVs:** ***(RVIA.org)***
- **Safety issues:** ***(RVSafety.com)***
- **Internet search for types of RVs**
- **To find out special driver licensing requirements (for larger vehicles) in all 50 states:** ***(ChanginGears.com/RV-Sec-State-RV-License.shtml)***
- **Jack and Danielle's excellent comparison of a medium duty truck and a heavy duty truck as a tow vehicle for a large fifth wheel:** ***(RVLifestyleExperts.com/Free-RV-Info/Getting-Started/MDT-or-HDT-Tow-Vehicle)***

NOTES

"Once upon a time is now."
Emilie Autumn

Chapter 11

What are my personal needs?

At this point you will need to do some exploration. Start by going to RV dealerships to see a variety of rigs. Read articles about RVs online or in RV magazines. Become familiar with the terminology.

Don't buy yet—even if they make you an offer you think you can't refuse.

The issue of assessing pros and cons is very individual. What is a bonus for one family is a definite liability for another. For example, people who want to travel easily to many destinations for sightseeing will want a small easy-to-handle rig. If you have off-road vehicles and spend a lot of time in designated wilderness areas, you will want a rig that provides sleeping and eating space but can also haul all your equipment—known as a toy hauler.

Another concern of course is cost and size. Are you just starting out and unsure of what will work for you? Are you retired and planning to travel occasionally, or will you sell your home and live in the RV full-time? Before you actually buy, talk to other RVers, rent an RV to get the feel of it, travel with a friend if possible, search out the new RVer websites, go to RV shows and dealers (BUT DON'T BUY YET—EVEN IF THEY MAKE YOU AN OFFER YOU THINK YOU CAN'T REFUSE!). When you do buy, we urge you to start with a used vehicle. No matter how careful you've been about assess-

First think about your own lifestyle and analyze your needs.

ing your needs, there are always nuances you don't realize until you start using your rig. A new rig loses thousands of dollars in value as soon as you drive it off the dealer's lot. A used rig depreciates very slowly.

MAKING A CHOICE

Think about your own lifestyle. Are you a weekend traveler? How many people will be traveling together? What do you plan to use the rig for? Will you be traveling full-time? Do you have any physical restrictions that need to be accommodated? Do you already have a truck? Are you an experienced RVer? What is your budget range? Talk with your partner about what you both envision for your travel experiences. Here is a list to get you started. If you'll be traveling with a partner, write down or discuss both your responses.

- Will I live in it full-time, seasonally or occasionally?
- Do I need room for more than two people occasionally or frequently?
- Will I use hook-ups or dry camp?
- Do I plan to spend a lot of time in National Forest campgrounds?
- Do I already have a pickup truck (for a fifth wheel)?
- How much load can the truck tow?
- Will I be parked more often than travel? Or vice versa?
- What can I afford?
- How much storage do I need for clothing and stuff?
- What kind of hobbies will I bring with me? How much room do I need for them?
- Do I have any physical restrictions that need to be accommodated?
- Am I handy?

- Do I like lots of windows or would they make me feel like I'm in a fishbowl?
- Do I plan to spend a lot of time in cold climates?
- Will I need to work on the road? Do I need space to carry a product with me?
- If a trailer, do I prefer a rear living room or rear kitchen?
- Will I have pets with me?

MAKE YOUR PRELIMINARY DECISION

Once you've analyzed your needs, it's time to decide on the type of rig you want so you can begin the more specific information-gathering detailed in the next chapter. Here are several stories describing the choices other newcomers made. **Doug and Rhonda Salerno** explain their reasoning for choosing a fifth wheel over a motorhome.

> "Rhonda and I began RVing full-time in August 2005 in a Montana fifth wheel (thirty-six feet, two slides) pulled by a Chevy diesel truck. Before our purchase, we researched the pros and cons of motorhomes and fifth wheels on the Internet and in magazines, visited several dealerships and talked with several private owners who had their rigs for sale. We thought going the fifth wheel route had one advantage in that we'd only have to maintain one engine rather than two.

Once you've analyzed your needs, decide on the type of rig you want.

> "As we continued looking at motorhomes and fifth wheels, it seemed that fifth wheel interiors looked more like home to us. They didn't have cockpits and steering wheels to remind you that you were living in a vehicle. In addition, the kitchen space seemed more plentiful in the fifth wheels we looked at.

"We considered buying a used rig and truck but couldn't find any that we really liked at what we considered a reasonable price. We wound up buying the Montana at a dealer who'd had it on the lot for a year and offered it at an attractively low price. It has the bells and whistles we wanted and some we initially didn't but now consider essential in any other rig we'll buy. We bought the Chevy from a dealer at a time when they offered employee prices, rebates and zero percent financing.

"Occasionally, for kicks, we visit an RV dealer to look at other fifth wheels, but we've never seen a model that we like as much as ours. Yes, I sometimes lust after a third slide (one that has a computer desk). Occasionally I even envy motorhome owners. Some of their rigs look so much sleeker than ours and I'm envious of their automatic leveling systems.

Choose the type of rig you'd be happy with after weighing the pros and cons.

"We knew that in buying a fifth wheel we would have some advantages and also some disadvantages over a motorhome. But that's life. Every decision you make involves gains and losses. Overall, however, Rhonda and I are very happy with our decision."

Larry and Adrienne Brauer, on the other hand, chose a motorhome over the fifth wheel.

"When we decided to become full-time RVers, for years before we actually did, we researched both types of RVs and looked at many different RVs. As full-timers, we decided that we would have either a Class A motorhome or a fifth wheel. We finally decided that for us a Class A motorhome made the most sense. Our first motorhome for full-timing was a 35-foot Winnebago Adventurer. It was actually our third motorhome, but the first for full-timing. The motorhome was great but as it turned out, the inside storage was somewhat more limited than we thought. After about four-and-a-half years, we decided to upgrade.

"Our second, and current, motorhome for full-timing is a 39-foot Winnebago Journey. The extra four feet allows for much more inside storage. There is a downside to that extra length. Some of the campgrounds that we like do not permit motorhomes that are 39 feet long. So we've had to give up staying there.

Longer motorhomes have more storage space, but may limit your parking options.

"If someone is looking at any RV, be sure to examine all the storage. Don't be swayed by how classy the motorhome looks or how fancy everything is. Look at the practical side of the RV. Also, don't be afraid to deal with the sales people. After purchasing three different motorhomes from dealers, we have learned you can always try to deal. Make a relatively low offer but be willing to negotiate."

Barbara Heller and husband, Alan Steinberg, make the case for a Class B, the van. They are not full-timers and as of this writing had only been traveling for four months in their van.

"My husband and I definitely DID NOT think of ourselves as RVers. We do own a small motor-sailboat, a 26-foot McGregor, and love traveling and approaching new areas via their waterfronts. But when we thought of taking an extended trip, I couldn't see myself onboard for more than the two-week length I'd already tried.

"That's about when the book *Live Your Road Trip Dream* by Carol White caught my eye. Actually, I was reading a copy of *Money* magazine at the local library and in a 'makeover' article there was a mention that the parents of the woman had traveled cross-country for a year and had written about their adventure. No book title was given. Yet in this Google era, the online search was easy and I ordered a copy of the book. From perusal to a second full read, the ideas in *Live Your Road Trip Dream* kindled my interest. Some of the planning info was helpful and some not relevant to our situation. For example, we didn't plan to rent or sell our home.

"We were most intrigued by the description of Class B RVs, which we had never heard of or seen before.

"While visiting relatives in Florida we went to our first and only RV show. The Class Bs were motorhomes closest in style to the small boats we were used to, except they had more amenities: more headroom, more kitchen appliances, a larger bed and a shower. I didn't want to drive a larger rig because of maneuverability and parking issues.

"Initially, when we returned home to New York State, we had difficulty locating a Class B dealer and were surprised when we found one only two hours from our home. We are now in California, having been on the road in our 2008 Roadtrek 210 Popular for four months. We love following the sun and visiting mostly national parks but also friends, family, and attractions along on the West Coast. It has been a great decision; this is a wonderful trip.

Class Bs offer better gas mileage plus more back road and parking flexibility.

"Our mileage is approximately 13 mpg. It's better when driving flat roads rather than curvy hills and mountains. Space could have been a problem, but as sailors we both like the simplification of Roadtrek's compact well-designed interior.

Of course, we are usually outdoors for hours a day. Also, we are small people, which helps (I am 5'2" and Alan is 5'8").

"Sometimes when we want privacy/separation, one of us sits in front with the two seats swiveled and the other is in the back. Especially if one of us has headphones on to watch TV or to listen to an iPod, it does the job."

Joei Carlton Hossack chose a truck camper after an accident.

"I had been on the road for many years and in many different types of RVs when I got rear-ended on the highway pulling a 22.5-foot fifth wheel trailer. The accident totaled the trailer, did very little damage to the truck, but hurt me badly enough to require months of physiotherapy. I knew that I didn't want anyone sneaking up on me again. I purchased my first truck camper and was delighted with it. It meant that I was one piece while I traveled and within minutes in a campground I could detach and have a run-around vehicle. I now have my second truck camper and it still works for me."

A truck and camper make a single unit for travel and can be separated when parked.

RESOURCES

- **DVD "Better Business Bureau: Buying a Recreational Vehicle," hosted by Chuck Woodbury: (*RVBookstore.com*)**
- **Information about RVs: (*RVIA.org*)**
- **Safety issues: (*RVSafety.com*)**
- **Internet search for types of RVs.**

NOTES

““Wisely, and slow. They stumble that run fast.” William Shakespeare

Chapter 12

How do I choose wisely?

Once you have become familiar with the variety available and have considered your personal needs, you can narrow down the field. Here are some areas to consider:

You have reviewed the market and your needs, now you can narrow down the field.

BUY SECONDHAND

In the more than fifteen years we each have been on the road, we don't believe we've met anyone who still travels in the first rig they started with. No matter how careful you are to predict what you want, there are bound to be issues that you didn't think of until you have lived in the rig for a while. The advantage of buying secondhand is that the rig maintains its value as opposed to a new rig that becomes secondhand as soon as you've driven it off the lot. Unless you are very handy, we suggest you buy from a reputable dealer and get a guarantee.

CHECK THE WEIGHT

An overweight vehicle can cause serious problems to the tow vehicle and your personal safety. Check the GVWR (Gross Vehicle Weight Rating), which is the combined weight of the rig, the water you are carrying (100 gallons will weigh 800 pounds), the kitchen stuff, your books and videos, clothing, the hand weights you carry, electric drill, and on and on and on. What is the rating for your tow vehicle? Most people's rigs are overweight! Be sure to become familiar with RVSEF (Recreation Vehicle Safety Education Foundation) listed in Resources at the end of this chapter. These days, things like the Kindle, Nook, iPods, iPhone apps, etc., can help cut way down on storage needs by reducing the weight of books and CDs.

Betty Prange describes how she gets her rig weighed.

> "It is easy to get your rig weighed. And don't just do it when it is new. I weigh in once a year to make sure I am not accumulating 'stuff.' I pull into a full service truck stop where I can fuel up (both propane and my gas), dump gray and black tanks, fill the fresh water tank and then pull through the scales. I simply pull onto the scale, punch the button that activates the intercom to the desk. They weigh, I go in and pay ($7.50 for the one I usually use) and get a printout. My car is hooked behind the motorhome when I do this. Now, if I can lose a bunch of personal weight, I can have more books!"

One RVer calls an RV a rolling earthquake. Be sure yours is built well enough to survive the road.

VISIT AN RV FACTORY

If it is at all convenient, take the time to visit. You will have more insight into how an RV is put together. The size and floor plan are important, but do not neglect the actual construction. Read about the pros and cons of roofing materials, chassis variations, aluminum vs. wood construction, and more. Your "house" will be bumping along the road at 60 mph, turning corners, making sudden stops. One RVer calls an RV a rolling earthquake. It must be well built. Check out the RV Buyers Guide and JR Consumer Resources websites listed at the end of this chapter. They are both excellent sources for learning more about RV construction.

RESEARCH CONSUMER GROUP EVALUATIONS

In the Resource section at the end of this chapter are two websites to use for independent evaluations: JRConsumer and RV Consumer Group. While they may seem expensive to purchase, they will save you in time and actual dollars by teaching you what to look for and are inexpensive in comparison to the money you will be spending on your RV.

The time you spend before you plunk down your money is invaluable.

TALK TO OTHER RVERS

You will have no problem finding people to talk about their RVs. They are happy to tell you the great things about their current choice and the horror stories about their previous choices (or, unfortunately for some, their present rig). Always take their comments with a grain of salt, but you can be sure that they will be more candid than an RV sales staff. Join forums for the brands you're interested in. You will learn a lot. The time you spend before you plunk down your money is invaluable. One of the best forums for research is *(RV.net/Forums)*.

Here are the experiences of a number of RVers. When we first went on the road 15 years ago, many of the younger RVers had inexpensive, smaller and older rigs. Alice remembers **Joanne and Nick Alexakis**' Holiday Rambler travel trailer very well. Joanne neglects to mention that they also traveled with two large dogs in that limited space.

> "Our first RV was a 17-foot Jayco travel trailer. It was a luxurious improvement over our previous pup-tent camping style. We used it for weekend camping trips and on our annual two-week vacation. It had all the necessities except a separate

bed. The couch made into a bed at night and then made back up into a couch in the morning—very inconvenient.

"We traded up to a 24-foot Holiday Rambler travel trailer with a bedroom. The bedroom gives a separate area for reading, studying, taking a nap, or even sulking. I believe this individual space is essential to preserve a good relationship with a traveling companion.

"Eventually we ran short on space and we purchased a 32-foot Alpenlite fifth wheel with two (count 'em – 2!!) slideouts. And, of course, windows—big windows! Now I could (and do) live in this rig with lots of open space, a long closet across the front of the trailer and much more storage.

"However, after the thrill of newness has worn off, Nick finds towing this 32-foot fifth wheel trailer a chore. He calls it a dinosaur. Nick misses our smaller 24-foot travel trailer and wishes we had it back at least once a month.

"Eventually we hope to set our Alpenlite in an RV park and use it as a home base. Nick wants to buy a camper for our Dodge ¾-ton truck for traveling. He figures we will be able to drive any road and park in the smallest of sites.

The most important first step is to fully define the RV lifestyle you want.

Juanita Ruth One traces the development of vehicles through the years according to the needs of her family.

"The most important first step is to FULLY define the RV lifestyle YOU want! Each of my RVing experiences required a vehicle adapted to a different purpose.

"In the 1940s, my family traveled in a Ford Sedan my father had modified to sleep our family of four. My journalist parents put in a typewriter, Ditto machine, fishing equipment, camp stove, icebox, minimal clothing and two preschoolers! For two years we toured (and wrote about) North America.

"In the 1960s, my own young family enjoyed tent camping. However, an extended autumn New England tour demonstrated that the frequent setting up and breaking camp was laborious. Therefore, we were thrilled to inherit my parents' Airstream, which made camping more fun and less work. It featured a double bed plus a large foldout couch that could accommodate our three girls.

"In 1989-90, Mom and I traveled in a 32-foot Class A towing a Chevy Nova for 18 months, visiting all 50 states while writing to homeschoolers and others. Our 1972 self-contained motorhome featured two single beds with individual storage areas above and below.

"I'm now retired into a 27-foot Class C that is just right for a single's 'home on wheels.' I've my own double bed and can accommodate short-term guests in the cab-over single or the 6' double-bed dinette conversion. I don't tow a car but carry a bicycle.

"Bottom-line considerations: size (for living AND driving convenience), affordability and planned usage of the RV. Decide this ahead of time, make your "must have/would like/optional" lists, establish your budget, then take your time shopping around (used is usually the better buy)."

Each RVer chooses based on individual considerations and budget—so will you.

Kimberly and Jerry Peterson made their choices based on their interests, life events and budget constraints.

"Our easiest part in the process was researching the many different types of rigs. This decision was almost instantaneous for us because we wanted a Class C motorhome. We were sure we wanted to purchase it from either a friend (best case scenario) or a very reliable source, not a dealer.

Prioritize your needs to find the best fit in RV type.

"Our highest priority was mechanical maintenance since in the many months of looking at rigs, we had never found exactly what we wanted that also fit our budget so we were certain we would be doing a major overhaul to the interior. We had always remodeled our homes and even though this home would be on wheels it did not make a difference for us.

"Jerry was the avid camper. In his younger days, he and his family camped all the time. I, on the other hand, had only tented two or three times in my entire life. When we ran into some financial difficulties and no longer had a rig, we found other arrangements. For the first few years we tented or found work that included housing until we were able to purchase our own 27-foot Class C motorhome that we still have.

"We also tow our Jeep, which we feel is a necessity for us even though many people do without. We even entertained the idea of going without for a brief moment, but decided it was worth the added expense of having a toad. We eventually would like to get a pair of motorcycles and tow them instead of our Jeep, which would be the fulfillment of another dream of ours."

Beth and Art Ramos downsized from a Class A to a Class B as their needs changed.

"As gas prices rise incrementally with summer temperatures and inverse to those in winter, many members of the Escapees RV Club (SKPs) are re-evaluating their lifestyle. Folks who full-time are staying longer in one place; others have permanently parked their vehicle somewhere as a vacation home.

"Our choice presented itself to us one day last January when the brakes on our 35-foot double slide, Class A motorhome froze on our way toward the Florida SKP resort in Wauchula, Florida. Wauchula looks like it's in the middle of nowhere, but it's only 45 minutes from the mechanic who had been doing the maintenance on the coach for the three years we'd owned it. He noticed as he filled out the paperwork that we still had two days left on our warranty. The cost of replacing the brakes would be covered!

Changing needs may result in a change in RV.

"Our mechanic also sold pre-owned RVs, and as we walked toward our 'Toad,' we poked our heads into a couple of class 'Cs' and 'Bs' on the lot, realized that a Class B could serve as a second car and returned to his office to put our 'A' on consignment.

"While this appeared to be a 'spontaneous' decision, it had been quite a while in the making.

"My husband's dream had been to retire to work as a street sweeper in Disney World; mine was to spend quality time in each of the contiguous forty-eight states.

"Until two years before his retirement we thought we'd go our separate ways, but on a tent camping trip through Civil War battlefields we met folks who lived in their motorhomes full-time and realized that we could have it all.

"In 2003 we sold everything we owned in Massachusetts and bought our Class A. The plan was to work at Disney during the winter, travel spring and fall and volunteer at a national park in the summer months. However, the Disney job was more fun than I imagined (we're not street sweepers!) so we lived six months as Florida residents, six months out traveling.

"The first year out we volunteered, the second year we toured the perimeter of the US and the third year we took advantage of campground memberships to live in several places for three weeks at a time and absorb the spirit of an area. We were sitting on the edge of Lake Champlain in August '06 when we admitted that we were bored without structure or direction. It seemed to us that we needed to make a choice: Become members of the full-timer RV community or put down roots and travel when the rhythm of our life allowed.

"We took full advantage of workshops and conversations to help us with our decision."

"The 2006 Escapees rally in Goshen, Indiana, was our last planned stop that season and we took full advantage of workshops and conversations to help us with our decision. Our commitment to the Escapees became even firmer when I joined the 'Penwheels' BOF and Art started the BOF 'Disney Lovers—Friends of the Mouse.' Full-timing would certainly give us a full and gratifying life, but was it the life for us?

"On our way back to Florida, we agreed to take the winter to make up our minds. We already owned a condominium in Celebration (15 minutes from Disney)—which is why the brakes froze on our motorhome that morning in January. The poor thing had been stuck in storage for four months! Despite our goal to 'go out often,' we'd become rooted, and finding a vehicle that would allow us to 'travel as the rhythm of our life allowed' was the logical and not really a sudden choice.

"The Class B facing us looked as if it had been custom designed by us. The passenger seats had been replaced with closets and the media system was state of the art, with the TV placed in just the right spot for my husband to watch comfortably while taking a nap. It also has the standard two-burner stove, camper's fridge, commode AND a shower.

An RV can be used to upgrade your life.

"Built on a Chevy Chassis, our traveling home is a van that we can park in front of the condo, use as a second car, and getting ready to 'go out' only involves packing our clothes and the fridge. Since buying it, we've traveled on short and long trips, visited family but could stay in our own space in their driveways. We can drive roads we couldn't have done before. By downsizing we have upgraded our lives."

As a solo woman traveler, **Carol Weishampel** prefers a smaller Class C motorhome.

"I have been RVing for about twelve years. When my children were young, we tent camped and backpacked with the Scouts. As the ground got harder I upgraded to an old Coleman pop-up tent camper. I took nine of my kids in a van pulling the pop-up from Texas to Canada. I threatened to leave them but we survived. Kids grown, I invested in my first motorhome and am now in my fourth. For a single senior female, there is safety in a motorhome. With keys in the ignition, I can drive off in the middle of the night, no levelers, no trailer to hitch up. Have potty will travel!"

JJ Dippel, also a solo woman traveler, prefers to go toadless. She provides suggestions for alternatives.

"I have been RVing since 2004 and I'm in my early 50's. I still don't have the nerve to pull a car behind me. Trying to navigate my 31-foot RV through gas stations is bad enough without having to deal with a car attached. So I do my sightseeing in the following manner:

- ➤Electric bicycle
- ➤Public transportation
- ➤Rental cars
- ➤Lots of walking

Electric Bicycle. I purchased this item from a company in Rhode Island called Ego Vehicles *(EgoVehicles.com)*. I use it to travel short distances. Since it runs off a battery, most states do not require any special license for it (but check with your state to be sure). Since this bike can only be used on surface streets, do not attempt to ride on freeways or busy highways. Its top speed is around 25 mph.

Public Transportation. If the city has public transportation, try to stay in an RV park along the bus line. This option sometimes is not readily available, but I have had a couple successes with it.

Rental Cars. Enterprise Rent-a-Car can deliver the car to you if you are staying within a reasonable distance from an office location. I have had success with this option in a few places. There have been other places where I rented cars from other companies, but had to walk to the pick-up location. One time I walked five miles to pick up a car.

Stay at RV parks that are close to activities you enjoy.

Lots of Walking. In this case, stay at RV parks that are close to activities you enjoy. State Parks are good for this. It is possible to enjoy RVing without the hassle of pulling a car behind you. It just takes a little ingenuity and planning."

RESOURCES

- **RV Consumer Group publishes *RV Rating Book*, also available in some libraries: *(RV.org)***
- **RVSEF for more information on RV weight and safety issues: *(RVSafety.org)***
- **Excellent article on RV construction at RV Buyers Guide: *(RVBG.com/Articles/?ID=2007793)***
- **Excellent resource for comparing RVs. Site includes free articles: *(JrConsumer.com)***
- **Links to clubs by RV brand name: *(RV-Clubs.US/RV-Clubs.html)***

NOTES

"A peacefulness follows any decision, even the wrong one." Rita Mae Brown

Chapter 13

Where would I buy an RV?

You have many options for buying an RV. Consider your prior automotive and RV knowledge if you are buying from a private party without a warranty. If you are inexperienced, be sure to have a knowledgeable friend or mechanic help you decide.

Betty Prange shares her experience.

> "Sometimes it helps to take along a friend who is an experienced RVer. That person is not making a decision for you, but he or she often knows the questions to ask and recognizes when the salesperson doesn't know the product. Since it is not a personal emotional experience for your friends (after all you are the one spending a lot of money and making a major decision), they can view the process calmly and rationally. As a single woman, I asked a friend to go along. I was glad he was there when the first dealership carrying the kind of motorhome I wanted was heavy handed in their sales approach. He gave me the perfect exit line. '*Let's go have lunch,*' he said. I later found a better dealer, a better price, and a better product."

You have many options for buying an RV.

OPTIONS FOR PURCHASE

Never buy at your first show.

RV Show. The biggest advantages are the variety available in one place and the added incentive of a special "show" price. Of course, those are the two biggest disadvantages as well. You can become overwhelmed by the sheer number of rigs and too pressured to make a hurried decision so you don't lose that fabulous, one-time only "show" price.

Never buy at your first show. Use it as an educational tool. Take clear notes or else it will all be a vague memory when you get home. However, if you've already done your homework and have a clear idea of what you want, you might get a great deal at the show. As of this writing, the RV industry is beginning to show growth again. Prices are down and good deals can be made (ONLY after you've done your homework so that you know you are really getting a good deal).

RV Mall. The same comments for RV shows apply to a mall. Particularly at the beginning of the process, it's a great place to learn about your options. You can be open with RV salespeople. They know RVers tend to buy several rigs over time. A good salesperson wants to build an ongoing relationship with you. They will be helpful if you don't monopolize their time pretending you are a serious buyer, ready to take the plunge today. Take a camera with you to help you remember particular rigs that you like. Be sure to have a notepad as well. After a while, the brand and model names and the dealer names get confusing due to the variety of rigs and dealers at a mall or an RV show.

Private Party. Buying through a private party—whether a friend or an advertiser in a newspaper, RV magazine, or Internet site—should only be done when you've completed your research and know what you want. Then you can get great buys. Don't buy sight unseen. If this great deal is far from home, it's worth the transportation to make sure it measures up to the ad. We've heard of too many disasters when friends have bought online without checking out the rig carefully first.

The key is your preparation.

HOW DO I PREPARE FOR THE SALES PROCESS?

If you have not had positive experiences dealing with car salespeople, you may find purchasing an RV an uncomfortable process at the beginning. Even if you had good experiences, working with RV salespeople is a bit different. The key is your preparation. First, become educated about the types of RVs, what your specific needs are, relative costs, and particular features of the RVs that match your needs. Second, understand the RV sales process to find just the right RV for you.

Become educated:

- **Refer to the analysis** you did in Chapters 10-12 to decide on the best RV for your needs. What features are critical to you? Once you know that, you can focus on the specific brands and models that have those features.
- **Determine your budget range.** Do the budget preparation in the next chapter (14) first.
- **Cheapest is not always the best.** The acceptable age and condition of the RV depends on your ability to remodel and repair. It may very well be cheaper in the long run to spend more money up front to have a more dependable RV and to purchase a long-term warranty.
- **Prepare a list of questions** to ask the salesperson about the features: weight capacity, payload, size of tanks, construction, insulation, etc.
- **Make a chart** to fill out as you gather your information so you can compare brands, models, features, and quoted prices using the criteria important to you. It's unusual to find everything

you want in one rig, but you want to come as close as you can, especially for those aspects that are non-negotiable for you.

➤ **Research the RV Consumer Group's rating systems.** They publish *RV Rating Book*, which is also available in some libraries. You will need to join the RV Consumer group to obtain it, but it is worth the fee to evaluate the differences among the brands you like. (See *RV.org)*

Understand the RV sales process.

➤ **Join discussion forums** on specific brands. *(RV-Clubs.US/RV-Clubs.html)*

➤ **For the many Canadians purchasing RVs in the USA, consider the following:**

★Ensure that the RV can be legally imported into Canada.

★Complete all appropriate forms. Often RV dealers have a good understanding and can supply these. See Registrar of Imported Vehicles. *(RIV.ca)*

Understand the RV Sales Process:

➤ **Build a relationship with the salesperson.** A good salesperson wants you as a long-term customer since RV owners tend to buy more than one RV over the years.

➤ **Speak with the sales manager first** to ask for a seasoned salesperson.

➤ **Set parameters:** Be clear about where you are in the sales process and indicate that at the beginning. Let the salesperson decide if this is a good time to spend with you when you are not yet at the buying stage.

➤ **Questions:** Good salespeople will want your repeat business plus the referrals you will make as a satisfied customer. Here are some questions they should be asking you to ensure you get the rig you need:

★What kind of trips will you be taking?

★How often will you travel?

★How far will you be going?

★Will you be staying in full-service campgrounds?

★Will you be living in it full-time?

★Have you had experience on the road?

★What is your budget range?

★Do you expect to keep it for a long period or change it out?

➤ **Test-drive:** Be sure to test-drive the vehicle. If it is a used vehicle, have it inspected by someone you trust.

➤ **Negotiate the price.** For a new vehicle, know the dealer's bottom line cost if possible, or at least other dealers' prices. Negotiate a percentage over their cost. For a used vehicle, become familiar with the wholesale and retail blue book suggested prices. Have a clear idea in your mind what your bottom line price is. If you are educated, you can be assertive about what you want. Do not let them pressure you with statements like "This offer is only good until today at 8 pm." See Resources at the end of this chapter for pricing information.

Do not make any major purchases until you have thought about it for 24 hours.

➤ **Follow the 24-hour rule:** Do not make any major purchases until you have thought about it for 24 hours. **Betty Prange** adds: "Sales people will try to tell you the deal may be off the next day. Baloney. Take your time. Chances are the RV you are looking at has been on the lot for weeks, maybe months. It's still going to be available."

Sharon E. Runyon, solo RVer and former president of Wandering Individuals' Network (WIN), reiterates our advice.

"The place to decide what kind of rig you want is at RV shows and campgrounds, NOT the sales lot. Make sure you've done your research prior to going to a dealer. When you get to the buying stage, you should know what you want and how much you will spend. And don't rely on the salesperson to assure you, for example, that the GVWR is not a problem. Check it out independently."

Bob and Ginny Odell discovered that their one-year-old grandson was a great sales tool when they bought their RV.

"Good friends wanted us to get an RV because we were retiring. Bob and I talked with them and looked at a few RVs. We knew nothing really and had never had one. On April 1, 1988, we headed for Scotts Valley (near Santa Cruz, California) to look at what a dealer there had. We were shown everything and continued to feel very vague. At noon we needed to leave to pick up Kevin, our one-year-old grandson. As we left the salesman said, 'Bring him back for a hot dog or a hamburger. We're about to begin the barbecue.'

Understand the RV sales process to find just the right RV for you.

"We three went back and enjoyed the hamburgers and then looked some more. Kevin was a doll. He smiled at everyone and enjoyed all the attention as he rode around in his stroller. There was one rig I really liked. Bob did too. The salesman took us for a ride in that rig along with Kevin and his car seat. He immediately went to sleep.

"We had a great ride. Back at the showroom two more salesmen took turns trying to close the deal. We did like the rig. We were feeling that we had just come to look. The offers of add-ons piled up. By mid-afternoon they would give us a set of special RV dishes, special RV sheets, four chairs, a pod for the top, an awning, and a hitch, but they would not lower the price.

"We could not believe that we drove back to our daughter's with a new 1988 26-foot Minnie Winnie. Kevin was tickled. We were shocked. Our engineer son-in-law could not believe that we bought it without further investigation. We have loved it. We have traveled in it for twenty years—many trips to Mexico, Canada and the East Coast. We tell Kevin it is all his fault that we bought it. If he had just misbehaved we would have had to leave with no RV. He laughs about that to this day."

Take your time. Do your research and choose wisely.

Remember, you are investing a lot of money. If you will be a full-time RVer, this is your only "house." Take your time. Do your research and choose wisely.

RESOURCES

- **RV Consumer Group. Independent group that rates all models. Fee to join: *(RV.org)***
- **JRConsumer.com– Rating guides, articles. Fee: *(JRConsumer.com)***
- **RV Safety Education Foundation (RVSEF). Excellent training in safety issues including overweight vehicles, tire safety, fire, propane, etc: *(RVSafety.org)***
- **RV Finder– Will give comparative prices: *(RV-Finder.com)***
- **RV Buyers' Guide: *(RVBG.com)***
- **NADA RV Pricing: *(NadaGuides.com)***
- **For used tow vehicles and rigs, buy the latest copy of your local magazines– *RV Trader* and *Truck Trader* or go online: *(RVTraderOnline.com)***
- **Recreational Vehicles Dealers Association: *(RVDA.org)***
- **RVIA (Recreational Vehicle Industry Association): *(RVIA.org)***
- **Do Internet searches for "new RVer" and "choose an RV" for links to many sites with more information on how to choose.**
- **For Canadians purchasing RVs in the USA, see Registrar of Imported Vehicles: *(RIV.ca)***

Section III: THE BOTTOM LINE—MONEY

Chapter 14

Can I afford the RV lifestyle?

The Budget! Yes, you have to do this step. But you'll be pleasantly surprised. The RV lifestyle is generally less expensive than living in a stix 'n brix house or apartment. This is especially true if do not have an RV payment, as we'll see.

YOUR RV BUDGET

Consider the amount that you spend now in each category. You'll discover that your expenses will be greatly reduced and you will have a good chance of living on your retirement income. You won't have to allow for work clothing, commuting, or restaurant lunch expenses. Living in an RV reduces your energy expenses: less electricity, gas, and water. Your reduced space limits the number of "things" you can buy.

The RV lifestyle is generally less expensive than living in a stix 'n brix house or apartment.

On the other hand, you will have to include RV-related expenses you didn't have before. We recommend you complete the budget worksheet at the end of this chapter. If you want a more detailed budget worksheet, see the Resources at the end of this chapter for a link to one at *(RVLifestyleExperts.com)*.

WHAT OTHERS SPEND

In a survey taken at our ezine (electronic magazine), *RV Lifestyle Ezine*, in 2010, sixty-five percent of full-timers live on less than $2000 a month. An additional seven percent spend between $2000 and $2499 a month and 72 per cent spend under $2500 per month. The cost of fuel along with the overall cost of living continues to rise. This could boost the amounts a little today.

When revising *Support Your RV Lifestyle! An Insider's Guide to Working on the Road*, Jaimie asked for some RVers to submit their budget. The six budgets included in the 3rd edition range from a low of $1,098 per month for a solo who received a free RV site where she Workamped, to a high of $5,046 per month. This last couple had an RV payment of $2,765 per month. The other couples, who had no RV payment, had monthly totals of $1,653, $1,703, $2,505, and $3,168.

You can plan your travels to minimize expenses.

Juanita Ruth One plans her travels to minimize expenses. For major trips, she takes along a companion who shares the expenses. This is how she does it.

> "My initial retirement into a Class C included a goal of extensive travel while returning to travel writing. However, the rapid increase in gas prices dampened the idea of constantly being on the go.
>
> "I've found that I divide my time in fourths. Some is spent in Charleston, West Virginia, where my 93-year-old mother lives with my brother and sister-in-law, while I cover her care to give them time to travel. Sometimes my RV is parked in my daughter's country yard outside of Lexington, Virginia, serving as a 'mother-in-law' cottage. Becoming a 'Workamper' allows me to choose two to three month assignments in de-

sirable locations, exchanging twelve to fifteen hours of work per week for a pleasant RV site plus amenities.

"I have also made some lengthy trips, always with a traveling companion sharing the expenses. My cousin and I toured Nova Scotia, my daughter and I spent January in Florida, and I took my mom to Louisiana for a summer family reunion. My developed routine included breakfast and dinner in the RV and lunches at inexpensive local restaurants as we toured. (Lunch prices are always less than dinners.) Keeping careful records, I totaled the cost of gas, tolls, ferries, campgrounds (with various discount programs), groceries, eating out, and admissions for sightseeing. Each trip included one-night free parking at a Walmart, Flying-J or a friend's driveway.

"In each case, I found that the TOTAL expenses for each trip averaged between $50 and $55 per day per person. You can't travel any cheaper than that!"

The RV lifestyle allows you to both reduce your expenses and add to your income.

GOOD NEWS FOR RVERS!

The good news for RVers is that spending can be much more flexible than in your former life. You have control of many items that will impact your costs. You have many options. Particularly in today's economy with reduced savings income, you can easily economize. The RV lifestyle allows you to both reduce your expenses and add to your income. In this chapter we'll look at controlling expenses. In Chapter 15: "What if I can't afford it?" we'll discuss ways to add to your income.

CONTROLLING EXPENSES:

Travel less. When people first start out, they think they have to see the whole country in one year. They are still operating on the two-week vacation syndrome, except now they have fifty weeks. Phew!

It's exhausting to travel that way, plus it's expensive. Take your time, stay in each area longer, take advantage of weekly or monthly campground rates, and lower your fuel bill considerably.

Eat at home: You have a stove, refrigerator, and cupboards in the RV. Use them. You can eat more simply. Then when you do go out, it's a real treat.

Volunteer: Spend some time volunteering at various local, national or private parks or places of interest. Although not paid, you will often be given a free campsite sometimes with hook-ups. (See Chapter 16: "How do I volunteer?")

Lower camping fees: In addition to volunteering, see Chapter 7: "Where will I go?" for ways to reduce your camping expense. **Kimberly and Jerry Peterson** explain how they have economized on camping.

> "We are determined not to allow rising gas prices to stop us from what we enjoy doing the most, and that is traveling. So we have learned to change other things, like where we camp. Boondocking has become much more comfortable for us, especially because we do it every time we are at a racetrack and learn something more to enhance our experience every time. We rarely stay at a Walmart, only because our dozen or so attempts ended badly. Carrying several discount camping memberships help for camping discounts. We stay at casinos as often as possible; even the parks at casinos are much less expensive than other campgrounds. Combining all of these help lower our camping expenses so that we have more to spend on gas to travel those roads less traveled that we enjoy tremendously."

Reducing expenses in some areas can allow you to do what you enjoy doing most.

Larry and Adrienne Brauer also have a handle on how much they spend on camping.

> "Costs for being on the road have gone up, but staying in one place for longer periods of time and cutting back on driving distances can significantly reduce expenses. We've never liked driving more than about 200 miles in one day. Generally we stay in RV parks but we do use our Good Sam discounts, Passport America parks, and Escapees parks to save fees. We have never had any issue where we felt our safety was threatened. Although we have never stayed in a Walmart parking lot, that's not to say we won't. Of course, we will ask permission."

Toys: Using a pre-paid cell phone plan or watching local instead of satellite TV can reduce these expenses.

Insurance and other fees: Your choice of domicile will impact how much your taxes, insurance and vehicle registration cost. (See Chapter 17: "How do I choose my domicile?")

Darlene Miller explains how she and her husband, Terry, can make adjustments to their budget to keep their expenses low.

> **"We do not pay much to heat our RV in winter or cool it off in summer."**

> "With the price of fuel so high, many people ask, *'Why are you RVing?'* When they learn that Terry and I have lived full-time in an RV for eleven years, some raise their eyebrows in astonishment and say, *'You must be crazy.'* Other people shake their heads negatively and say, *'It must be impractical or even immoral to drive that huge bus-type RV.'* A few people look wistful and whisper, *'You are living my dream but I can't afford it.'* Yes, fuel costs are high but during the scorching summer days in Arizona, we live in Alaska. When it is cold and dark in Alaska, we sunbathe by the pool in the temperate winter of Arizona. We do not pay much to heat our RV in winter or cool it off in summer.

"In fact, we spend ten to twelve weeks each winter boondocking on free BLM (Bureau of Land Management) sites in Arizona and California. Boondocking means that we aren't connected to electricity or water or sewer. We use six solar panels on our RV roof connecting to batteries that transfer energy to the inverter/converter to produce electricity for appliances, TV, and the computer. The chest freezer and all our lights are 12-volt so the energy goes direct from the batteries to the freezer and the light fixtures. The two satellite dishes bring the TV and computer signals to us.

"We have learned to use the free solar power conservatively.

"Our refrigerator and hot water heater switch to propane from electricity while our stove is always on propane. We have learned to use the free solar power conservatively and don't plug in the hair dryer, the coffee pot, toaster and microwave at the same time. If it rains for a week, we use the generator. The BLM rules say that you are only allowed to stay for fourteen days. That's okay, because after two weeks, it's necessary to get fresh water and dump your tanks at a campground, rest stop or fuel station.

"Yes, life has changed a little since fuel prices became so high. We stay longer in each location. We use the 'green toad' (our towed Suzuki) more often because it gets better mileage. Terry runs a computer program on the laptop on the dash of our RV, to show how many miles per gallon we are getting. (I love it when we are going down a mountain and the screen says that we are getting 256 mpg!) By slightly adjusting the fuel pedal and not re-accelerating until the crest of the hill, he increases our mileage. Terry has always checked our tires to be sure that our tire pressures have proper inflation levels for optimal mileage. Now he has a gauge, which alarms if the tire pressure changes. If there is a headwind, we wait a day or two for the next trip. Terry uses the computer to check online for fuel prices.

"When we review our total energy expenses for electricity, heating and cooling in a stick-built house plus gasoline for our car and compare it to our energy costs in our RV and green toad, we use less energy in our present lifestyle.

"Terry and I will continue to RV. It is our lifestyle. We feel that our RV gives us the freedom to live fully as we explore the world around us."

Peggi McDonald, RV author, writes about the impact of the economy and how RVers are still finding ways to RV. The "staycation" is one way. The tips that occasional or part-time RVers would use can also apply to snowbirds and to full-time Rvers.

"Times are changing for all of us RVers. Costs of everything seem to be rising at each turn. But we RVers simply love to take off in our RVs, so giving up the lifestyle is not really an option. Loading up to embark on a short or maybe a longer getaway to enjoy a freedom adventure can be exciting—unlike few other forms of travel. Yes, with the increases in gas and fuel you might be discouraged from traveling cross-country, but RVers still come up with an abundance of creative ways to continue RVing without breaking the budget.

Loading up to embark on a getaway to enjoy a freedom adventure can be exciting.

"A new term surfaced this summer—'Staycationer.' Going on a vacation translates as vacating your home, but a staycation escape translates as you stay in one spot while you enjoy your RV outing. The two main pleasures of vacationing are to take a break from work and to hang out with the family. An RV Staycation satisfies these needs plus it cuts fuel costs. Look for a park close to home, and make plans for a real vacation—not just a makeshift, no-money-available substitute. Activities such as a bus trip, a city tour, or a day at the beach may help you stay within budget, but the Staycation adventure should be less than most getaways due to limited traveling.

Staycation—stay in one spot while you enjoy your RV outing.

"Your perfect summer holiday may include swimming in clear blue water at the beach or the park pool. Adding a round of golf, tennis, or biking the local trails adds to the experience. Eating some meals out is fun, but so are barbecued/picnic style feasts. Entertainment can vary from park entertainment, to a community concert under the stars, taking in a ball game with fireworks, or even a museum or show garden visit. Pick up the local travel guide to check out the many local attractions you may have forgotten about, or never knew existed. Take time to explore places you don't usually have time for.

"With a few simple modifications to your travel plans, it is not too difficult to find a way to enjoy the amazing, contagious life experiences we find in our RVs that we love.

"Numerous snowbirds, especially full-timer RVers like John and me, usually book a summer season in a park near family or friends. We generally look for a place near our doctors, dentists and vets etc. Seasonal camping rates cost much less than daily or weekend rates plus there will be no added gas/fuel costs.

"Fellow full-time RVers and good friends Norm and Linda Payne *(Seeya-DownTheRoad.com)* offer this suggestion on their website for extensive RV travelers who want a change of 'backyard'—to stretch dollars, travel slowly and stay in an area longer. Why not drive 100 miles and stay a week, then drive 100 more and stay another week? During winters, consider spending several months in one spot in the sunny south, and gravitate north in the summer for several more in one park. Ignore the price of gas/fuel since there's no way we RVers can change it, but we can control the cost of our RV travel. We alone can decide how we spend our cash

"With a little creativity, we can continue to enjoy the pleasures of the RV lifestyle."

"Take a long look at all options. With a little creativity, we can continue to enjoy the pleasures of the RV lifestyle."

RESOURCES

- **Budget worksheet– see page 154. For a more detailed budget worksheet, see: *(RVLifestyleExperts.com/pdfs/Budget_Worksheet.pdf)***
- **For more articles on budgeting, see "RV Retirement Basics" section at: *(RVLifestyleExperts.com)***
- **Chapter 3, "How Much Money Will You Need?" in *Support Your RV Lifestyle! An Insider's Guide to Working on the Road*. Pine Country Publishing, see: *(RVLifestyleExperts.com/RV-Books/Books-for-Working-on-the-Road/Support-Your-RV-Lifestyle)***

DEVELOP A BUDGET FOR LIFE ON THE ROAD

A budget is essential for knowing how much money you require. This will give you an idea of what you can afford and whether you need to reduce expenses or generate more income. Figure your expenses per month, then multiply the total by 12 to get the yearly amount.

	Now	Full-timing
➤ RV payment/housing	$	$
➤ Food, including restaurants	$	$
➤ Health		
★ Medical insurance	$	$
★ Other medical expenses	$	$
➤ Camping Fees		
★ Membership parks & campground fees	$	$
➤ Transportation		
★ Fuel	$	$
★ Insurance, incl. towing	$	$
★ License & reg.	$	$
★ Maintenance	$	$
➤ Communication		
★ Telephone and Internet	$	$
★ Mail service	$	$
➤ Other		
★ Clothing	$	$
★ Gifts	$	$
★ Laundry	$	$
★ Life insurance	$	$
★ Memberships- clubs	$	$
★ Federal/state taxes	$	$
★ Propane	$	$
★ TV/satellite	$	$
★ Misc.	$	$
Total	$	$
Annual Total	x 12=______/yr	x12=_____ /yr

NOTES: See Chapter 17 on Domicile for RV insurance companies. You can get a ballpark estimate by getting a Quick Quote from these sites.

"Stop worrying about the potholes in the road and celebrate the journey."
Fitzhugh Mullan

Chapter 15
What if I can't afford it?

We looked at ways you can control your RV budget in the last chapter. In this chapter we look at increasing your income.

There are hundreds of ways RVers can add to their income.

ADD TO YOUR INCOME

There are hundreds of ways RVers can add to their income. Working on the road, or Workamping®, as it is often called, can take many different forms. **Barbara Bowers** wonders if they'd be Workampers and full-time RVers, and decides they are.

"I am a full-timer. Sort of. I am a Workamper®. Sort of. Why 'sort of?' My husband and I have lived exclusively in our fifth-wheel trailer since May 14, 2006. We also work full-time, E.K. at the same place he has been for more than a dozen years.

"The term 'full-timer' has nearly as many definitions as there are people who claim the lifestyle. The thing they all have in common is that a full-timer is someone who lives in an RV all of the time. *Workamper News* defines Workampers as 'adventuresome individuals, couples and families who have chosen a wonderful lifestyle that combines ANY kind of part-time or full-time work with RV camping. If you work as an employee, AND you sleep in an RV, you are a Workamper!'

> Based on these definitions, we are both full-timers and Workampers, although many in the RV lifestyle might disagree.
>
> "Because our home is a classic recreational vehicle, we do not often travel in it (we have stayed in only five different campgrounds). We choose instead to attend rallies in a tent. It is amazing the number of people one meets when sleeping in a fabric house surrounded by 1000 recreational vehicles.
>
> "As a person with three college degrees and former careers in management, I do not believe that we are 'trailer trash,' but I am sure there are people who would look at our housing situation and disagree. The difference is heart. Our hearts are in the RVing community. We are never more complete than when we are with other Escapees and would not trade in the RV lifestyle for any amount of money.
>
> "So, are we full-timers? Are we Workampers? Decide for yourself. For now, I will call us that rare breed called a 'sort of.'"

Many opportunities are available to you as a Workamper.

If you are a Workamper, many opportunities are available to you. You can often apply your skills from your avocations as well as your vocations. Or you can learn new skills. Employers like to hire more mature workers for part-time or seasonal work to take advantage of their reliability and sense of responsibility. If you are at all interested in making money on the road, you must read *Support Your RV Lifestyle! An Insider's Guide to Working on the Road* (see Resources at the end of this chapter). It will help prepare you to find the jobs and apply for them.

Canadians are restricted from working in the United States (and vice versa). A Canadian will need a green card to work as an employee. You could have your own business and some volunteer opportunities are open to Canadians. Canadians sometimes work out an exchange of labor for an RV site too. Check to see what income tax issues could affect you.

EMPLOYMENT OPPORTUNITIES

Workampers often choose these types of employers:

RV parks, campgrounds and resorts: These jobs are good choices for RVers because an onsite RV site is usually provided. Sometimes the Workamper pays nothing for the site; sometimes they work a certain number of hours per week for their site. Other perks may also be included such as free or discounted laundry, propane, store or food purchases, WiFi and others. Often area businesses will provide complimentary tickets to their attractions so workers can tell guests about their attraction.

You can work in beautiful places and get a free or low cost RV site.

State and national agencies: State and national parks and forests, Army Corps of Engineers, wildlife refuges and other government agencies hire RVers or use RVers as volunteers. You work in beautiful places and usually get a free or low-cost RV site.

Concessionaires: In many national parks and forests, concessionaires operate the campgrounds and services offered within the boundaries. In a national park like Yellowstone or the Grand Canyon, concessionaires hire hundreds of workers for stores, campgrounds, gas stations, hotels, restaurants and other services. National forests often contract the operation of their campgrounds out to concessionaires. You usually have an RV site or housing there and also get to work in a beautiful area.

Temporary jobs and special events: Companies often contract with agencies when they need workers for short periods of time. Though an RV site is not usually included, this can fit an RVer's travel schedule. If you have a skill, more lucrative short-term assignments can be found in your specialty. Nurses, tax preparers and other skilled workers can take advantage of these jobs. You might also find opportunities at events like NASCAR, spring training, state or county fairs, golf tournaments and other special events.

Brooks Rimes has found contract computer work on the road. He was able to use his prior background and training to find well-paying assignments in his travels. While he and his wife are not retired, the RV lifestyle allows them to combine travel and earning an income.

> **You can use your prior background and training to find well-paying jobs in your travels.**

"I received an early start in computer programming when I was 17 years old in 1970. My high school (H.C. Technical H.S. in Buffalo, NY) was the first, or one of the first in the country, to have an IBM mini-computer. FORTRAN, a scientific language, was the first I learned and later used at my entry-level computer job at the gas utility in Buffalo. My second language was COBOL, used for business, and I worked on IBM mainframes at several large companies including Electronic Data Systems (EDS), run by Ross Perot at the time.

"In 1989, I became a self-employed consultant, moved to the client server platform and learned Microsoft Visual BASIC and Access, the desktop database. After study and exams, Microsoft awarded me Certified Professional status. A year or two later I became a certified trainer and traveled the East Coast teaching several hundred students to program in Visual BASIC and Access. Following the teaching, I concentrated on solving customer business needs with Access database systems.

"In 2004, we started full-timing. With today's connectivity, computer work can be done almost anywhere. I traded my desktop computer in for a laptop. I use a Sprint aircard to connect at EVDO data rates, which approaches cable modem speed. I can exchange emails with customers and send them finished projects as email attachments. I also speak to customers by phone when needed and sometimes have meetings when in their area. I use Quickbooks for accounting and a great little program called TraxTime to keep track of the hours I work.

"This summer I had more projects than usual, including an asset rotation program for a certified financial planner, a contractor requisition system for a major bank, a project tracking system for a construction estimating firm, a retiree medical benefits application for a county government, a laboratory reporting program for an engineering company and did some IT management consulting for a guardianship agency.

"At 55, I'm not really retired, I just changed my residence from a house to a motorhome."

"Access is a part of Microsoft Office and is included with the Professional edition of Office, but my customers do not need to own Access to use the programs I create.

"At 55, I'm not really retired; I just changed my residence from a house to a motorhome. My wife, Brenda, and I enjoy traveling the USA and being in warmer, southern states during the winter. We are up to 42 states visited and plan to see them all."

The experiences that **Joanne Alexakis and her husband, Nick,** have had show the great variety of jobs RVers can find.

> **"We've had lots of work opporunities and lots of traveling experiences, all in our RV."**

"Nick and I started full-time RVing in April 1994 and wholeheartedly enjoy this gypsy lifestyle. We have worked seasonally at state parks in Minnesota and South Dakota. We have been assistant managers at a New Mexico RV park. We have been parked on construction sites in Texas, Arizona and California, acting as 24-hour security. Nick assisted in building fiber optic networks in Illinois, Michigan, North Carolina, Georgia, Colorado, and from Florida to Texas, moving from work site to work site in our fifth wheel. Our German Shepherd dog and I traveled along, of course. We've had lots of work opportunities and lots of traveling experiences, all in our RV."

John and Kay Hasty have worked in customer service jobs, both for government agencies and businesses that cater to tourists. For them, Workamping is how they live the RV lifestyle.

"Workamping has defined our lives for 12 years. Being seasonal Workampers has enabled our full-timing lifestyle. Part of 'who I am' is 'a Workamper.'

"All of our experiences have been in customer service, with working at the front desk and continental breakfast in seasonal hotels being among our favorites. Working as assistant innkeepers at a B&B was a lot of fun, too.

"We've experienced several disappointments by going to jobs where the work description was changed after our arrival. Sadly, when this couldn't be reconciled, we've had to give our notice and move on.

"Most of our exciting and interesting experiences as full-time RVers have been on jobs! On a job at the gatehouse of a large forest service campground we often had to direct emergency vehicles into the campground. Memorial Day weekend there was a houseboat fire in a cove adjacent to the campground. We could see the explosion from the gatehouse. We directed emergency vehicles down a dirt road to access this cove. Luckily, there were no serious injuries.

"At our job at the B&B, we had many international guests. Part of our job was to visit with and give information to these guests. We learned a lot from these people about their home countries. One young couple wanted to have dinner at a nice restaurant, but he didn't bring a jacket and tie. They were surprised and delighted that my husband was happy to let him wear the jacket and tie out of his wardrobe. Providing this USA hospitality was rewarding for us."

Decide what you want out of Workamping.

HOW TO GET STARTED

Here are five steps to get started finding jobs to add to your income.

1. **Set goals:** Decide what you want out of Workamping. Some people want to earn a certain amount of money. Others want to try something new, like work at Disney World. Still others want to be in a certain part of the country to be near relatives or explore the area.
2. **Get information:** We recommend a subscription to *Workamper News*. This publication comes out every two months and has advertisements for hundreds of jobs in each issue, plus informative articles. Their online bookstore has a number of books on the subject. Participate in forums on working on the road. Workamper, Escapees and *(RV.net)* have forums on working on the road.

3. **Prepare your resume**: Prepare a one-page resume, focusing on the skills that a seasonal employer would need. Even without Workamping experience, you have undoubtedly worked with people, dealt with customers, handled money or done maintenance. Include any work experience that applies, as well as community work and hobbies. For example, if you have maintained your home, you have used a number of maintenance skills you would need in an RV park.
4. **Find job openings:** Besides *Workamper News*, other sources of potential jobs include *Caretaker Gazette* and *(Coolworks.com)*. Campground directories list potential employers. Temporary agencies have all types of work from general to professional. Specialized directories can help you find venues like fairs or flea markets to sell products. To work in a certain area, check with the Chamber of Commerce or Tourist Bureau for employers. Most RV magazines have help wanted ads in their classified sections. Other Workampers are also good sources of job openings.

Ask a lot of questions since your interview is usually by phone.

Betty Prange adds her experiences.

> "If you have a specific geographic area in mind, use the Web to do your research. Many tourist areas, major parks, etc., have websites. Check the homepages and look for a listing for jobs. I've found a couple of jobs that way. As a solo, I have had better luck with that than *Workamper News*, which has more ads for couples."

5. **Apply to many jobs:** The more employers you interview, the more you'll learn about Workamping. It is important to ask a lot of questions since your interview is usually by phone and you may have never seen the location. Besides questions about job duties and compensation, you'll want to find out about the RV space, what's in the area, availability of cell and satellite

signals, etc. Some employers offer perks such as free or discounted propane, store discounts or tickets to area attractions. If you only apply to one or two jobs and they don't work out, you'll be left with nothing. If you apply to 15-20 jobs, you're more likely to end up with two or more job offers.

PUTTING IT INTO PRACTICE

Dick and Rhonda Salerno explain how they have found their jobs:

"We subscribed to *Workamper News* a few months before we hit the road in August 2005. In July, we put our resume online on the Workamper site and within two days received our first offer. After a telephone interview, we accepted the job at a commercial RV park. The next month, before we'd even arrived at our first job, we received two more offers: one for a state park in early spring 2006 and another for the summer season. A flood wiped out the state park gig and in January 2006, we backed out of the other gig, taking a position instead at a BLM day-use park.

"*Workamper News* has been our main source for jobs. At first we felt like kids in a candy shop as our resume resulted in many tempting job offers. So far, only our first gig came from a solicitation from the employer. The rest we've researched and applied for ourselves. Most of our leads come from *Workamper News*. The Forest Service position was obtained by cold-calling the volunteer director. It was a park we'd visited a few times and really liked.

"It's easy to get a job, but a bit harder to get a good job."

"Our experience has been that it's easy to get a job, but a bit harder (but not too hard) to get a good job. About eighteen months ago, we actually changed our online resume to discourage employers from calling us because we are getting pickier about the kind of work we want to do and where we want to be and for how long.

"Now we decide what part of the country we want to be in and then start researching jobs. In the future we may just decide on a particular area and, once there, use our resources to find work.

"We like to use email to tie down job duties, hours, etc. That way we have a written record of what was said and expected. A few times we've signed contracts. We had one situation where after several email exchanges, we were sent a contract that contained duties that hadn't been discussed through the email. We declined that job offer!

"All of our experiences have had both advantages and disadvantages to them. We've never had a really awful experience. Rhonda is particularly good at compartmentalizing the negative stuff and dwelling on the positives.

"When we began our adventure, we were impressed (and shocked) that many people (RVers and employers) planned more than a year in advance. We applied at one park in November for the following summer and were told that all positions had been filled. That got us thinking ahead, planning where we wanted to be a year in advance. But now we're less concerned about having our lives planned out that far in advance. Our most recent summer job was applied for about two months before we started work. With more than three years under our belt now, we don't feel quite as anxious about having a job (and we're grateful that we don't need to work for pay or site exchange). Our main concern is to be in a place that's fun to explore, where we are doing

"We like to use email to tie down job duties, hours, etc."

something interesting, learning new skills and meeting new friends and interesting people."

The interview is the most important part of the process.

BEFORE TAKING THAT POSITION

The interview is the most important part of the process. You are not only selling yourself as the best candidate for the job, but you must also find out all about the employer and the job. Most interviews are done via the telephone or Skype, since you will want to line up a job before traveling a great distance to work there. These are a few of the things you should find out, plus add any specific concerns or questions you have:

- **Duties:** get as specific as you can so you are clear on expectations.
- **Hours and length of season:** if a bonus is involved, clarify exactly how it is achieved.
- **Compensation:** if you are working some hours for your site, make sure it is a fair amount and clarify pay for additional hours.
- **RV site:** Will your RV fit? Will you have cell phone and satellite TV reception or WiFi in your site? 30- or 50-amp service? Sewage disposal at the site?

If possible, talk to other Workampers who have worked there before or, if you are a subscriber to *Workamper News*, you can check the Workamper Experiences forum for reports on that employer. You may also need to set limits when you are working. **Fran Vogt** and her husband found out after they were hired that more was expected of them than they had thought when they accepted.

> "My husband and I trained for a month to be Workampers in Livingston, Texas, at Rainbow's End. The person responsible for the training had been there for years. In addition to the training, she had us 'volunteering' to do things like straighten up the product inventory shelves, sand and paint benches, and do other work that we didn't consider training. Com-

munication was not the best, and information given to one group did not always get to the next since we worked in shifts on different days. Nevertheless, we passed the muster and were given an assignment at The Plantation, an Escapees park in Summerville, Alabama.

"In Alabama, we worked with excellent managers, enjoyed all of the sights in the area, and made more good friends. But, as in the training, we were required to volunteer additional hours that did not count as part of the time we had agreed to work, doing jobs that should have been done by paid staff. This company was started as a 'mom and pop' operation depending on volunteers to do much of their work. Unfortunately, it still runs on that premise in our experience.

"I look back on our training and two months of Workamping as good experiences and I'm glad we tried it."

"I look back on our training and two months of Workamping as good experiences and I'm glad we tried it. We did not take another assignment after that first one. We love hearing from and seeing some of our fellow trainees and friends that we met in Alabama.

"My feelings about it are mixed. I really don't have any other Workamping experiences to compare, since that is my only one. I had both positive and negative feelings about the job and am thankful for the experience though I would not want to work for them again."

MORE EXPERIENCES

Dick and Rhonda have had a variety of assignments. Part of their concern in choosing assignments was taxes. When they worked for their first employer, they did an exchange. The second job was outside an RV park.

> "Before hitting the road full-time, Rhonda and I decided that to live as frugally as possible we'd try to swap work for an RV site. We knew that it made more economic sense to work a paying job and pay for our own site but we both were retired, planned to do a lot of traveling and didn't want to get involved in the hassle of multiple tax returns each year.
>
> "Our first gig was at a commercial RV park. For working six hours per week (each), we received a free site. Recently, we worked part-time at a gift store in a resort town unconnected with an RV park. We had to get our own site accommodations and pay a monthly rent.

"It took us about a week and a half of work to earn enough to pay our monthly rent."

> "It took us about a week and a half of work to earn enough to pay our monthly rent. The job was interesting and—like all the other work we've done since hitting the road—we've learned some new skills and have been able to explore a new area of the country.
>
> "Before we accepted our first paying job, we got a written response from the state tax authority clarifying our situation. We both receive pensions, which are not taxed by the state in which we have residence and we don't want them taxed in another state because we earned income there. The state tax authority assured us in writing that our pensions would not be taxed and so that was a big relief."

Note: If you work in a state that has state income taxes, you will pay income tax on that money earned. See Chapter 17: "How do I choose my domicile?" for more information.

Betty Prange not only works on the road for money or an RV site, she has found a new calling. She loves what she does! Here is her story.

> "I was in my mid-50s when I found my true vocation. Don't get me wrong. I didn't go back to school, start a new career, and devote all my waking hours to it. I found something, facilitated by being a full-time RVer.
>
> "Some kids knew at an early age what they wanted to be when they grew up. By high school many had clear career plans. Not me. I fell into things, taking classes that interested me without goals in mind. Eventually those classes shaped themselves into a career, which was fine and gratifying. But 'fine' is a word that lacks excitement.
>
> "I was on a leisurely fall trip with RV friends along Highway 395, where the Sierra Nevada Mountains meet the high desert of eastern California and Nevada, when I suggested a detour to Bodie. Kept in a 'state of arrested decay' by the California State Parks Department, Bodie is a gold and silver mining ghost town, set in a treeless, high desert bowl with views toward the Sierras. Its weathered buildings, rusted cars, and mining equipment are ideal photographic subjects. My late husband and I, avid photographers, had visited many times. I always wished I could stay overnight, be there for dawn and dusk lighting, and see it covered in snow. But the park is day-use only.

"I found something, facilitated by being a full-time RVer."

> "On this visit, I spied my chance. A flier announced openings for Seasonal Park Aides for the next season. I applied and was hired. I was to spend three seasons living and working in Bodie.
>
> "In preparation for giving history talks and walking tours of the stamp mill (where equipment crushed the ore to extract

the gold and silver), I was sent to a superb workshop on interpretive skills led by the park ranger at nearby Mono Lake.

"Photographing in dawn and dusk lighting came to pass. So did photographing the buildings in heavy snow. I was allowed to enter buildings where the public never goes. I saw my first badger, watched coyotes grow from clumsy pups to experienced hunters, and reveled in electrical storms. Several of my photographs appeared in Bodie calendars. But most of all, I discovered I loved sharing what I had learned about this place with visitors.

> **"Eventually wanderlust caught up with me and the time came to look for another interpretive opportunity."**

"Eventually wanderlust caught up with me and the time came to look for other interpretive opportunities. For six weeks I volunteered at Heceta Lighthouse in Oregon. Then, behind the wheel of a vintage red 'Jammer' bus in Glacier National Park, I drove the narrow, winding, spectacular Going to the Sun Road, took visitors to Waterton National Park in Canada, and through the Blackfeet Reservation narrating as we traveled and at stops on the way. Next, I applied to drive Yellowstone's recently refurbished, yellow, vintage, White Motor Company touring buses.

"Xanterra, my employer, provided a full month's training, including a 32-hour National Association for Interpretation certification class. Serious about their training, the transportation department did a daylong evaluation of my skills.

"Each workday I saw wildlife, wildflowers, superb scenery, and geothermal features. I learned about and explained geology, fire ecology, wildlife habits, and the area's human history. I met people from diverse backgrounds and made friends among the staff. In addition to Yellowstone National Park I drove visitors to Grand Teton National Park and Beartooth Mountains. I was thrilled to answer questions about my assigned classic 1936 bus.

"Yellowstone is a big place and it may be several seasons before wanderlust sends me to a new interpretive job. There are plenty of paid jobs (to fun overseas adventures) and volunteer positions with RV space to keep me happy for years to come.

"I would not have considered these jobs when I had a full-time career. As an RVer, the logistics of accepting seasonal jobs are easy. This lifestyle has provided a time to experiment, try new things, and in my case, find a new vocation as an interpretive guide."

RESOURCES

- ***Support Your RV Lifestyle! An Insider's Guide to Working on the Road*** **by Jaimie Hall Bruzenak. It includes how-to's, legal issues and more than 350 opportunities for jobs, volunteer assignments and for your own business on the road. See: (*RVLifestyleExperts.com*)**
- ***Workamper News.*** **Find links to Workamper Store and forums: *(Workamper.com)***
- **Coolworks: *(Coolworks.com)***
- ***Caretaker Gazette: (Caretaker.org)***
- **See articles on working with more information on how to find a job: *(RVLifestyleExperts.com)***

"Spend the afternoon. You can't take it with you." Annie Dillard

Chapter 16

How do I volunteer?

Many opportunities exist for people who want to volunteer, and you will usually save money by having a free or inexpensive site. Since you'll be in one place for a while, you'll save money on fuel. You might also be invited as a guest to places of interest nearby.

In addition, you'll experience the joy of sharing your time and knowledge with others. One additional benefit: the camaraderie among the volunteers often provides deep and lasting friendships.

Many opportunities exist for people who want to volunteer.

VOLUNTEER OPPORTUNITIES

Here are just a few volunteer opportunities.

- **Habitat for Humanity.** Promoted by former president Jimmy Carter when he volunteered for them, the organization has helped numerous families gain low-cost housing. Volunteers (and the recipients) literally build the housing. Men and women participate and learn the skills as they work. RV-Care-A-Vanners is the sub-group just for mobile volunteers.
- **US Fish and Wildlife Service.** Imagine being in a beautiful environment AND doing service to maintain it for current and future visitors.

- **National Parks VIPs.** VIP stands for Volunteers in Parks. A volunteer can do almost any job except law enforcement.
- **State Parks.** State parks rely heavily on volunteers. Some state parks are popular with RVers, like along the Pacific Coast in California and Oregon, so contact them early.
- **American Red Cross Disaster Services.** Since 9/11, people have become more aware of the need for disaster workers.

HOW TO FIND VOLUNTEER OPPORTUNITIES

Check the Resource section at the end of the chapter for links to some of the above government and nonprofit agencies. You can always contact the agency or the location directly and see if they use volunteers and how to go about applying. Some positions are competitive!

You may be able to create a volunteer assignment if you have special skills.

You might be able to create a volunteer assignment if you have special skills. This could work well if you want to stay for a short time, rather than a full season. Skills in computers, photography, skilled trades could all be useful for projects.

Use your imagination. One of our friends ushers at nonprofit theaters in return for seeing the production at no cost. Another RVer was able to get a two-week assignment as a camp host in a dispersed camping area in order to stay and do some four-wheeling in the area.

GETTING A POSITION

Many agencies have application processes in place to select volunteers. Direct contact with the supervisor you will be working for is another way, particularly if it is a commitment of less than a month. If there is no procedure in place, send a resume and photo along with a cover letter to the volunteer coordinator or supervisor with your related qualifications and experience. (Previous public contact and willingness to work and enthusiasm are usually the most important!)

Before committing, you will want to talk to your contact to find out what you can expect in terms of duties, hours for your site (if one is provided), and other perks or compensation, length of your commitment, and what your site is like. Most any of the questions you would ask of a paying employer should also be asked of the volunteer coordinator or your supervisor. That way there are no surprises on either side. If you have physical limitations, stress what you can do, but also make sure they are aware of what you cannot or are unwilling to do.

Before committing to a position find out what you can expect.

Canadians can become International Volunteers in Parks (IVIP) through a specific application process. *(NPS.gov/oia/Topics/IVIP/Application Process.htm)*

Dick and Rhonda Salerno, who described their paid jobs in the last chapter and how they found them, have also completed several volunteer assignments. This narrative picks up after their first paid job at an RV park.

> "We heard about a volunteer opportunity at a state park/arboretum and were accepted there. We each had to work twenty hours per week for our site. The work was fun and it felt good to be helping out. We also were one of six Workamping couples and the chemistry among us was just right. In all, it was an unforgettable experience. But even though we were considered 'volunteers,' the situation didn't meet our personal definition of the term. To us, volunteer means doing something and getting nothing (except a good feeling) in return. Here we essentially were swapping work for a site.

"Since that first 'volunteer' gig, we've worked at a BLM day-use site, another state park, the US Forest Service and a Non-Governmental Organization (NGO) wildlife refuge. In all cases, we worked between sixteen and twenty-four hours per week each in exchange for our site."

As Dick and Rhonda found, often governmental agencies do provide a site, usually because there aren't other options nearby and you are more readily available. Often you do work more hours for the agency than you would for a comparable job with a commercial park. That is your "donation."

Many governmental agencies provide an RV site.

Camphosting can be paid or volunteer. **Diana and Allen Storm** were full-time RVers and camp hosts for eight years. At the encouragement of a friend, they wrote *The Adventures of Campground Hosting*, which was published in 2005. Here is one adventure from their book, a humorous experience—at least in the retelling—by Diana.

"Why do Men make it sound and look so hard...?

"I am a woman of few words, a 'Jack-Of-All-Trades and Master-At-Absolutely-None-Of-Them.' On top of that, when it comes to Women's Lib—look out Joan Baez you'd better move over. If a job needs to be done and a man isn't around, no matter how disgusting it might be and doesn't weigh over 20 pounds (I've gotten a bad back due to my Women's Lib attitude) I'll do it! And, yes of course, show me how to do a job once and naturally I know it all—yea, right!

"With all that said—before my husband and I started full-timing I had been camping in an RV three whole times in my entire life. During those three camping trips I left all the outside work to my then 'boyfriend' (I didn't want to scare him off by letting him know what kind of 'real woman' I was). What I really knew about RVing you could put on two pieces of paper and scratch out half of it, because I really knew next to nothing.

"We are now full-timing two whole weeks and I am trying to get our 'little home on wheels' ready for a dinner party. My now husband still thinks of me as his 'little lady' (boy, do I have him fooled). I have the whole day and a wonderful meal planned well in advance. Oh yes, we have also been campground hosts for two whole weeks by this time and our black water holding tank has been doing its job quite well—it hasn't either leaked or been emptied once! Yep, it has been holding all that 'stuff' wonderfully well for two full weeks.

"Since I am such a clean fanatic and want to have everything perfect for the party I decided, *'I should clean that darn black water holding tank—I don't want the house "to smelling" while our company is here, now do I?'* Of course not.

"Did I mention that at the campground where we are doing our hosting job the number one critters in residence are raccoons? I didn't? Well, let me tell you if we have one of those critters we have 500 of them! Every night, they make it a point to come and visit us personally—ALL 500 OF THEM!!! You see, before we got here there was no host living here. So, someone who felt sorry for the raccoons from a local bakery brought over their day old bread at least three times a week. When the rangers came by (before we got here) they would find anywhere from 150 to 200 plastic bread wrappers left in what is now our campsite. So, we had all these raccoons visiting us every night looking for a meal. Did I mention that raccoons have three-inch long

Camphosting whether paid or volunteer can be full of adventure.

fingernails on all four of their paws? *'The better to climb with my dear!'* Now, back to the holding tank.

"There I am getting ready for this wonderful dinner party, the steaks are marinating, the refreshments are ready, the ice cubes are freezing (in this lifestyle you don't keep ice cubes laying around you know), the fancy salads are prepared, the table is set, I have showered and am 'dressed to kill' and I get this brilliant idea to clean the black water holding tank. After all I have one hour before the guests will arrive, a half hour before my wonderful husband is due home from his other job and I have nothing else left to do. It can't be hard—right? It can't be messy—right? All I have to do is go behind the trailer, open up that little door, pull on that little handle to release the valve, listen until I can no longer hear anything draining, push the little handle to close the valve, close the little door then go inside and put two ounces of the toilet chemical and some water in the toilet and the job is done—right? Why do men make it sound and look so hard?

"So, there I go—in my nylons, three-inch high heels, dangling jewelry and of course mini skirt (that is the latest fashion you know—forget the fact that I am too fat and too old for it). I open the little door—no problem. I try to pull on the little handle to release the valve. It won't budge. Because the DRY sewer hose is in the way, I am standing off to one side. I try pulling the handle again. It won't budge. Well, am I (the world's #1 Women's Libber, remember) going to let this handle get the best of me? Of course not! No one is looking. I straddle the DRY sewer hose—you know the kind they sell at Walmart for $3.99, the plastic sewer hose that is so thin you can see thru it. When my husband set up the sewer hose he attached

"Why do men make it sound and look so hard?"

one end to the trailer, the other end to a pipe coming out of the ground and left the middle laying on the ground. I am now straddling the sewer hose and I pull on the handle again. It won't budge. Now I am getting mad—my Women's Lib attitude is getting the better of me and I am not going to let any *#&$^&&$%($# handle get the best of me! Now I bend my knees, dig in my three-inch high heels, grab the *$&(#)@)&$ handle and pull with all my might. The handle comes loose, the valve opens up and the 'stuff' starts flowing down the sewer hose. The thin plastic sewer hose. The thin plastic sewer hose the raccoons have been crawling all over for the last two weeks—with their three-inch-long claws!

"Yes sireeeee folks—now you can see it—there I am straddling this wonderfully ventilated sewer hose with my nylons, three-inch high heels, dangling jewelry and mini skirt (which don't forget I am too fat and too old for) and getting a shower I will never forget! Now I push the handle to close the valve—it won't budge! I push harder—it still won't budge! Now I put every bit of strength I have left behind it and push even harder—it finally closes, but not before I noticed there is no longer any 'stuff' coming out of the hose! Guess where it went?

Some RVing adventures are more memorable than others.

"The dinner party—it was cancelled and we went out to dinner (after I got my third shower of the day and threw away my entire outfit). The smell was so bad the three campers we had in the campground all found excuses to leave for a few hours. Two campers who were trying to decide if they were going to stay found excuses to find accommodations elsewhere. The raccoons completely disappeared from our campsite for two months! And my husband—well, let's just say he now knows that 'his little lady' has a complete dictionary of her own words when they are needed!"

Volunteering can have many rewards. You experience an area in depth and get a behind-the-scenes look, seeing things the average visitor never sees. When George, Jaimie's husband, volunteered at Big Bend, he was told about petroglyphs, springs and primitive sites that were not on visitor maps. You may be included in special training sessions that are provided for paid employees, giving you a depth and insight you would otherwise not have. In some cases you also receive propane or an allowance for propane plus uniforms. And, the best is that you are helping a worthwhile cause or agency.

The best is that you are helping a worthwhile cause or agency.

RESOURCES

- **Habitat for Humanity Care-A-Vanner: *(Habitat.org/RV)***
- **US Fish and Wildlife Service: *(Volunteers.FWS.gov)***
- **National Park Service VIP program: *(NPS.gov/Volunteer)***
- **National Park Service IVIP program for international volunteers: *(NPS.gov/oia/Topics/IVIP/Application Process.htm)***
- **American Red Cross Disaster Services. Contact your local chapter to find out about training and opportunities to help: *(RedCross.org)***
- **DVD: "RV Volunteers Make a Difference." All about volunteering, including dozens of volunteer opportunities: *(RVLifestyleExperts.com/RV-Books/Audio-Visual-Courses)***

"You are never too old to set another goal or to dream a new dream."
C.S. Lewis

Chapter 17

How do I choose my domicile?

Disclaimer: This chapter is provided for informational purposes only so that you are aware of issues that may impact your finances. Nothing written here should be construed as legal or financial advice. Remember, the burden for compliance with these laws rests with you and not your tax preparer, IRS employees, or authors of any books or articles you might read. Since these issues can have considerable ramifications, if you are in doubt, see your legal and tax advisors to determine the effect on your individual situation.

WHAT IS THE DIFFERENCE BETWEEN YOUR DOMICILE AND RESIDENCY?

Domicile and residency are often confused. If you live year-round in a house, they are, for all intents and purposes, the same. They do not, however, have the same legal meaning. For an RVer, your domicile and residence will coincide, at least part of the year, but as you travel in other states, the two will differ.

Domicile and residency do not have the same legal meaning.

Domicile: As a full-time RVer with mobility, you have the opportunity to choose your legal domicile. This is your "home" state or where you are domiciled the majority of the time. Your domicile is the place where you intend to remain permanently. It is your true and principal establishment, to which whenever you are absent, you "intend to return." You have only one domicile. If you are domiciled in a state, you must establish this by your subjective intent as well as by actual residence.

Residency: When you are physically present in a state that is where you are currently residing—even if only a day as you travel through. In the course of a year, you can, and probably will, reside in more than one state. You may own an RV lot or property. You could reside there part of the time, but maintain your domicile elsewhere.

States will consider you a resident after a certain number of days; requirements vary by state. (Taking a job in a state may be evidence that you are a resident.) However, if you have spent time in a state, and did not earn money in that state, or from a source in the state, you will not have to file an income tax return there.

Some states make it easy for full-time RVers to establish a domicile.

ESTABLISHING YOUR DOMICILE

Some states make it easy for full-time RVers to get a driver's license, motor vehicle registration and tags, as well as to register to vote. RVers have reported that South Dakota, Texas and Florida have reasonable costs and are easy to work with to establish your domicile. Texas is where the headquarters of the Escapees RV Club is located and many RVers use their mail-forwarding address as their legal domicile. Florida is home to the Good Sam's mail-forwarding service. South Dakota is RV friendly and has two mail-forwarding services used by many RVers: Alternative Resources and America's Mailboxes. These states are also popular because they have no state income taxes. (Alaska, Nevada, Washington and Wyoming are the other states with no state income taxes.)

Establishing your domicile is more than simply driving your RV to a new state, registering it there, and establishing an address and declaring it so. If you don't clearly establish one state as your domicile, more than one state may conclude they are your domicile at tax time or at the time of your death. Some states, California, New Hampshire and Ohio in particular, are very aggressive about claiming you have tax liability even when you thought you were a casual visitor. You will want to read "How to Become a Real Texan," no matter which domicile you choose to learn more about this important choice. (See Resources at the end of this chapter.)

Your choice of a domicile will have a financial impact.

FINANCIAL IMPACT

Your choice of domicile will have a financial impact. Laws in states vary on these issues and cost can be dramatically different from one state to the next.

- Vehicle license and registration fees
- Vehicle insurance rates
- Income taxes
- Sales tax
- Inheritance taxes
- Real estate taxes
- Personal property taxes
- Health insurance costs

There is no one-size-fits-all. Before you choose a new domicile, you will want to talk to a legal and a tax professional.

Vehicle fees and insurance: RV Insurance is somewhat different from traditional vehicle coverage. Make sure your policy is from a credible RV insurance company. General insurance companies do not have the same years of experience in the RV world. In addition to the usual vehicle requirements, the policy must include specific elements relevant to the RV lifestyle: awnings, satellite dishes, and special antennas, for example. Also, if you are a full-time RVer, you need "full-time" insurance, which covers your personal effects. If you are not full-time, personal effects should be covered in your homeowner's policy. You may need additional coverage for electronics, musical instruments or other items of value.

Make a chart of the features you want included in your policy.

Make a chart of the features you want included in your policy. Compare the availability of coverage and the cost among the major insurance companies. See sample chart at the end of this chapter.

You can get quick quotes or estimates from several of the RV insurance companies that insure full-time RVers. (See Resources at the end of this chapter.)

Working on the road and state income taxes: If you work in a state that assesses state income taxes, you will owe money on the amount you earn there. You will have to file an income tax return in that state. Some states would like a portion of all your income while you are residing in that state, so check with a tax preparer before taking the job to find out how (and if) you can limit your taxable income to what you earned there.

There are several scenarios to explain to which state you would owe state income taxes. To totally avoid state income taxes, you must be domiciled in a no-income-tax state and work in a no-income-tax state. Here are two more situations you could encounter:

1. If you work in a no-income-tax state but are domiciled in a state that has income tax, your domicile will collect taxes on your earnings.
2. If you work in an income-tax state and are domiciled in an income tax state, you pay the tax to the state where you earn the money and get a credit in your domicile so you don't pay taxes on that income twice.

Is your RV site taxable when you work? If you receive an RV site as part of your compensation, it is considered barter income and could be taxable. To avoid being taxable, the exception is if your employer requires you to live there. According to IRS Code Section 119, if you are required as a condition of your employment to stay at the premises, the value of the lodging which you receive, qualifies as "excludable income." Be sure to get a statement in writing to this effect and a brochure from the employer showing his rates.

If you receive an RV site as part of your compensation it could be taxable.

RESOURCES

- **Federation of Tax Administrators website: Compare state taxes in several categories: *(TaxAdmin.org/FTA/Rate/Tax_stru.html)***
- **RetirementLiving.com gives the overall tax burden for each state, broken down by tax. Excellent resource for choosing a domicile: *(RetirementLiving.com/RLTaxes.html)***
- **"How to Be a Real Texan," free download for members at Escapees RV Club's website. Or purchase booklet at their store for $2.95: *(Escapees.com)***
- **Choosing Your RV Home Base. See Recommended Books: *(RVLifestylEexperts.com/RV-Books/Recommended-Books)***
- **RV insurance companies:**
  - ★**PoliSeek: *(PoliSeek.com)***
  - ★**Foremost Insurance Group: *(Foremost.com)***
  - ★**Progressive Insurance: *(RV.Progressive.com)***
  - ★**GMAC Insurance: *(RVInsurance.com)***

FEATURE	#1	#2	#3
Colision			
Convenient payment plan including electronic funds transfer			
Deductibles			
Discounts for safe driver, mature driver, AARP			
Driving record			
Natural disaster coverage: Fire, Hail, Earthquake, Hurricane?			
Online Internet access			
Personal effects			
Personalalized service			
Rental reimbursement			
Replacement coverage (purchase or full)			
RV Claims Experts			
Suspension of coverage when not traveling			
Theft			
Toll-free numbers			
Towing reimbursement			
Travel in other countries (covered in Canada? Mexico?)			
24/7 claims service			
Other			
Other			

"If you rest, you rust." Helen Hayes

Chapter 18

What about health insurance?

One of the biggest concerns full-timers have is how they are going to obtain quality health care on the road and how they can get affordable health insurance. At our website, *(RVLifestyleExperts.com)*, we share information articles, links and other resources that should help you achieve your health care and insurance goals. Provisions of the Patient Protection and Affordable Care Act (PPACA), as they take effect, will make it easier for RVers under Medicare age to find adequate insurance.

Obtaining affordable health insurance and quality healthcare on the road are big concerns of full-timers.

FINDING HEALTH INSURANCE

Until then, please refer to the following links for Jaimie's excellent three-part article that takes you through the steps of researching and choosing health insurance when you are not yet eligible for Medicare. You'll find other helpful articles there too.

- Health Insurance Options Part 1 Choosing a state *(RVLifestyleExperts.com/Free-RV-Info/Health-Insurance/Health-Insurance-Part-1)*

- Health Insurance Options Part 2 Choosing a policy *(RVLifestyleExperts.com/Free-RV-Info/Health-Insurance/Health-Insurance-Part-2)*
- Health Insurance Options Part 3 Reducing medical expenses *(RVLifestyleExperts.com/Free-RV-Info/Health-Insurance/Health-Insurance-Part-3)*

COVERAGE OPTIONS

- **COBRA.** If you are just leaving your job, you may be able to pay the group rate of your current policy for 18 months (or more) under COBRA coverage by your current employer.
- **Veterans.** If you served in the Armed Forces, you may be eligible for health care through the Veterans Administration (VA).
- **Associations.** You may be able to join an association that has group coverage.
- **Individual Insurance.** If you are in good health, you may want to just purchase catastrophic insurance. You would pay routine costs out-of-pocket, but have coverage for a major illness.
- **No insurance.** Some people have chosen this option. Often they will get lower rates from doctors and hospitals if they pay in full. They use health fairs and clinics staffed by nurse practitioners for routine care.

There are ways to reduce medical costs.

REDUCE MEDICAL COSTS

If you have no health insurance or have a large deductible, here are some ways you can keep your costs down:

- **Comparison shop** when your insurance doesn't cover it. Ask for a cash discount.
- **For regular female checkups** and for other more routine exams, use a nurse practitioner or physician's assistant. Or check on state clinics, local clinics, or Planned Parenthood.

- **Ask for the Medicare rate** if you have an operation or procedure.
- **Participate in a clinical trial** related to your diagnosis. At one website, (*CenterWatch.com)* you can sign up for email notification for new trials or medications in specific health areas.
- **Negotiate with the hospital.** See if you can have the procedure done on an outpatient basis.
- **See if the hospital has interest-free loans** to assist patients. They may have an obligation to provide free services in some instances to low-income patients under the federal Hill-Burton Free Care Program. 800-638-0742 or at *(HRSA.gov/HillBurton).*
- **Check your bill carefully** to make sure you weren't charged for items or service you did not receive. Also look for "upcoding," where the patient is charged for a similar but more expensive procedure than received.
- **Research the newest techniques** if you need an operation. Sometimes the newer technology is less invasive and less expensive.
- **Check with Medicaid for your state.** Find information and links at *(64.82.65.67/Medicaid/States.html*). In New York, for example, single seniors with incomes up to $35,000 can get help with prescription drugs.

RVers can find ways to reduce prescription drug costs.

REDUCE DRUG COSTS

RVers can find ways to reduce prescription drug costs. A number of generic drugs are available at Walmart, Walgreens and other pharmacies for $4 or $10 per prescription. Here are some ideas to help curb prescription drug costs:

- **Ask your doctor for samples.**
- **Check with pharmaceutical companies;** most have established programs to assist low-income patients. Ask your physician about them.

- **Compare prices at pharmacies.** In some cases buying a larger dose and cutting the pills in half saves money too.
- **Some RVers purchase certain prescription drugs in Mexico** at a savings.
- See **RVLifestyleExperts** *(RVLlifestyleExperts.com/Free-RV-Info/Health-Insurance)* for more articles on saving money on prescription drugs.

FINDING CARE ON THE ROAD

When we live in one place, we generally have a community of doctors and medical support. On the road we need to develop the appropriate resources. In an emergency, people of course seek emergency help. With a serious illness, many will often head "home" to their familiar doctors or call to ask them for recommendations. Others will use the computer either to search for the best options or to communicate on travelers' bulletin boards for their suggestions.

Develop appropriate medical support resources for emergencies while on the road.

Larry Brauer describes their experience at City of Hope (Southern California) when his wife, Adrienne, was treated for cancer.

> "Health insurance is important. Fortunately, we have a nationwide Preferred Provider Network and the number of hospitals and doctors that are preferred providers is extensive.

> "Near the end of February, we returned to City of Hope. Fortunately, we were able to get into the very small RV Park on the grounds of the City of Hope. We had actually been able to stay there for about 10 days in January. It's very small and maneuvering a 39-foot motorhome into our assigned space was not easy. However, even with its shortcomings, it is very

convenient and, if you have to be a long-term patient at City of Hope and you are mobile, it's a good place to be living.

"After another surgery in February to get a Port-a-Cath—the means by which Adrienne would receive the chemo drugs, and several more tests—Adrienne started her chemotherapy treatments on March 18. Although there has been some variance during Adrienne's chemo treatments, a typical day goes like this:

1. Adrienne first goes into the clinic to have her port accessed and have blood drawn.
2. Then she sees the doctor who gives her an examination and asks some questions. He also checks the results of the blood tests
3. Anywhere from an hour to more than two hours later, she goes into the infusion area to have two of the Chemo drugs administered.
4. The infusions all start with saline and toward the end of the series of chemo sessions, other drugs were added to relieve some of the side effects. About an hour after the IV is started, the two chemo drugs are started. It takes another two hours to administer those two chemo drugs. Finally, a third drug is administered by means of a pump; a portable, self-contained machine given to Adrienne in a pouch (kind of like a fanny pack) that Adrienne will wear for two days. So after about three hours in the infusion room, we walk back to the RV.
5. Forty-six hours later, we head back to the clinic to have the pump disconnected.
6. Adrienne then has about eleven days to recover, enjoy life, and get mentally prepared to continue the treatment.

"It will probably be another month before we are able to leave the City of Hope. We will be back for periodic tests and doctor's appointments, but those should all be short-term stays. I can't say that it has been a great place to spend nine months; it certainly isn't where we wanted to be. But, given the circumstances, I am very grateful we are here. I appreciate our chosen lifestyle even more than I did before. Because of our chosen lifestyle we were able to stay here, take advantage of the various classes and support groups, meet some fantastic people (both staff and patients), and learn more about this wonderful place."

WHAT ABOUT CANADIANS?

Canadian RVer and author **Lynne Benjamin** has researched this issue and written about it. She advises Canadians to purchase travel medical insurance, in fact, don't leave home without it for the following reasons:

1. The cost of medical care outside the country—particularly in the United States—is far and beyond what the province pays.
2. Even if you are in excellent health and have provincial medical insurance, what would you do if you break a leg?
3. You can avoid paying out-of-pocket expenses if you seek medical treatment while out of the country.

Check to see if you are already covered, but if not be aware that a number of factors will affect the cost of your premiums, according to Lynne. Research policies carefully, making sure you understand what you are getting and how extensive the coverage is. Sometimes there are "catches" in policies—like whether your maximum coverage is per trip or per claim or there are exclusions you were not aware of, so read your policy carefully all the way through.

Purchase travel medical insurance when RVing in another country.

RESOURCES

- ***The New Health Insurance Solution: How to Get Cheaper, Better Coverage Without a Traditional Employer Plan*** **by Paul Zane Pilzer.**
- ***Drugs for Less: The Complete Guide to Free and Discounted Prescription Drugs*** **by Michael P. Cecil, M.D.**
- **See Lynne Benjamin's article, "Travel Medical Insurance: Don't Leave Home Without It," for more details for Canadians traveling in the U.S. Look under health insurance: *(RVLifestyleExperts.com)***
- **Additional articles on this topic can be found at: *(RVLifestyleExperts.com)***

NOTES

Section IV: SPECIAL SITUATIONS

Chapter 19

How can I travel with my children?

Many families travel together. One father, who works seasonally, says that he jumped at the chance to travel full-time. "I want to know my children really well. We travel without a TV and spend our evenings playing games, reading, and talking." Another parent says that the way she sees it, "We have a small home but a very large yard."

Some items to consider:

HOMESCHOOLING

The RV lifestyle is a good way to really get to know your children.

This type of education has become so prevalent now that there are numerous homeschooling courses of study you can purchase, as well as books, magazines, websites, and local organizations to support you. Be mindful of the state rules you must follow.

Writer **Ted Kasper** has been RVing for 18 years, much of it with his family. Here he explains how your RV can be a classroom on wheels.

> "By learning and exploring, your RV is a classroom on wheels! RVs can be both a playground and a classroom for our kids. And this year more families with school-aged children will learn and play like never before. An ever-increasing number of families are making their RV travels as much a field trip as vacation.

"What to do on a rainy day? Sure, TV and video games will fill the kids' time. How about visiting one of the many interactive, hands-on children's museums across the state? It will not only provide hours of fun and enjoyment for the kids, but the activities are designed to teach children. Not only might they 'drive' a spaceship but they may be able to 'invent' a toy.

"The nature centers at Michigan's state parks are fantastic educational tools that are often overlooked. Some of the parks offer interpretive nature programs for children. Oftentimes, they include the history and attractions of the area. Many of these programs are hands-on, interactive fun for kids (and for adults too!)

"How about taking a walk with the kids through the woods to see who can spot the most kinds of wildlife? Bring along bug jars and see who can catch the 'yuckiest' looking creature—or the one with the most legs! Or collect different kinds of leaves on your walks through the campground? Or just talk, share stories, spend time and bond with the kids?

"Adults who camped as kids will tell you that camping helped them develop an appreciation for nature."

"It's a safe bet that the overwhelming majority of adults who camped as kids will tell you that camping helped them develop an appreciation for nature and the outdoors. And a healthy respect for both!

"Bringing along a notebook or journal for the kids to write in only reinforces what they have seen and experienced. How about collecting postcards and starting a scrapbook of all the places they have visited? It's excellent for reinforcing those learning experiences (and for those famous 'what I did on my summer vacation' assignments in the fall).

"Kids can learn about history, as no book can convey, by visiting historical sites and seeing recreations of times past. The many historical markers throughout the state are excellent props to start discussions with kids.

"Most parents will tell you that the kids are enjoying themselves so much that they do not even realize that learning is taking place. We, as parents, are helping to create memories that will last a lifetime. Not only is there the opportunity to make RV trips educational experiences for our kids, but there are some important skills being practiced that will help to make them successful later in life—things like the teamwork learned in setting up and tearing down camp and the tolerance of other's views and behaviors learned on rainy days.

Find an RV that ensures that each family member has some spot to call "home."

"Michiganders live amid many wonders of nature. Our state's varied landscapes include sandy beaches, expansive forests, and emerald waters. Through their 'classroom on wheels,' Michigan children are enjoying their state's magnificent scenery, the healthy benefits of outdoor recreation as well as getting the opportunity to learn and have fun at the same time."

FINDING AN APPROPRIATE RV

Depending upon the ages and number of children, this critical step ensures that each member has some spot to call "home." A number of RVs are now available with second bedrooms or bunkrooms. One couple found the Titanium 36E41, a fifth wheel with three bedrooms and two baths! It is 41 feet long, however. Often the toy hauler trailers and fifth wheels have beds that lower when the "toys" are out.

KEEPING TRACK OF "THINGS"

Storing each person's things in buckets and cloth bags helps keep the rig organized and as clutter-free as possible. **Samantha Eppes** contributed this to *RV Traveling Tales: Women's Journeys from the Open Road.*

> "I first began traveling when I was three months old. Fourteen years later, I'm still traveling and still loving it. We currently live in a motorhome, the better to hold all my "stuff." My parents and I are very close because we live in close quarters. Some see this as a difficulty, but it doesn't bother us; we're used to it. My theory is simply this: RVs aren't small; houses are big."

A few years later, **Samantha** contributed this piece for Alice's column in our *RV Lifestyle Ezine*. Unlike what you'd expect, Samantha is the neat one in her family! She says:

> "My parents find it funny that my teenage way of rebelling is to keep my room clean, and I'm always picking up their stuff.
>
> "My family has absolutely no control over our stuff. It spills out of drawers and cabinets, hides under beds and tables, and is strewn hopelessly on the floor. Well, not really. Anything on the floor we pick up and put on the nearest piece of furniture. When we're expecting company, the stuff is forced out of sight, but within twenty-four hours it's back with a vengeance.

"My theory is simply this: RV's aren't small; houses are big."

> "We stay at my grandparents' house every summer, and store some of our stuff there. Last summer I couldn't take it anymore. I attacked the black hole under my bed, pulling out stuff and carting it off to my grandparents' house to be furi-

ously sorted. Then I started on the cabinets. It was invigorating. I was overcoming my stuff. I was throwing things out, I was giving things away, I was leaving things at the house. Then I took what I wanted to keep back to the RV, and I ORGANIZED IT. My room was CLEAN!

"Now I had a new problem. The stuff clogging my parents' room saw how much space there was in my room and began to migrate. Their shoes were on my floor, their radio was on my table, their papers and clothes were on my chairs. I grabbed the stuff and hauled it back to where it came from. But it kept finding its way back.

"Now I stand here, an army of one, fighting desperately to keep the small space of organization I worked so hard to get. It may seem like a losing battle, but in the face of stuff, clean will always prevail. Okay, not always, more like half the time... Maybe a third... I have to go; I can see my mom's sneakers hiding under my chair. Clean will triumph one fourth of the time..."

Communicating is even more critical to a family's mental health on the road.

An update: Samantha traveled with her parents from three months of age until she left for college. Before that, her parents worked at Disney World several winters. Samantha insisted they return the year she turned 16 and was eligible to work there too for one more season.

ENCOURAGE COMMUNICATION

Communicating in a family is essential to its mental health. On the road it is even more critical since everybody is living in each other's pocket. After doing some research, each family member should decide if they could see themselves in the lifestyle, what their needs would be, and what they hope to get out of the experience. One suggestion is to try it out first at a nearby campground before selling everything.

Years ago, we met an RVing family with a two young girls. It was the first family Jaimie had met who was full-time RVing. The husband told us they often stopped at playgrounds in their travels so the girls could get exercise and play with other children.

Ted Kasper touts the advantages of camping with your family in a place where the children can play outdoors.

> "Remember as a child, getting home from school and bursting out the back door into the back yard, field, or woods to climb high up in the trees, dig in the dirt, or go exploring? Maybe there was a tree fort, or there was digging in the dirt to do (while looking for squirmy, icky things) or a creek that needed to be checked out.

> "Today, a child's life after school more often than not means sporting events, dance class, clubs, church and social events and activities. All these have value and contribute to the development of the child, but leave children with little free time. The mantra that many of us heard while growing up, *'Go outside and play,'* has been replaced with *'Get in the car. We're going to be late.'* Even when kids are home, and could be playing outside, computers, TV, video games, and cell phones seem more compelling to them.

Children who often play outdoors are smarter, more cooperative, happier, and healthier.

> "There is a whole raft of recent studies and research that shows us children are smarter, more cooperative, happier, and healthier when they have frequent, and varied, opportunities for free and unstructured play in the out-of-doors. With the number of reasons for deciding to purchase an RV being as varied as the seasons in Michigan, using your RV for camp-

ing can provide your children with many opportunities for playing in nature.

"Whether the kids are making up games or tossing bugs into a spider's web, playing freely in nature allows kids to make their own rules, dream up their own stories and experiment and come to their own conclusions—all at their own pace. And unlike playground equipment and some toys that respond the same way every time they are used, nature changes at the whim of the life that inhabits it. An overturned log may reveal a nest of bugs on one day. Another overturned log on another day may harbor a humongous spongy mushroom. Meeting small challenges like climbing a tree or crossing a stream on a log bridge can help to build confidence and self-esteem.

Nature is an ever-changing playground for kids big and small.

"Some ideas to encourage play in the out-of-doors for kids who are unsure about leaving the comfort of the your RV:

➤Leave most of the kids toys out-of-sight when camping, especially video games & DVDs, and save them for rainy days only.

➤How about venturing into the woods to see who can spot the most species of wildlife? Bring along bug jars and see who can catch the 'yuckiest' looking creature … or the one with the most legs.

➤Take a walk through the campground property and collect different kinds of leaves or unusual rocks.

➤Bring along a disposable camera and have your kids take photos of wildflowers or wildlife for a scrapbook.

"Remember the mantra of parents of day's past: Go outside and play!"

It is probably easier to travel with younger children than teens. **Ted Kasper** has advice for keeping older children interested in RV camping.

> "One of the reasons that you made the decision to purchase an RV was to take trips together as a family. Spending time together as a family, doing things as a family, creating life-long memories was what you envisioned when you took the step and became an RV owner. It is a gratifying and wonderful feeling when your older kids/teens ask, '*When are we going again?*'
>
> "According to a number of parents who RV with teenagers and pre-teens, the number one thing that parents can do to keep their older children wanting to come with the family is involving them in the planning of the trip or the weekend camping outing. This keeps their interest up and lets them know that they will be having some fun once you arrive at your destination.
>
> "What about planning your trip to include some of the things that the kids want to do? Like camping near amusement parks, water parks, resort-type campgrounds or visiting places of interest to them? Doing things that you would not normally do as a family, like catching a matinee or going bowling, is essential in keeping the kids interested in going along with the family.

Involve older children in the planning of the trip.

> "Trying to think like a teen (remember, you were once a teenager!) definitely helps in planning. Knowing their likes and dislikes makes things easier for everybody. With work, school, after school activities, maintaining homes/cars, etc., we are all so busy, it is very easy to fall into a routine of not spending time together as a family and really getting to know our kids.

"Think about having your child bring a friend along. Let them camp in their own tent. It gives them some privacy. It is amazing how well children can get along with other people around.

"Believe it or not, doing things together as a family is important to kids. They may seem to want the opposite at times, but knowing your kids well will let you know how much "together time" they need. Some families may make it a habit to play a board game together after each dinner while camping. Others make the campfire the time to be together. But make sure that kids get some private time—many teens can't stand being with the family every minute. They need time to be alone.

With just a little effort you can hear your older kids say, "When are we going to go again?"

"The length of a trip can make or break your trip with older kids. A week or two away from their friends is easier to take than a four to five week trip!

"Also, having an Internet connection available to kids on longer trips allows kids to chat with their friends.

"Lastly, all families come to a point when the older kids can't go along or would rather stay at home. Hopefully, these tips will help you hear from your older kids, '*When are we going to go again?*'"

RESOURCES

- **National Home Education Network: (*Homeschool-Curriculum-and-Support.com/National-Home-Education-Network.html)***
- **Families on the Road: *(FamiliesOnTheRoad.com)***
- **Judith Waite Allee: *(DreamsOnAShoestring.com)***
- **Homeschooling: *(Home-Ed-Magazine.com)***
- **Find a play area as you travel: If you are traveling with kids, check out this resource for finding a great play area in your travels: *(PlaySpaceFinder.Kaboom.org)***
- **Pit Stops For Kids- Fun places, adventures and road trips that will interest children: *(PitStopsForKids.com)***

"There is only one success—to be able to spend your life in your own way."
Christopher Morley

Chapter 20
How can I travel by myself?

A number of singles groups and websites will give you the support and knowledge you need. You can find this information in the Resources section at the end of this chapter. Many of the traveling issues (choosing a rig, maintenance, communication on the road, to name a few) are detailed in other chapters in this book. This chapter is devoted to some of the specific concerns of traveling solo.

Successful solo RVers are comfortable being alone.

AM I SUITED FOR SOLO TRAVEL?

In their book, *RVers: How Do They Live Like That?*, **Judy Farrow and Lou Stoetzer** (full-timers as well as psychologists) identify four characteristics successful solos have.

Successful Solo RVers:

1. Are comfortable being alone.
2. Have access to a supportive community.
3. Maintain connections with family and/or friends from the road.
4. Possess resources to manage health issues while traveling.

LONELINESS

Perhaps the biggest concern for men and women is loneliness. Many singles solve this by traveling side by side with one or more rigs, particularly in the beginning. When they feel more comfortable in the lifestyle, singles appreciate the solitude.

As **Betty Prange** said in *RV Traveling Tales: Women's Journeys on the Open Road*: "There is no one in the passenger seat to point out you made a wrong turn, scraped a low-hanging branch, or hit a curb pulling into a gas station."

Being alone does not necessarily mean being lonely. People can be fulfilled being by themselves; others can be lonely in a relationship or in a crowd. They are two separate issues.

If you are lonely because you're alone, decide what you need to improve the situation. If it's a momentary feeling, as in many cases, let the moment pass, giving it the respect it deserves, but knowing that it WILL pass.

If you want more people to socialize and travel with, consider getting involved with social groups, including the many singles groups. Join groups that share some of your interests, like hiking, biking, playing bridge, church groups, or get involved with the many volunteer groups.

Being alone does not necessarily mean being lonely.

MEETING PEOPLE

Meeting people on the road is a critical skill for all people—single or coupled. The change from the old familiar routines is drastic. Unless you've been a person who has moved frequently, you've usually been with the same circle of friends for a long time. After you start traveling, you will probably feel the loss of old friends and experience uncertainty as you make new friends.

For the solo traveler, this may even be more difficult at first since you don't have the comfort of at least one familiar face with you. How do other solos handle this experience? Even if you are not a joiner, keep your options open. Finding congenial and interesting people along the way is one of the great attractions in the RV lifestyle.

One of the great attractions of the RV lifestyle is finding congenial and interesting people along the way.

- **Join singles groups.** They provide an easy venue for meeting people. Members are already on the road so you don't have to explain your lifestyle choice. Since the others are joining for companionship as well, they are open to making new friends. Groups have different cultures. You will need to pursue several to find the ones that meet your needs. See Resources at the end of this chapter for a list of RV singles groups.
- **Practice conversation starters.** An icebreaker may be a license plate from a previous state you lived in, a shared club sticker on the windshield, the same make of RV that you have had or currently occupy. Leave a note on the door of your neighbor's camper to join you for cocktail hour, a campfire or a morning coffee.

  One reader received a rather large white plaster of Paris duck, complete with outfits for every occasion, and some non-occasions. She promptly dubbed her Gertie A.F.Lack and dressed her for Christmas, setting her outside on the patio. People came by and stopped to comment on Gertie and her outfit. Others did too and before she knew it, Gertie and she had chatted with about twenty different folks who were contentedly strolling through the park, and she had made about twenty new acquaintances.

  Not everybody would own an artificial duck, but what about meeting people through your dog or other "yardart?"

- **Pursue your interests.** Within the larger RV organizations, there are sub-groups based on similar interests: Beading, birding, bicycling, boondocking (dry camping), writing. The list goes on and on. In the Escapees RV Club, these groups are called BOFs: Birds of a Feather. The focus is on sharing the interest, not necessarily whether one is single or coupled. Other interests you had in your pre-RV life have national websites informing you where you can travel to meet others all over the country to pursue your hobby: hiking clubs, square dance festivals, bridge tournaments, vegetarian groups. Do an Internet search to find the websites of your choice.

> **In an RV, you can travel to meet others who share your interests.**

- **Follow up on your new contacts.** When you meet people, get their information and immediately transfer it to your email address book. Don't wait for others to contact you. Send a short email note saying how much you enjoyed talking to them about whatever. Use your computer to print up business cards with your name, cell phone, Facebook and email address. If you have particular interests, add those so that somebody looking for a bridge or square dance partner will think of you. Add a photo of you and/or dog, rig, favorite hat with election campaign buttons on it—whatever makes you unique.
- **Volunteer.** When you volunteer, you not only enrich the lives of the people you help, your own life becomes richer. You also create special friendships. People who have worked together on volunteer projects often form a bond with each other that transcends the miles and time they are apart until they see each other again. (See Chapter 16: "How do I volunteer?" for more about volunteering.)

INEXPERIENCE

Women have added concerns. Because they may not have grown up with the experience of tinkering with cars and trucks, many women feel apprehensive about relying on their vehicle. Some men have those same doubts. (See Chapter 23: "I'm not handy—should I travel?") In reality, women on the road do learn the skills and feel stronger afterwards. Many RV rallies offer such classes designed strictly for women, single or married, to help them become more independent.

You can get more comfortable traveling in your RV by first attending an RV event, such as an educational rally, chapter trip, or traveling in an RV caravan. That way if something goes wrong, you have others to give you advice or help. You'll gain confidence before traveling totally on your own.

SAFETY

Another concern is safety. Women who travel alone must use their common sense. They do not park by themselves in an unknown area. Some classes on women's safety have recommended buying the biggest pair of men's galoshes they can find and set them outside the rig at night or have a giant dog dish with the name "Killer" emblazoned on the lip. When all else fails, travel in a motorhome with the ignition key always in place so that at the first sign of danger, you just start it up and leave. There is a risk to everything, but if you take precautions, go by your gut, and use common sense, you can avoid most bad situations.

The first step to staying safe is to start with a reliable rig and keep it that way.

Make your rig safe. The first step to staying safe is to start with a reliable rig and keep it that way. If you buy a used RV, make sure it is safe. Get it inspected by a mechanic you trust. Each time you drive your rig you should do a safety inspection. Keep an eye on the tires particularly, both for wear and proper tire pressure. Make sure everything is stowed. Be sure the refrigerator is off whenever you fuel your vehicle. Don't exceed the gross vehicle weight rating for your vehicle, or you will add unnecessary wear and tear or even damage your engine. If you are driving a motorhome and towing another vehicle, periodically check the hitch and "toad."

Be safe as you travel and park.

- **Cell phone:** Have a cell phone with you. A used cell phone that has been activated but has no service will work for 911 calls.
- **Driving:** Keep your fuel tank at least half full. Stop well before dark and choose where you'll park for the night carefully if you do not stay in an RV park. Many RVers park in truck stops and Walmarts overnight because they are lighted and patrolled to some extent. If you park in a more remote area, check your cell phone signal.
- **Lock your doors:** Lock your doors whether in or out of the rig including when you are traveling. At night, close any sliding windows. Jalousie windows can be safely left open.
- **Anticipate problems:** Think about how you will get out of a location before you drive in and always park heading out. Think of how you could handle situations like someone following you or deliberately causing an accident.
- **Be cautious:** Don't let people know you are traveling alone or tell them too much about yourself. When solo Kim leaves her rig, she shouts something back inside to her "husband."
- **Share your travel plans:** Someone, a relative or friend, should know your general travel plans. Check in with them on an agreed upon schedule.
- **Carry ID:** When you leave the rig, make sure you have ID and a card with your rig's location.

Betty Prange suggests a simple but more complete solution for carrying your ID.

> "Pick up one of the very cheap thumb drives (often at the checkout counter in the large office box stores). Look for one that has a hole in the end so you can put it on your key chain. Then use your computer to list important information, such as emergency contacts, medical insurance data, drug allergies, prescriptions you take, etc. Transfer those files to your thumb drive. Often I go out for walks and don't take my purse, wallet, etc. But I always have my key chain to lock and unlock my motorhome door. If, like me, you forget to update and give the exact information about where you are parked, at least put a notice on the drive that you are an RVer and give your rig's and toad's license plate numbers and let them know an RV is in the vicinity. Of course, your emergency contact person will also know that you travel in an RV and can share that information, but having it on the thumb drive makes it handy for law enforcement officials if there is an emergency. Will someone who finds your lost keys use this to break in? I'll take the chance, which I think is minuscule."

If an area looks unsafe or there are suspicious people about, don't stop there.

- **Trust your instincts:** If an area looks unsafe for any reason or there is any suspicious looking person, do not stop or park overnight there.

Adrienne Kristine recommends having a redundancy plan.

"The first, second, and third rules of computer operation are back it up, back it up, back it up. The same should be true of your gear/equipment/stuff: you have a flashlight. You drop it, it breaks. Now what? Yes, I have three flashlights. I carry a Coleman to the campground store so when I walk back to the motorhome, I can see the path. The back-up in the backpack is a mini-Maglite a little larger than a roll of quarters (also good for defense in a pinch)."

A safety course can help you avoid or be prepared for unsafe situations.

Should I take a safety course? A personal safety course can help you both avoid unsafe situations and be prepared for them if they occur. You can find courses at RVing Women *(RVingWomen.org)* events. Courses are sometimes offered at other rallies. Check with community colleges and police departments also.

Should I carry a weapon? This debate rages between couples as well as solos. If you decide to carry a weapon or even something like Mace, get the proper training and practice regularly. Most police officers advise that if you do not have the personality to use it in a life-threatening situation, you are better off without a weapon. Most RVers never find themselves in a position to need a weapon IF you follow two rules: go by your gut and use common sense.

In general, use four of your senses as a warning system. Whenever something is suspicious (a different sound, a different smell, a different look, a different feel), stop and investigate. Make it second nature so you don't have to dwell on safety issues and can enjoy the freedom and lure of the open road.

Joei Carlton Hassock, solo, shares her thoughts about safety as a solo.

"Yes, I feel safe. I try not to drive after dark. I want to be in a campground or truck stop early. I do from time to time stay in Walmart lots but I prefer truck stops where I can do my laundry, have a bite to eat, work on my computer or just relax in front of the television set. No, I'm not a truck driver but who's to know. There are a lot of old ladies like me on the road and we go pretty much where we like. And I NEVER stay overnight in rest areas."

DRIVING ALONE

The thought of driving a large RV can be intimidating. Like anything else, knowledge and practice are the keys. It is important to learn to drive your rig, knowing what it will do, and where it can go. Women who have a partner should drive enough to be able to take over if something were to happen to their partner.

When you choose your rig, consider how easy it is to drive. **Donna Sauter's** husband passed away, leaving her with a 26-foot Itasca Class C motorhome that she'd never driven. She decided to downsize. "I knew that for my own peace of mind I had to buy a smaller motorhome, one that I felt I could handle. I needed to prove to myself I didn't need to give up the RV lifestyle altogether." She ended up with a 1986 20-foot Coachmen micro-mini.

The keys to safe RV driving are practice and knowledge.

Here are some ideas to get you started:

- **Take an RV driving class.**
- **Practice in a large parking lot.** Become aware of where the RV is in relation to white lines and learn to maneuver. Learn to use your side mirrors.
- **Drive on Interstates to get a feel for the RV** without having to worry about turns.
- **In a motorhome, you'll need to stay closer to the white line** than in a regular vehicle. Use your left side mirror to stay no

more than 12" off the center line (to your left). Do this consciously until it becomes automatic.

- **Take your time and don't let other drivers intimidate you.**

More driving tips:

- **Swing wide around curves.** Remember the back end takes extra space.
- **Leave plenty of space between you and the vehicle in front of you.** Slow down well in advance of your turnoff. It takes a lot longer to stop an RV.
- **If you are in a multilane highway, stay in one of the middle lanes** until it is time to turn or get off.
- **Anticipate lane changes** and move over well before necessary.
- **Go slow on curves and slow down for any bumps.** Your rig is top-heavy so bumps, fast stops, and fast turns will throw things off their resting place.
- **Watch for overhead obstacles.** Trees and signs sticking out could damage your rig.
- **Memorize the height of your rig.** Mary was driving her Bounder and saw a sign on a bridge—11 feet 10 inches. She couldn't remember the height of her rig. She wisely decided to back up. Her rig was 12 feet 2 inches.

More advice from solo drivers:

- **Plan your route** ahead of time.
- **Write out the turns** on a sheet of paper and have it handy.
- **Keep maps close by.**
- **Check your route in a map program.** *(Mapquest.com)* and *(GoogleMaps.com)* are free.
- **Use GPS (global positioning satellite) devices** that pinpoint locations via satellite to map your route.
- **Have a backup plan.** As much as possible, be aware of alternate routes in case you encounter construction.

- **Learn proper braking techniques** and use of your transmission in going up and down hills. Brake assists are available for diesel engines.

Investigate RV Driving Courses:

- **RVing Women** *(RVingWomen.org)*
- **RV Driving School** *(RVSchool.com)*
- **RV Trainers** Northern California *(RVTrainers.com)*

TRANSITIONS

Remember—the joy of traveling outweighs the fear of doing it alone. Both **Annise Miller** and **Betty Prange** began their lives on the road traveling with their husbands. After they were widowed, each opted to continue on her own. Here are their stories.

Annise

"When Jaimie and Alice requested articles on transitions, I thought, *'That should be easy after five years of nothing but that.'* This followed the loss of my husband of 30 years to lung cancer in June, 2003. Transitions showed up on all levels. I needed to restructure my finances as our Massachusetts pension plan necessitated a doctor at its head. A deceased doctor didn't cut it.

> **The joy of traveling outweighs the fear of doing it alone.**

"I would continue full-timing and would need to learn 'his' jobs. The lesson here is to be capable of doing all the rig jobs. Trust me when I say you're not going to want to become more familiar with the care and feeding of your internal combustion engine(s), electrical system or rubber roof while preoccupied by grief. Necessity, being the mother of mastery, increased competence (or at least its appearance). I garnered the admiration of male neighbors and the silent resentment of their wives.

"The lack of invitations to couple activities from the cocktail hour gathering to dinners out often resulted and signaled the social transition into the single's role while still in a seascape of couples. For me, being viewed with suspicion by other women was a particularly difficult adjustment. Not only did this diminish the opportunity for new friendships, but it also stood in such contrast to who I am. These exchanges left me lonelier than when alone. Couple this with the lack of validation as reflected in the loving eyes of someone who really knows me made this change more disconcerting.

"Five years out, I now spend entire seasons in one location instead of a couple of weeks. I have a maintenance schedule and follow it. Most importantly, I rest in a deeper spiritual center trusting that the ongoing transitions are all part of our divine journey. And so it is now. I am again able to celebrate and enjoy life. I wish you the same blessings."

The RV lifestyle is adaptable to changing situations.

Betty

"Then came another change. Lin was diagnosed with cancer. Circumstances forced us to base in one place. We lived in the motorhome and made short trips when we could. I drove some while he was healthy. Now I took on most of the driving and hooking up. When treatment ended, we hit the road again, but it didn't last long. The treatments had not given us the hoped-for remission. In less than two months, I was a widow.

"Nine years later I am still full-timing. I don't do it quite like I did when Lin was alive. I love winters in the Southwest where my RV friends gather. Widowed, orphaned, and with no siblings, my family now consists of RV friends and a couple of second cousins. Summers turned out to be hardest for me.

Friends disperse then, and places to stay, especially free and economical ones, are more crowded. I like to amble and don't like keeping to reservation schedules.

"A new pattern evolved. Now I hang out in various desert locations in winter, meander the open roads in spring and fall, and work summers as an interpretive guide. I am off the road, but in a campground in a spectacular spot. I give driving or walking tours where I experience the best a place has to offer. I've made new friends with co-workers. RVers and not, we share an appreciation for our work locations.

"With summer earnings I take vacations. After all, even RVers need vacations from their homes on wheels. One fall I took a train journey from Beijing to St. Petersburg, stopping to explore the Great Wall, Mongolia, and Siberia. Between the first and final draft of this article I booked a trip to Morocco and Spain. One spring, I rafted for eight days on the Colorado River between winter in the desert and a summer job at Glacier National Park.

"Is this what I will be doing five or ten years from now—I don't know."

"The mix of summer seasonal jobs, wandering in spring and fall, hanging out with friends in the Mojave and Sonoran deserts in the winter, suits me now. Is this what I will be doing five or ten years from now—I don't know. And I'm not worried about it. Change happens when it happens."

RESOURCES

- **Loners on Wheels:** ***(LonersOnWheels.com)***
- **RVing Women:** ***(RVingWomen.org)***
- **Wandering Individuals' Network (WIN):** ***(RVSingles.org)***
- **RV Singles Discussion Forum:** ***(Groups.Yahoo.com/Group/RV-Singles)***
- **Solo-Net:** ***(Skally.net/Solo-Net)***
- **Thousand Trails has several singles groups:** ***(ThousandTrails.com)***
- **Escapees RV Club singles group:** ***(Escapees.com)***
- **Loners of America:** ***(LonersOfAmerica.net)***
- **PoliSeek offers excellent free articles about safety and other issues:** ***(Poliseek.com/RV-Insurance-Articles)***
- **More free articles on travel, vehicle safety, etc:** ***(FunRoads.com)***
- ***RVers: How Do They Live Like That?*** **Judy Farrow and Lou Stoetzer:** ***(RVLifestyleExperts.com/RV-Books/Life-on-the-Road)***
- **Maintenance- home study course on RV maintenance for ladies and other courses:** ***(MobileRVAcademy.com)***

"All of the animals except for man know that the principle business of life is to enjoy it."
Samuel Butler

Chapter 21

How can I travel with my pets?

People travel with all sorts of pets. One woman loved horses. She traveled in a slide-in camper on a truck and towed a small horse trailer for her two horses. Her dog and cat rode in the camper. She worked part-time on the road and selected her jobs based on corral space for her horses and interesting places to ride.

Some people travel with more than one. **Alice** relates the time she and her late husband, Chuck, pulled into a campground just before dusk.

> "After we set up, we were sitting outside enjoying the ambiance when I noticed a man handing two little dogs to his wife who was just inside their motorhome. I looked away to watch the beginning of the sunset and then noticed that he was handing in those two dogs again. Well, I thought to myself, I wonder why they put them out again. So I watched some more. He handed two more little dogs, then two more, then two more, then two more … I had to go over and find out what their story was. They raised dogs and showed them and were down to thirteen (!) at the moment. *'Oh,'* I said, *'So you have a home somewhere and travel around to the different dog shows?'* No, they told me. They were full-timers and did it all from their

People travel with all sorts of pets.

> motorhome. They had taken out their couch and used the space for their little dog kennels."

Yes, of course you can travel with your pets. **Joanne Alexakis,** a long-time RVer, did.

> "Nick and I full-time RVed with our two German shepherds for years. People would ask us if the dogs were good travelers. Our response was that these dogs are happy as long as they can be at our side, wherever it may be. They'll go anywhere we go and often voiced their opinion if they weren't included in our comings and goings."

Of course you can travel with your pets.

SOME CONSIDERATIONS

Here are some things to consider if you travel with pets:

- **Your pets will need time** to become accustomed to different environments.
- **Be aware of coyotes and other wildlife**, particularly at night. Keep your pets inside at night or when you are gone.
- **Check the temperature inside the rig** to avoid extreme heat or cold when you are gone for the day. **Joanne Alexakis** shares how that affected their travels.

> "Traveling in a RV with pets can be more difficult than caring for pets back in your 'stick-built' home. Since the RV is rather like a metal can, it can heat up quickly. And when the RV is closed up, the temperatures can build up to be hotter than outside temperatures, just like an automobile. Pets need special consideration. We passed on viewing some attractions because the dogs would not be comfortable or safe left alone while we saw the sights.

Outside, rural outings worked better for us than big city, downtown or amusement park visits. Lots of walking was very necessary for all of us."

- **If you travel to Canada or Mexico,** you will need to show documentation of your pet's shots. (See Resources at the end of this chapter.)
- **Be a responsible pet owner.** Train your pet not to bark and be sure to pick up their waste. **Carol Weishampel** gives some practical advice.

"I traveled for ten years with two Shelties, and now travel with a collie, Sassie, and a cat, Frizbee. The following note was in a baggie with a couple of dog treats received in a campground:

Here's a little treat

For our four-legged campers

And a gentle reminder

That they don't wear Pampers

"Along with current rabies certificate, leash, plastic bags, food, and water in gravity feed bottle in the shower, I carry a collapsible kennel for the dog and a cat carrier. A baby gate keeps Sassie off the bed. Frizbee hides under a chair skirt or in the overhead, so I keep windows closed. A squirt water bottle or water gun taught the cat to stay away from the screened door."

Sometimes it's hard to decide whether to take a pet with you when you travel.

TRAVELING WITH A PET

Sometimes it is hard to decide whether to take a pet with you when you travel. The Brauers' dog adapted, but also had a sabbatical from

RVing so **Larry and Adrienne** could enjoy their trip to Alaska. If you lose your pet, will you get another?

> "When we retired, we still had Whitney, a medium-size Norwegian elkhound. She was already 13 years old when we started full-timing. She had gone with us before in a motorhome but we wondered how she would do if we were full-timing. Well, she loved it.
>
> "Whitney was with us when we took our first long motorhome trip along the coast of the Gulf of Mexico. She loved exploring new places.
>
> "When we drove to Alaska, we decided to give her a vacation at our daughter's house in Oregon. We wanted to be free to spend long days away from the RV to explore the beautiful state of Alaska.

"We wondered how she would do if we were full-timing. Well, she loved it."

> "When we returned to the lower 48 after six months of traveling, Whitney was ready to come back to the motorhome. We enjoyed traveling with Whitney for another two years before her health declined.
>
> "It was hard letting go of Whitney. Despite the companionship that Whitney provided, we made the decision not to get another pet."

JJ Dippel shares a humorous look at traveling in an RV from her cat's point of view as "Kitty" takes her first RV trip.

> "Mrrrrooowww. I'm ten years old and have owned a human named JJ most of my life. We started out in a nice big house, with a big back yard where I stalked big game (tasty mice

and a few bugs) and chased butterflies. And when I got 'cat crazies,' I could do the ten-yard dash in less than a second! When I was six, all that changed, and I became an RV traveling cat.

"JJ came home all excited about something called an 'RV.' Yawn, hopefully this doesn't pertain to me. Hold it! Why is JJ bringing the carrier out? *'NO! NO! Don't put me in the carrier! Nothing good EVER happens when cats are put in carriers! MRROOWW!!!!'*

"When I was six all that changed and I became an RV traveling cat."

"Oh good. I'm being let out! Hmmmm … it doesn't smell like the veterinarian's office, and I don't see anyone with things that poke and those horrible sticks that get put in my…. well, never mind! This kind of looks like our home but it's quite small. *'MROW, MROW, this simply will not do! I cannot run the ten-yard dash in here!'*

"Whew, JJ is coming to her senses. She is putting me back in the carrier. We are getting out of here.

"All is back to normal, or so I thought. The next morning, JJ brought the carrier out again. Nothing good EVER happens when cats are put in carriers! JJ is taking me out to the house in a box again! *'Hey! I thought we had a deal! No house in a box!'*

"JJ let me out of the carrier. I walk around. Whoa! What's happening? The house in a box started to move! *WAAAHHHH!' What is happening? Is JJ trying to get rid of me? She did seem disappointed when I refused to cuddle. Cuddling is for wimps! I'm an attack cat! I stalk big game! 'Mrrrow…. please JJ, please don't get rid of me, please, please, whatever I did to upset you, I can change….. Mrrrroooowwww…….'*

"Ok, she wins; I'll cuddle and sit on her lap. Wait, why is she pushing me away? Something about…. running off the road? What kind of a silly excuse is that? I jumped on her lap again, and again she pushed me away. Third time is a charm. I jump again. I hang my paws over one of JJ's arms and look out the side window.

"Why does JJ keep saying, 'I can't drive up narrow winding mountain roads with one arm?' I don't understand! Why is JJ muttering something about 'that deep ravine?' What is a 'deep ravine?'

"The house in a box stops. JJ gets out and goes somewhere. Is this where JJ is going to get rid of me? *'WAAAAAHH!!!'* Wait a minute. JJ is back, the house in a box moves again, and stops again. JJ is re-arranging and fumbling in the house in a box. Now she has the TV on. I'm still here! Hey, look at all these trees, out this big window in the back! I can sit on the bed and look out the window! And finally, JJ explained to me that getting this 'house in a box' was to allow her to bring me on her vacations! Well—why didn't you say so before?

"Then JJ went to something called 'Life on Wheels' and after that, I had to ride in the carrier."

"JJ and I have taken many RV trips since then. At first, JJ used to let me hang on for dear life buried in the bed sheets while she drove. That's my favorite place! Then JJ went to something called 'Life on Wheels' and after that, I had to ride in the carrier. Nothing good EVER happens when cats are put in carriers!"

"Kitty" is a Siamese/Tabby mix. Kitty's favorite places are state parks because of all the trees and little animals. Kitty's favorite pastime is to snooze either in a sunbeam or burrowed in JJ's bed. Kitty wishes that JJ would quit driving on winding roads because Kitty gets car-sick and has to sit in the carrier with "car-sick mess."

Simple modifications to your rig can make travel with a pet more convenient.

WHERE DO YOU PUT THE LITTER BOX?

Speaking of cats, where do you put the litter box? Some people use the shower so the litter is contained when the cat scratches. Our friend Betty made an opening just inside the rig by the doorway. There she installed a swinging cat door into the bin below. The litter box was in the bin; the cat happily climbed down to use it and had a dark space to explore. It was easy to access the litter box to clean it and kept any smells out of the rig.

LOSS OF A PET

Pets are beloved members of the family. Losing a pet is hard. Both **Nick and Joanne Alexakis'** German Shepherds passed away while on the road. Here is how they commemorated them in a place where they had special memories.

> "During the summer of 1996, my husband, Nick, and I were working as summer help at Custer State Park in the Black Hills of South Dakota. Our travel trailer was parked on a large site in the employee/volunteer RV campground. We had just begun full-time RVing and I missed the gorgeous autumn colors of back home, Minnesota. So, with approval of our supervisor, I bought a red maple tree from Kmart in Rapid City to contribute to the park. I can still remember driving from Rapid City thirty miles south back to the park

with that ten-foot sapling hanging out the back window of our station wagon and flapping wildly in the breeze. We planted it on our lot and watered it often.

"Our old, old German shepherd died that summer at the park. She was the best dog ever. We had her cremated and we scattered her ashes around our little tree. Four years later, when we were traveling in Florida, our other German shepherd got old, old and died, too. We had her cremated also and brought her ashes back to the little tree that was now growing tall. We knew our dogs brought nutrition to the maple and it is a fall foliage beauty now."

Some RVers commemorate pets in places that hold special memories.

RESOURCES

- **U.S. and Canada Dog-friendly Campground and RV Park Guide:** ***(DogFriendly.com/Server/Travel/Guides/Camp/Camp.shtml)***
- **PetFriendlyTravel.com:** ***(PetFriendlyTravel.com)***
- **Documentaton for pets traveling into Canada:** ***(CanadaWelcomesYou.net/TravelReminders.html)***
- **Documentation for pets traveling into Mexico: (*MexOnline.com/Mexpets.htm*)**
- **Documentation for pets traveling into or returning to the U.S.** ***(CBP.gov/LinkHandler/cgov/Newsroom/Publications/Travel/Pets_Wild.CTT/Pets.pdf)***

Section V. LIFE HAPPENS

Chapter 22
What if I'm disabled?

As a result of the ADA (American Disabilities Act) in 1990 and increased awareness, campgrounds have built more ramps, paved more pathways, and created handicapped-accessible bathrooms and showers. The RV industry offers wider doorways, wheelchair lifts, and barrier-free floor plans in their RVs.

You can join the legions of disabled RVers and enjoy the outdoor life and the freedom of the lifestyle. A huge network will help you make the transition and provide ongoing support.

Like life, the only limits we have are the ones we put on ourselves.

One RVer, who is legally blind and traveled by himself for years until he met his new wife, used a transportation company to move his RV from campground to campground when he traveled solo. He tended to stay in one place longer than most RVers, but enjoyed the activities and camaraderie of his fellow campers.

Soon after **Judith** and her husband went on the road, she caught a virus that attacked her heart. She received a heart transplant and after her six months recuperation period, her husband left her! Her kids begged her to stay with them and live out her days there. She refused and took off in the truck and trailer. About five years later, she finally acquiesced to her family and traveled in a motorhome, which is easier to handle. Judith lived for eight more years making the most of the gift of time her new heart had supplied.

Another RVer, who had lost part of one arm, still leads singalongs at RV parks and plays the electronic autoharp with her other hand. Like life, the only limits we have are the ones we put on ourselves.

THE HANDICAPPED TRAVEL CLUB

The Handicapped Travel Club *(HandicappedTravelClub.com)* was formed in 1973 to encourage RV traveling for people with a wide range of disabilities. They currently have more than 250 active members, publish a newsletter, have local get-togethers and sponsor an annual rally as well as an occasional regional rally.

Finding a rig that accommodates a specific disability is one of the biggest challenges.

Check out their resource information and links for a comprehensive view of the lifestyle from lists of companies that modify rigs, listings of used rigs for sale, traveling suggestions, and general support so the disabled traveler is never alone out there. This excellent club, whose fee is $12 to join and $8 a year thereafter, is probably the best bargain in the RV world for the support and friendship they offer.

HOW TO FIND A MODIFIED RV

For those traveling in RVs, one of the biggest challenges is to find a rig that will accommodate a specific disability. Many companies will make conversions, depending on what modifications people need. Some manufacturers will build to individual specifications or change a floor plan to make a unit accessible. The needs differ so much that it would be impossible to build an accessible RV that would work for everyone. Some units just need an assist bar at the door, others need a wheelchair lift, some furniture removed, dinettes shortened for a wheelchair to access a rear bath, etc. Some require a track system in the ceiling to move the individual from the front to the rear.

For more information on companies that customize RVs, visit:

- *(RV-Info.net/RVSpecialty.html)*
- *(GoRVing.com/Where-to-Find/Manufacturers)* Search: "By RV Type" click on "RVs for Disabled"

WHERE TO TRAVEL

Another challenge is finding places to travel that have accessible sites. Most campgrounds now provide sites for disabled campers. In Alice's brief experience in a wheelchair one year, she discovered that despite all good intentions, some details are always overlooked. For example, although the spaces are flat and wide enough to accommodate a unit and a lift, the utilities may be surrounded with railroad ties or crushed rock, or the office is not accessible for check-in. On the plus side, people are most gracious about lending a hand when needed.

Since 1990, there is a greater awareness of the need for access to the beautiful sites in our country. One summer when **Alice** and her husband visited Olympic National Park, they went to the Visitor's Center as usual to find out where to go. The ranger recommended a beautiful waterfall that required a half-mile hike to get to it. "I can't walk that far," Alice said, the disappointment showing on her face. "No problem," the ranger said and guided them to another waterfall that was easily accessible from the parking area. Alice learned a valuable lesson that day: Even though accessible places may not be clearly marked in the written material, speak to the rangers or campground hosts to find out what may be available.

There is a greater awareness of the need for access to the beautiful sites in our country.

Fortunately, more books are being written about accessible places to travel:

- *Wheelchairs On The Go: Accessible Fun in Florida*, by Michelle Stigleman
- *Barrier-Free Travel: A Nuts and Bolts Guide for Wheelers & Slow Walkers*, by Candy Harrington
- *Guide for the Wheelchair Traveler*, by Patricia Smither
- *Walks in the Northeast for the Not So Young and the Disabled*, by Marina Harrison

MEDICAL RATES

Sometimes RV parks will provide special rates if RVers need medical treatment. When **Nancy's** husband was temporarily disabled while traveling, she discovered that the local KOA only charged them $9 a night while her husband was undergoing physical therapy as a result of his accident. Nancy says:

> "I would advise any RVer who needs medical treatment to call all the RV parks in the area and find out if any offer medical rates. And if the RVer needs hospital treatment, then I would suggest the RVer contact Hospital Admissions and find out if the hospital has any relationships with RV parks where the RVer can stay at a discounted rate while he or she is undergoing treatment."

Some RV parks provide lower rates for RVers undergoing medical treatment.

RESOURCES

- **Travelin' Talk Network– An international information network providing assistance to travelers with disabilities: *(TravelinTalk.net)***
- **Access-Able Travel Source– Information on accessible attractions and HTC-identified accessible RV parks: *(Access-Able.com)***
- **For hearing and vision impaired– The Sidekick II Signature Series, by Silent Call Communications, monitors doorbells, telephones, smoke detectors and fire alarms within 2,000 feet and alerts people with hearing problems that there is a visitor, phone call or danger. They also make devices for visually impaired that vibrate: *(SilentCall.com/Catalog/Index.php?Intro=1)***
- **Links to access travel guides throughout the country: *(DisabledTravelers.com/Access_Guides.htm)***

NOTES

"Stop worrying about the potholes in the road and celebrate the journey."
Fitzhugh Mullan

Chapter 23

I'm not handy—should I travel?

The main advantage to being a handy RVer is that you save money by doing your own repairs. However, many people on the road rely on assistance from various sources. They also educate themselves by learning about the potential problems. Even if they can't fix it themselves, they have a better idea of what needs to be done.

Many people on the road rely on assistance from various sources.

EDUCATE YOURSELF

- **Read your manuals.** For many people, this is usually the last step—when all else fails. It's not a bad idea to do this at the beginning.
- **Attend educational sessions.** At most large rallies there are sessions focused on specific RV systems like batteries, waste disposal, electrical.
- **Build a relationship with service managers.** If you buy from a dealership or consistently use one for repairs, rely on the service manager as one of your technical experts.
- **Read and save articles.** Every RV-related magazine and website publishes technical articles.
- **Use Google and other Internet search engines** to locate your specific problem.

- **Talk to others in the campground.** Almost everybody has already experienced your problem. Listen to their stories about what happened and how they solved it. Besides talking about it, they often offer to help you.
- **Join RV forums and ask questions.** Many experienced, knowledgeable RVers participate in RV forums. Often they can help diagnose problems and offer solutions. You may get different ideas from different participants, but you can get ideas to try.

FOLLOW A MAINTENANCE SCHEDULE

By maintaining your rig, you can avoid many repairs as well as improving your own safety on the road, plus keeping up the resale value of your RV. Buy the proper tools: a set of metric or standard sockets and wrenches (depending on what your RV requires), crescent wrench, pipe wrench, torque wrench, pliers, channel locks, vice grips, standard and phillips screwdrivers, hammer, tire gauge, and valve extenders if you have dual tires. Having a collection of various screws, nuts, bolts, washers, and nails comes in handy, too.

Maintaining your rig helps avoid many repairs and improves safety on the road.

Follow the maintenance program in your owner's manual.

Keep records. Know exactly when you need to do the next scheduled servicing. If your owner's manual doesn't have a chart, make one for yourself, showing what has to be done, how often to do it, and a place to note the date when you did it

Consider the following maintenance areas:

- Lubrication.
- Wheels and tires, including inspection, rotation, inflation pressure, balancing and replacement.

- Engine oils.
- Fuel and air filters.
- Air cleaner replacement.
- Coolant system, including checking coolant levels, appearance, strength; checking hoses for signs of damage or deterioration (hoses should be firm not soft).
- Transmission, including fluid level, smell and color (should be pink not amber and burnt), plus signs of deterioration of the oil cooler, electrical and vacuum lines. Changing the transmission filter and fluid is one of the best things you can do to prolong the life of an automatic transmission.

Find trustworthy repair people.

- Heating and air conditioning, including lines, surfaces, drive belt.
- Front and rear suspension and alignment.
- Brakes.
- Drive belts, look for fraying and cracks.
- Propane tanks and lines.
- Exterior, including checking stains, sealant, roof, locks and hinges.

FIND TRUSTWORTHY REPAIR PEOPLE

How to find repair people:

- **Call your manufacturer or dealer for a recommendation** or for an authorized dealer. If the work is under warranty, this is an absolute must to maintain your contract.
- **If you are in a campground, ask for a recommendation** from the office and from fellow campers.
- **RV Repairs**: Find RV repair facilities in any state or Canada. *(MotorhomeDirectory.com/RV-Services)*

- **Camping World**: The biggest advantage for the traveler is that any Camping World store will honor work done in a different store and they are scattered throughout the United States. (*CampingWorld.com)*
- **Email your RV friends** to see if anyone can recommend a repair shop where you are.

Joei Carlton Hossack has chosen to stick with her dealer for repairs.

> "I take my vehicle to the dealer, whether I'm in Canada or the United States. I'm on the road too much to trust it with just anyone. I know if the last dealer didn't fix it properly, the next dealer will be able to pull up the record and see what's been done. Yes I pay more for the service but for the piece of mind it's worth it. My truck is eleven years old, a diesel, and I love it."

The choice is yours; choose what you're most comfortable with.

How to communicate with repair people:

- **Ask them for their shop labor rate** (about $80 seems to be the going rate as of this writing).
- **A good shop will not charge for every minute.**
- **Get an estimate.** They need to call you if it exceeds the estimate. On the authorization should be a not-to-exceed amount.
- **Put everything in writing.** Make two copies of your own list of necessary repairs. If possible have them initial it and keep one copy. It's easy to forget one of the details when you don't write it down.
- **Assume that it always takes two visits** to make sure something has been fixed.
- **Do not allow them to intimidate you**. Remember that you are in charge; you're paying their bill.

- **An honest repairperson will LISTEN to you**, be knowledgeable, and not try to sell you additional fixes.
- **If you are away from your usual trusted repairperson**, call and ask for guidance about what might be wrong and what you should be charged.
- **Determine the problem area and write down all the symptoms** you've noticed. That way you won't forget a crucial clue while you are talking to the service manager.

A final tip

Check it out before you start down the road.

Be alert to any changes in your systems that might indicate problems: uneven wear on your tires, for example, indicates a problem with alignment in a motorhome or truck or axle problems in a trailer. Knowing your vehicle will help you identify anything that seems out of the ordinary. Check it out before you start down the road. Check it out before you start down the road—it's worth repeating.

RESOURCES

- **We recommend that you order appropriate e-books by Mark Polk. Mark has done an outstanding job of providing detailed technical information for almost every aspect of RVing. If you are a neophyte to RVing, you might want to order the videos for your type of RV in his RV 101 series: *(RVLifestyleExperts.com/RV-Books/RV-Education-101)***
- **Check out service facilities before you make an appointment: *(RVServiceReviews.com)***
- **Maintenance– home study courses on RV maintenance: *(MobileRVAcademy.com)***

NOTES

"Ninety percent of all those who fail are not actually defeated. They quit."
Paul J. Meyer

Chapter 24

What do I need to know about RV systems?

Your safety may depend on reading the manuals and taking the warnings and cautions seriously.

This chapter is an introduction to the systems in an RV. A few basics and cautions are included. It is not designed to replace becoming thoroughly familiar with your owner's manuals. There are aids to learning how to operate your systems mentioned in the resources; however, each RV has unique features so read the manuals. Study the warnings and cautions and take them seriously. Not paying attention to them can cause personal injury, damage to your rig, even loss of your rig or your life.

We'll be looking at the following systems: vehicle, electrical, LP gas, fresh water, and wastewater.

THE WALK-THROUGH

When you purchase an RV from a dealer, make sure a knowledgeable representative does a walk-through with you to familiarize you with your RV and its systems. To get the most out of the walk-through and learn to operate your rig quickly:

- **Take notes.**
- **Stay in the area** or park near some other RVers so you can get further help and instruction if needed.

- Be sure to **perform each procedure yourself** as well as watch so you remember how to do it.
- If you have a video camera, **film the process** so you can watch again.

VEHICLE

Be familiar with the capacities for your vehicle and service it regularly. Pay attention to all weight ratings that apply to your vehicle such as Gross Vehicle Weight Rating (GVWR), Gross Combined Weight Rating GCWR (if towing), Gross Axle Weight Ratings (GAWR), tongue weight, etc. Do not exceed them. Overloading a rig or your tow vehicle can be dangerous. Towing adds a strain on the systems, which requires more diligent attention to service and monitoring your vehicle.

Overloading your rig can be dangerous.

Your driving habits also affect vehicle life. A driving class can help you acquire good driving skills.

Pay particular attention to:

- **Fluids:** Monitor and change oil, transmission fluid, and other fluids according to manufacturer's recommendations. Changing your oil and filter at the recommended interval is key to long engine life.
- **Tires:** Look for visible damage and uneven wear every time you drive. Check pressure regularly and make sure lug bolts are tight. Feel wheel hubs for excessive heat when you stop for rest and refueling to keep on top of bearing or brake problems.

ELECTRICAL SYSTEM

Your RV has two electrical systems: 12-volt (12V) and 120-volt (120V). It primarily operates on a 12V Direct Current (DC) system, using battery power. The 120V Alternating Current (AC) system requires a source of 120V power provided through a power supply cord ("shore power") or a generator. Since most lights and many appliances run on 12V power, a converter is almost always included to change 120V to 12V. The converter also charges your batteries when you are plugged in or your vehicle engine is operating.

Unless you have training, it is best to let trained service representatives handle electrical problems.

Some appliances, such as a microwave, will need 120V power to operate. They will only run on battery or 12V power if you have an inverter, which changes 12V power to 120V power and DC to AC.

Some rigs have built-in inverters, or you can purchase an inverter to fit your needs at a camping supply store or a store like Walmart. A small one will plug into a cigarette lighter receptacle and easily run a laptop computer. Excessive use of power when not plugged in can quickly deplete your batteries. To charge your batteries when not hooked to a power source, you can use your generator or install solar panels. See Generator on the following page. **CAUTION:** Unless you have training, it is best to let a trained service representative handle electrical problems.

- **Maintenance:** Regular maintenance is important. The most critical consideration for battery maintenance is to add distilled water when needed. Monitor your batteries closely.
- **Plugging in:** Before hooking up to shore power, use a voltage meter to make sure you have adequate power, a ground, and that the polarity isn't reversed. Check your voltage meter periodically to make sure power levels are not too high or too low, especially if you are running your air conditioning.
- **Adapters:** Your RV will come wired for either 30-amp or 50-amp service. RV parks or houses you visit may only have 15-amp service. Purchase adapters so you can plug in no matter what the situation. Be aware that with 15-amp service you will be limited on what you can run. (Running your refrigerator on

propane will reduce your electrical draw so you can run something else.)

- **Generator:** A generator can supplement your power when boondocking. If you plan to use your generator, park well away from other RVers and run it for limited time periods, respecting quiet hours. Do not run your generator if plugged into shore power. Smaller, quieter generators, like the Honda 2000, are fairly quiet and power all but things like your air conditioner.

LP GAS SYSTEM

Liquid propane gas (LPG) is highly explosive! Take every safety precaution when dealing with it. Since propane has no odor, it is treated to have a garlic-like odor to aid in detecting a leak. It is also heavier than air and can collect in pockets. If you have a leak, any flame can cause it to ignite. You'll find many safety precautions in your owner's manual. Read them.

Leak detectors: Every RV has an LPG leak detector. (If you purchased an older, used rig, make sure one is installed and still operable.) If it detects the presence of propane, the alarm will sound. Turn off the propane, open doors and windows, and vacate the rig until it is safe. Sometimes other substances like alcohol, cleaning agents and the propellants of aerosol cans will set off the detector too. **CAUTION:** If you have turned off the main power switch for any reason, your propane detector will not work. A green light on the detector indicates when it is on.

Take every precaution when dealing with the highly explosive liquid propane gas.

If you have a fifth wheel or trailer, when you reattach the filled bottle, you should test the connection: test with a portable propane detector or sniff the connection for the telltale propane odor, and also put soapy water on the connection. Bubbles indicate a leak.

FRESH WATER SYSTEM

Your RV can either use water from your onboard water tank or from a city water connection. Most RVs have a water pump to make your onboard water available. A switch, usually on your monitor panel, turns the pump off and on. Always turn off the pump when you are traveling or out of the rig for any length of time.

If you leave your rig for any length of time, drain your water system, especially in cold climates.

- **Water filters:** Most RVers filter their water before it enters the rig. In-line filters can be purchased from RV supply stores, Sears, Walmart, and others. You may also want to add an additional filter at the kitchen sink to provide better drinking water.
- **Filling the tank:** Fill the tank slowly and keep an eye on it. The tank must vent as you fill it or it may become pressurized and damage internal plumbing from excess pressure.
- **Winterizing your rig:** If you will leave your rig for any length of time, especially if the temperatures may drop below freezing, you must drain the water system. See your owner's manual. Sometimes it may help to evacuate water from low spots in pipes with an air compressor.

WASTE SYSTEM

You have at least two waste water tanks: a gray water tank for waste water from sinks and the shower, and a black water tank for toilet waste. Use recommended toilet tissue, a brand that breaks down readily.

- **Odors:** After emptying the tank, add a chemical and a couple of gallons of water by way of the toilet. Or use the toilet two or three times before adding the chemical. Note that most RV parks do not allow products with formaldehyde.

- **Hooking up:** Do not leave the valve to the black water tank open. Wait until it is at least half to three-fourths full and dump it all at once. Otherwise you will have a buildup of solids you can't get rid of. A day before you are going to dump, close the gray water valve and let it partially fill so it flushes out the hose when you empty the tanks. Dump the black water first.

Your monitoring panel is your friend.

- **Packing up:** When you leave, double-check that the valves are closed and the drain cap secured.

ITEMS YOU SHOULD CARRY WITH YOU:

- **Voltmeter:** The best ones show line voltage, frequency and warn if there is no ground or if there is reversed polarity.
- **Electrical Adapters** for different services.
- **Heavy-duty extension cords.**
- **Hydrometer** for checking batteries, if recommended.
- **Hoses made specifically for potable water,** white in color.
- **Filters at the connection,** optional at kitchen sink.
- **Pressure reducer** (optional).
- **Y connection:** Use at city water outlet so you can have a second hose to wash off with or to use in case of fire.
- **Tools:** channel locks or adjustable wrenches come in handy.
- **Disposable rubber gloves.**
- **Different hose than your fresh water hose** for washing out your sewage hose.

MORE TIPS

- **Your monitoring panel is your friend.** It lets you know the status of many of your systems. Check it frequently. Your owner's manual will explain what is there and how to interpret it.

- **If your generator** uses fuel from the main tank, make sure it can't drain your tank and leave you with no fuel.
- **A surge protector** will protect all your electrical appliances and equipment from damaging power fluctuations.
- **Some RVers install a catalytic or ceramic heater**, which is much more efficient than an RV furnace. It runs on propane, and uses no electricity. Be sure it is professionally installed and then operated according to manufacturer's instructions.
- **Before opening the black water tank**, first release a little gray water to test for hose leaks and secure connections.

RESOURCES

- **RV education 101– DVDs and e-books that explain RV systems and teach you about all aspects of RV operation:**
  - ★***How to Operate a Class A Motorhome***
  - ★***How to Operate a Class C Motorhome* (renters or buyers)**
  - ★***How to Operate a Travel Trailer or Fifth Wheel Trailer***
  - ★***The Three Primary Systems of an RV* (e-book)**
  - ★**Find these and others: *(RVLifestyleExperts.com/RV-Books/RV-Education-101)***
- **RV Safety– Under Articles/safety read about propane safety and other safety issues. See also Tech Notes: *(RVSafety.com)***
- **RV magazines like *Motorhome* have helpful articles each month. Use the article index to locate articles of interest: *(MotorhomeMagazine.com)***
- **See *Trailer Life* Magazine's website for articles on various systems under "Trailer How To:" *(TrailerLife.com)***

NOTES

"Don't wait around for our life to happen to you.
Find something that makes you happy and do it.
Everything else is background noise."
George Mason

Chapter 25

Will I be safe?

A number of questions often go through people's minds as they contemplate this lifestyle. Will I be able to drive a big rig? Is this a safe lifestyle? A number of safety issues were addressed in Chapter 20: "How can I travel by myself?" Even if you are traveling with a partner, go back and read this chapter.

The first step to staying safe is to start with a reliable rig and keep it that way.

RV SAFETY

RV safety begins with purchasing your rig. The first step to staying safe is to start with a reliable rig and keep it that way. If you buy a used RV, make sure it is safe. Get it inspected by a mechanic you trust. As soon as you notice something is wearing or not sounding like it should, have someone check it and get it repaired. You'll not only save money, but you may avoid a more serious problem or an accident.

Often other RVers are happy to assist with diagnosis and repair. Raise the hood on your RV and men will gather! Also, post your question in an RV forum. Many experienced RVers are more than happy to suggest solutions. Of course, you'll want to double-check this information since not all are experts.

Each time you drive your rig you should do a safety inspection. (See Chapter 24: "What do I need to know about RV systems?") Use a checklist every time you hook up and set up your rig. Keep an eye on the tires particularly, both for wear and proper tire pressure. Make sure everything is stowed. Be sure the refrigerator is off whenever you fuel your vehicle. Don't exceed the gross vehicle weight rating for your vehicle, or you will add unnecessary wear and tear or, in all likelihood, damage your engine. If you are driving a motorhome and towing another vehicle check the hitch and "toad," when you stop for fuel or a break.

Driving an RV is a matter of getting used to driving a larger, longer rig plus practice.

DRIVING

Driving an RV is a matter of getting used to driving a larger, longer rig plus practice. Keeping in mind the extra width, length and height is important as you make turns, pull into fuel stations and campgrounds, and drive on certain roads. Stopping takes more time when you have all that weight and needs to be accounted for. You can practice on back roads and large parking lots when most businesses are closed. Actually Jaimie first drove her motorhome on a divided highway with two lanes each way that didn't have a lot of traffic. The road was fairly straight and other drivers could get around her. It helped her learn where to position the motorhome in relation to the two white lines.

An RV driving course is an excellent idea for those new to driving a motorhome or pulling a fifth wheel or trailer. Some RV rallies offer these courses. They are also offered in some locations in the winter in the Southwest. Check the driving schools mentioned in Chapter 20: "How can I travel by myself?" to see what their schedule is. You learn in your own RV, which is important.

JJ Dippel, a solo woman RVer, shares an account of taking her Class C on a Washington ferry. She was apprehensive about her ability to get into a tight space.

> "If you have wanted to take your RV to an island getaway but the thought of driving it onto a ferry is intimidating, well, it's as easy as taking a small car!
>
> "I had driven my RV down Interstate-5 through Seattle and all the traffic in the past. I swear the freeway lanes are claustrophobically narrower through Seattle than on the rest of I-5. I certainly didn't want to repeat the experience of having an 18-wheel truck on both sides and very little breathing room. I decided I'm going back home a different way! Let's check the map. The alternative is to go back via US-101 and board a ferry at Port Townsend. A FERRY? I CAN'T DO THIS! THEY PACK THOSE CARS IN TIGHTLY! AND WHAT IF I'M THE ONE WHO SINKS THE BOAT?
>
> "After having a panic attack trying to decide between the ferry or a hair-raising trip back through Seattle on I-5, I chose to brave the ferry. At Port Townsend, I paid my fare and was directed to Lane 4. There were five lanes total, with Lane 5 on my left. I surveyed the situation. PANIC! How am I going to make a very sharp 90-degree left turn to get on the boat without hitting the lead car in Lane 5? The ferry workers had this under control. They know how to direct the vehicles to board. RVs are spread out so the weight is distributed and not concentrated in any one spot. In fact, there were three other RVs and a delivery truck that were bigger than my vehicle aboard the

Following the experts' advice helps when driving in unfamiliar situations.

> ferry. When it was my turn to board the boat, the ferry workers made sure there were NO cars in Lane 5 for me to hit.
>
> "WHEW! I'm on the boat. We are packed in like sardines. Now I have 30 minutes to be scared to death about how I'm going to get off. Again, the ferry workers knew exactly what to do. I was directed off and went on my way! After that, I decided that riding the ferry is worth it to avoid Seattle's traffic."

Driving in a city can be downright scary too. Bridges, traffic, one-way streets are intimidating to some and make it difficult to move easily through congestion. And sometimes, you take a wrong turn. Here is **Kimberly and Jerry Peterson's** experience on the streets of Chicago.

> "We usually stay at RV parks or casino parking lots where security is ever-present. We have always been the type of people who lock doors and are very aware of our surrounding area, which we continue doing as we travel. There was one time when we were concerned about our safety and that was when we were driving through Chicago and made a wrong turn into not the greatest of neighborhoods. Many of the houses were boarded up or burnt down. The roads were very narrow to the point that we had nowhere to go if the person in front of us would not move over; we could not back up, after all, since we are a motorhome towing a Jeep. It was the longest hour of our lives that seemed like we would never make the right turn to get us out of there. Eventually we did and had a great laugh about it. Otherwise, we usually feel very safe during our travels and our overnight environments."

Oops! Sometimes you take a wrong turn.

Global Positioning System (GPS) devices have made travel in new locations much easier. For solo drivers they make driving not only easier but safer since you don't have to take your eyes off the road. **George**, Jaimie's husband, resisted getting one for several years. Now that he has one, he wouldn't be without it. It has taken us right to places without having to print out our own map and, occasionally, he has fun arguing with it. He says, "I have two women in the truck. One I can argue with!"

Now that he has a GPS, he wouldn't be without it.

Occasionally, though, things can go wrong. George and Jaimie's Garmin has taken them unnecessarily around a block making three right turns instead of indicating one left turn. The GPS maps are not always up to date, which can lead to frustration and wrong turns. **JJ Dippel** tells how her GPS occasionally leads her astray.

> "The RV driver's best tool is a portable (or built in) Global Positioning System (GPS) unit. This nifty gadget will give you turn-by-turn instructions to get to your destination. My experience with GPS units is that they will get you there, but not necessarily by the best route. And, once in awhile, a GPS unit will lead you astray.
>
> "My first GPS unit had difficulty providing directions in cloudy or rainy weather. It would either lose the signal or tell me I was 'off the road,' and include a stern warning about doing that kind of driving. One time I was driving on a 'freeway up in the air on stilts' through a large city on a cloudy day. The GPS unit showed that I was traveling on a surface street and insisted that I make a turn. *'Um, I don't think so.'*
>
> "When the prices came down, I bought a newer model. This one had no trouble with cloudy weather, and it could even plot my location under covered RV storage. However, I was led astray with this unit. I was attempting to get to an RV

park in Grants Pass, Oregon. The GPS told me to turn left. I obeyed, and when it told me that 'I had arrived,' I found myself not at the RV park, but on a steep and narrow dead-end road. (I should have gone straight instead of turning left.) There was no place to turn around. I had to drive backwards down that steep and narrow road, including going around a sharp, blind curve. If you are a solo driver, this can be a terrifying experience.

"When I finally got to the RV park, I jokingly asked what the 'body count' was for making the grievous error of obeying one's GPS. The check-in employee shook her head and said, *'Too many to count.'* Apparently, for employees of that RV park, it is now standard procedure to inform customers who make phone reservations to ignore their GPS and to drive straight instead of turning left.

"GPS units are great tools, but they are not a substitute for good map reading and navigating skills."

"GPS units are great tools, but they are not a substitute for good map reading and navigating skills. So keep some maps handy and learn to use them."

Myrna Courtney offers another piece of advice for using your GPS.

"Some GPS devices now have a menu to 'avoid' certain things, such as u-turns. Mine would do ANYTHING to avoid a u-turn until I unchecked it."

PERSONAL SAFETY

As we mentioned in Chapter 20: "How can I travel by myself?" the key things are to trust your gut and to use common sense. Don't park or stay overnight in any location where you don't feel safe or comfortable.

Nick Russell, publisher of the *Gypsy Journal*, confronted an armed robber in the process of robbing his RV. He and his wife had returned to the yard of the repair shop where it was parked after taking people to the airport. They saw the hole in the door window and, at first, didn't realize someone was still inside. The man stepped out of the rig with one of Nick's guns in hand. Nick was able to get the gun from him while Terry called the police. A number of items were stolen; more were stacked up ready to remove. We are so glad they only lost possessions and were not hurt. Neither of us was there nor knows what we would do in the same situation.

We no longer stay in rest areas along the Interstates.

Without trying to second-guess the situation, it does bring up some points to consider.

- **Where you park:** Often repair facilities are in industrial areas and not well patrolled at night. If possible, see if you can park in a secured area or even bring your RV inside the garage at night. If you pull over at night for a rest, choose a well-lighted spot around people. That's why Walmart parking lots are so popular. They are patrolled. We no longer stay in rest areas along the Interstates because of the many incidents that have happened to people parked there.
- **Don't open the door:** Never open the door if someone knocks at night. We keep a flashlight by the door that we can shine in the visitor's face through a window to see who is there. We also do not have our names showing on the outside where someone who means you harm could knock and call you by name, making you think you know them.
- **Firearms:** In this case, we don't know if the robber was armed, but he did use a gun he found inside. Decide if carrying firearms is to your advantage or the robber's.

- **Reaction:** In hindsight, it probably would have been better to drive a short ways from the area and call 911 and wait for the police. If Nick hadn't reacted quickly and slammed the door on the gunman's hand and disarmed him, he could have been shot with his own gun. Unless you are absolutely certain the robber has come and gone, call for help.

In spite of all this, RVing is relatively safe. Things can happen like accidents or fires. Being prepared and not taking chances can avoid most of them. A few other tips:

- **Keep your RV ready to drive away.** This is easier in a motorhome than a towed rig. In a fifth wheel or trailer, make sure it is safe to get out and get to your tow vehicle before leaving your rig.
- **Park where you have a cell phone signal** so you can call 911 if necessary.
- **Pay attention to your surroundings** when you park and if you walk outside your RV. Avoid bushes, parked vehicles, a person standing outside. Have your keys ready and stay in well-lighted areas.

RESOURCES

- **PoliSeek offers excellent free articles about safety and other issues: *(Poliseek.com/RV-Insurance-Articles)***
- **More free articles on travel, vehicle safety, etc.: *(FunRoads.com)***
- ***RVers: How Do They Live Like That?* Judy Farrow and Lou Stoetzer: *(RVLifestyleExperts.com/RV-Books/Life-on-the-Road)***

"It takes some couples two years or more before they find stability or a sense of community."
from– RVers: How Do They Live Like That?

Chapter 26

Can my partner and I survive?

Living with a partner twenty-four hours a day, seven days a week, requires that both (or more when it's a whole family) master the art of communication and negotiation skills.

How good your relationship is before you hit the road will be a factor in how you live together 24/7.

How good your relationship is before you hit the road will be a factor in how you live together 24/7. **Kimberly and Jerry Peterson** make this observation:

> "Whenever we talk with wannabes, one of the first subjects we bring up is how good your current relationship with your companion is; this makes a major difference. Your relationship has to be strong, open to change and very forgiving. Ours is challenged all the time and if we did not have a strong and firm foundation, there is no way we would have survived the constant togetherness that is a fact when you live in such a small space. Many folks need those breaks from one another, but we have always worked together so this lifestyle fits perfectly into our lives and has actually brought us much closer than we ever imagined."

Myrna Courtney tells how she and her late husband would handle her need for "private space."

> "When I thought I needed my 'space,' Gerry would drop me at a bookstore, library, pet shop, tea shop, mall, etc. By the time he came to pick me up, I was SO ready to see him again! When you're on the road, there's no one else to use for shoulder crying-on. You gotta deal with your traveling buddy."

PRACTICAL TIPS

Here are some practical tips for keeping your relationship on an even keel:

- **Practice relaxation breathing.** When too much is happening and it's starting to get to you, remove yourself from the situation for a few minutes (or longer if possible). Breathe deeply and slowly using your diaphragm. Actually feel your midsection expand. Hold the breath. Breathe out slowly. Your midsection should contract. Let yourself go-like a rag doll-and melt. Do this several times. Now you are ready to calmly find a solution.
- **Listen to the message behind the words.** Sometimes we are so busy trying to get across our own message that we literally can't hear what the other person means. Paraphrase what is said to check for meaning. "When you say you are sick and tired of traveling, do you mean that we've driven too many miles this week or do you want to get off the road entirely?"

"You gotta deal with your traveling buddy."

- **Give clear messages.** Say what you want. Don't expect your partner to read your mind. Use an "I" message when being critical. Describe how the other person's behavior is affecting you. "I feel overwhelmed when I spend time cleaning up the rig while you're swimming and then you come home and leave your wet towel on the floor."

- **Focus on finding solutions to problems.** Don't meet resistance with unyielding resistance. Agree whenever you can even if it's only that you agree there is a problem. Finally, discuss current issues, not personalities or ancient history.

Kimberly and Jerry follow these ground rules.

> "Emphasizing some of the ground rules we made when we first married has truly helped us in this lifestyle. They are simple, yet not always easy to follow. For this lifestyle to work for us, we adhere to them as often as possible. Some of those rules include:

Communication and a sense of humor are essential.

> 1. We both cannot be unreasonable, angry, or spiral down at the same time. If one goes down that path, the other must stay focused on staying upbeat.
> 2. Communication and a sense of humor are essential. We have to be able to talk to one another and most importantly, listen to what the other has to say and laugh about it often.
> 3. Pick our battles, not waste time on the 'small stuff,' and nitpicking is just not allowed.
> 4. If either of us do not like the way the other is doing it, either suck it up or do it ourselves without an attitude. We both have certain jobs around the rig to do but if necessary, we could switch at any time so we have learned to do it all. Not only do we feel it is essential to know how to do it all ourselves, just in case we ever have to, but also that we each can understand what the other goes through while doing their tasks.
> 5. The obvious, yet hardest thing at times to do is to always respect one another and greet each day and each other with a smile."

Joanne Alexakis suggests two necessities for long-term traveling with a companion.

1. A bedroom. Besides sleeping quarters, it lends a separate area for reading, writing, late-morning sleeping in, nursing a headache, pouting, or just plain vegging out. This individual space is valuable for maintaining a good relationship. Sometimes you just have to be by yourself.
2. Camping in areas that have good/great/fantastic weather so that you can spend lots of time outdoors. It's like adding a whole huge room onto your rig. And having an RV with windows on all four sides of the rig allows you to enjoy that "big room" outside from indoors. You can see out, take pleasure in the view, watch what's going on, and not feel closed in.

Having alone time is important.

Joanne's advice suggests that having alone time is important. **Sharon Vander Zyl** explains how she and her husband find their own time to renew, thus strengthening their relationship.

"*'Isn't it about time for you to go on another retreat?'* my husband, Rollie, asked with a wink as he dried the last of the dishes I had washed. We were four weeks into our volunteer assignment at Aransas National Wildlife Refuge in Texas. Except for a few separate work duties we'd been together 24/7 during those four weeks, so I knew exactly what he meant. It was time for some separateness in our togetherness.

"A wise person once said, *'Too much of a good thing is NOT a good thing.'* The togetherness in our 42-year marriage has been a good thing because we have always tempered it with times of separateness.

"When we were both active in our careers and with the National Guard, the separateness came naturally. Even then, I found that taking time alone (I call the time a 'retreat') every four to six weeks replenished both of us and revitalized our relationship. So it was a natural to carry that practice into our RV life.

"As we travel to a new state I computer search for retreat centers in that state and select one that interests me and that fits our location and schedule, making a reservation for two to three days. Other ways to take time away are to use resorts, hotels, or bed and breakfasts. A friend of mine cuts the costs of a time away by using a single friend's apartment when the friend travels for business."

Time alone can replenish and revitalize your relationship.

Here are **Sharon's** suggestions for a personal retreat.

"For me, the focus of a retreat is more BEING than DOING so I mostly follow my internal prompting. Sometimes I sit in silence, sometimes I read, sometimes I walk, sometimes I journal, sometimes I pray, sometimes I nap, sometimes I take a hot, soaking bubble bath (no tub in our fifth wheel).

"Here are some other suggestions for a personal retreat:

➤Slow down and rest

➤Sleep

➤Take a leisurely walk, preferably in nature

➤Do nothing

➤Pamper yourself with a manicure or pedicure

➤Write yourself a letter

➤Do a life review or inventory

➤Write prose or poetry

➤Read

- ➤Make a list of your values
- ➤Do some artwork
- ➤Listen to tapes or CDs
- ➤'Dialogue' with your body
- ➤Journal
- ➤Do a cleansing juice fast
- ➤Practice yoga or tai chi

> "Whatever the activity, the focus should be just being with the experience."

For those who can't imagine themselves in solitude there are other types of "retreats" that can provide spaces in couple-togetherness. One of my friends goes on a "sister weekend" every year with her four sisters. They take turns planning the weekend each year. Another friend takes her grandchildren to a resort that caters to children each year giving her daughter and son-in-law some alone time in the process. Other possibilities: educational workshops, health spas, weight loss spas, yoga or tai chi retreats, archaeological digs, birding, distance hiking with a group. The possibilities are only limited by the imagination. These types of "retreats" do not provide all of the benefits of solitude but they can give other benefits such as changes of pace and perspective, new knowledge, enriched family relationships, and improved health. **Sharon Vander Zyle** discusses the benefits she and her husband get from "retreats."

Possibilities for "retreats" are only limited by the imagination.

> "After Rollie drops me off for a retreat, he enjoys his alone time in our trailer with our dog. He, too, does 'whatever, whenever.' One of our friends joked that one day he might not pick

me up. But so far he always has and I think when he does, it is with renewed appreciation of me and of our relationship."

Not everyone travels with a spouse. **Carol Weishampel** has traveled with grandchildren and pets. Guess which one she finds easier!

"Grandkids. Love 'em or Leave 'em. I took one grandson to Alaska twice, and two grandsons to Alaska once. I'm either getting very forgetful or…

"Dogs and cats are more complacent companions and easier on the nerves than grandkids! I traveled with two Shelties for about ten years. Now I travel with a collie, Sassie, and a cat, Frizbee."

Some privacy is essential.

Good relationships often improve or get closer on the road. Even the closest of couples do need a break from one another. You can take a retreat as Sharon suggests but even a few hours or a day away from the RV and your partner can do wonders. Kay Peterson, co-founder of the Escapees RV Club, called these "Kay Days." Spouses understand the term, knowing that you aren't leaving them in anger, but that you need some space.

Other tips

- **Get a pair of headphones** for the TV and anything else that makes noise—radios, stereo, computers, etc. That way the one spouse does not have to listen to the other spouse's programs.
- **Respect each other's space.** Have personal areas for each, where the other would never go unless invited. Some privacy is essential.
- **The five most essential words** for a healthy and vital relationship are "**I apologize**" and "**You are right.**" Three words to avoid: **always, never, should.**

RESOURCES

- ***RVers: How Do They Live Like That?*** **by Judy Farrow and Lou Stoetzer available at:** ***(RVLifestyleExperts.com/RV-Books/Life-on-the-Road)***

"Travel is glamorous only in retrospect."
Paul Theroux

Chapter 27

What happens if I get sick?

If it's an emergency call 911. For routine treatment, check with your insurance for approval and providers.

Even if you take care of yourself, there are times when you get sick or you may have a chronic condition that needs treatment. Now is the time to reach out to others. RVers in the area and residents can often recommend physicians and other health care professionals. The Internet is also a source for locating doctors and checking their training and standing. If it is a true emergency, do not hesitate—call 911. Your cell phone will connect to local 911 operators.

CHECK WITH YOUR INSURANCE COMPANY

Unless it is an emergency, if you have medical insurance, make sure you know their policy about treatment that is out of their coverage area and if getting authorization prior to treatment is necessary. You may need to select a member of their network, if available, for full coverage.

In most cases, for Canadians, policies are set out quite clearly on the card your insurance company provides for you. Insurance companies have been known to increase your deductible if you do not contact them before seeking medical treatment.

CARRY YOUR MEDICAL RECORDS

Make sure you have your records, X-rays, and copies of recent tests with you as you travel. By law, hospitals and physicians must provide copies if you request it. These provide a baseline for the medical staff to use when comparing your current tests and symptoms. It's a good idea to have a record of your prescriptions with you, including correct name, dosage, and frequency of use. Invariably, if you're not feeling well, you won't remember all that information. If you have a specific illness or allergic reaction, you should be wearing a medical alert bracelet, since you may not have anyone with you who knows that information to give the medical staff.

> **Make sure your partner knows where to find your medical information.**

If you are traveling with a partner, make sure he or she knows where that information is in case you are not able to give that information. Here are some options:

- **Vial of Life** is a form you can obtain at no cost. Complete it and keep it in your refrigerator. A sticker alerts paramedics that your information is there.
- **A Care Memory Wristband** contains all your medical information on a wristband with a flash drive that can be accessed by the hospital or physician on their computer.
- **Make a medical ID card** for your wallet at no charge at Medical Identification Online. (Refer also to Chapter 20: "How can I travel by myself?" where Betty Prange recommended putting your ID and medical information on an inexpensive flash drive with a hole on the top to attach to your key chain.)

FINDING A DOCTOR OR HOSPITAL

The biggest problem is knowing who to go to if you don't have an emergency, but you do have an urgent problem or an ongoing medical situation. If you are in a campground, the host should either have some recommendations for medical assistance or know some local people who can give you that advice. If you have been in the community for a while, you may have made your own local contacts. Ask several people for recommendations. If two people mention the same doctor, follow that lead.

While you may be a patient, you are not a victim. Be assertive.

A number of websites rate physicians. Some are free; some have a charge. In some cases you can find out if disciplinary action has been taken. See Resources at the end of this chapter.

REMAIN IN CHARGE

When you do go to the doctor or hospital, remember that you may be a patient, but you are not a victim. Be assertive about what they will be billing you for. If you need one type of blood test, make sure that is clearly stated so that you are not charged for other tests. Find out how much the procedure will cost and get that in writing. If this visit will not be covered by your insurance, offer a cash payment and ask for their Medicare rate (even if you are not Medicare age).

MEDICAL EMERGENCY INSURANCE

For a backup in case you need to be evacuated in an emergency situation, you may want to consider supplemental insurance from one of these companies:

- Medical Air Services *(MedAirServices.com)*
- SkyMed 800-475-9633 *(SkyMed.com)*

Canadians should check Chapter 18: "What about health insurance?" for information about Canadian travel health insurance. Canadians may be able to include this coverage in their policy.

TRAVELING WITH CHRONIC ILLNESSES

Just because you have a chronic illness doesn't mean you can't travel. You need to know your limitations and monitor your medical needs carefully. You will also make some accommodations to your traveling style as well as your rig. People carry oxygen tanks with them, wheelchairs, back pillows, to name a few.

> **If you need to get off the road temporarily or permanently, give some thought to what you'll do.**

GETTING OFF THE ROAD

You may need to get off the road temporarily to deal with an illness. You can find an RV park where you get a long-term rate, perhaps near where you'll be getting treatment. Other RVers have moved into an apartment or house, at least temporarily.

One younger RVer with no insurance took a job with health insurance so she could get treatment. They stayed in that area for a few years until the treatment was finished and their finances had recuperated.

Escapees RV Club CARE Center: Members of the Escapees Club can stay at the Escapees CARE Center. CARE is the result of Kay Peterson's dream, which is based on this very issue: What do you do when you need assistance and you don't want to or can't leave your rig? One solo, for example, appreciated the opportunity to recuperate from foot surgery in her own rig with assistance from the CARE center.

The CARE center is located at Escapees headquarters in Livingston, Texas. A nonprofit corporation, it provides a safe haven with professional assistance at affordable prices for Escapees RV Club members whose travels are permanently ended or temporarily interrupted because of health problems. Residents continue to live in their RVs.

HANGING UP THE KEYS

At some point you may make the decision to get off the road for good. Whether you decide the RV lifestyle is no longer for you because of health issues or you are ready for a change, give some thought to what you'll do. Chapter 29: "Is the RV lifestyle for me?" lists a number of possibilities.

RESOURCES

- **DocFinder– Physician Profiles provides information about physicians including education, training, specialty, malpractice and disciplinary proceedings: *(DocBoard.org/DocFinder.html)***
- **Vitals.com– Free site with physician ratings: *(Vitals.com)***
- **HealthGrades.com– Rates both physicians and hospitals. Find the best hospital for your condition: *(HealthGrades.com)***
- **Care Memory Wristband: *(CareMemoryBand.com)***
- **Medical Identification Online: *(MedIDs.com/Free-ID.php)***
- **Vial of Life: *(VialOfLife.com)***
- **ICU in FL– In Florida if you have a driver's license, you can enter your emergency contact information online so it is available to police and emergency personnel: *(Services.FLHSMV.gov/ECI)***
- **Clinical trials– Free treatment for certain conditions if you participate in a study:**
  - ★***(CinicalTrials.gov)***
  - ★***(TrialCheck.org/Services)***
  - ★***(BreastCancerTrials.org/BCT_Nation/Home.Seam)***

NOTES

"I am prepared for the worst, but hope for the best." Benjamin Disraeli

Chapter 28

How do I handle an emergency?

Prevention is the key to avoiding many emergencies.

We don't like to dwell on bad things happening, but they do and they might happen to you. That's the reality. So you must prepare for that possibility. This chapter provides information that will enable you, even if you are alone during an emergency, to deal effectively with the situation.

PREVENTION IS THE KEY

Many emergencies can be avoided if you follow the other tips given throughout this book:

- **Keep your rig and tow vehicle in good repair.**
- **Maintain your vehicle-servicing schedule.**
- **Take a safe driving course.**
- **If you sense any danger or if something isn't "sounding right" as you're driving, stop and evaluate the situation.**
- **Follow your safety checklist before you start out** to make sure your tires are correctly inflated, lights are working, bike is secure, etc.
- **Check periodically that you have enough fuel.**
- **Pull over if you feel tired or not fully alert.**

EMERGENCY ROAD SERVICE

No matter how careful you are, accidents do happen. If it happens when you are on the road, make sure you have an emergency road service policy from a good RV company. That way you will never be alone any longer than the forty-five minutes to an hour it takes them to get to you. In the Resources section at the end of the chapter are several companies that provide excellent service. Do your research as thoroughly as you did for RV insurance.

Have an emergency road service policy from a good RV company.

Here are some of the features you want included in the policy:

- **Covers you anywhere in U.S. and Canada.**
- **"Sign and drive:" No cash is exchanged during an occurrence.**
- **No limit to number of occurrences.**
- **Includes towing, providing any fluids needed, changing flat tires, jumping dead batteries, lock-out service, etc.**
- **No limits to towing.**
- **Provides Travel Delay Assistance Program:** If accident happens more than 300 miles away from home base, company will provide up to $150 per day for lodging, meals and rental car for up to eight days.
- **Provides an extra person for transport if necessary.** In response to the concern, "What if a solo traveler's tow bar was damaged and both motorhome and toad had to be driven separately to repair facility," the company would provide an extra person to do the transporting.

EMERGENCY AIR AMBULANCE

For peace of mind, especially if you become very ill far away from your home base, consider membership in an organization like SkyMed or Medical Air Services. Some of the benefits include evacuation in an air ambulance to your home base as well as return of your stranded RV and vehicle. Ask about a discount if you belong to an RV organization. For example, Escapees members save about $80 on an annual family membership.

When an accident first happens, check first on the condition of the people involved and then the safety of the rig.

WHAT TO DO IN CASE OF A VEHICLE ACCIDENT

If an accident of any kind happens, determine if the damaged vehicle can be driven or moved safely without doing additional damage. If you drive or move a vehicle that results in additional damage, your insurance policy may not provide you protection for this additional damage.

When the accident first happens, check first on the condition of the people involved and then the safety of the rig. Be sure you always have your cell phone near you so you can dial 911 if you need that assistance. If you are able to move, do the following:

- **Get out**
- **Make sure everyone's okay and out of the vehicle(s)**
- **Turn off propane if you had traveled with it on**

Whether to travel with your propane on or off is a continual debate in the RV community. Here are **Betty Prange's** thoughts on the subject:

> "Traveling with it off, as I always do, means one less thing to remember in the trauma of an emergency. And if it is an emergency where I cannot get to the turnoff, I know it is off. Refrigerators will stay cold for a long time if doors are closed. If I am traveling in warm weather for extended times, I still turn off the propane. I can turn it back on when I stop for lunch."

- **Disconnect toad if there is a fire (if safe) or danger of one**
- **Call 911 for police or emergency vehicles if necessary**
- **Note the exact location** (and mile post markers if applicable)
- **Call your emergency road service** (see next section about towing)
- **Call your insurance company's hot line**

If you need to be towed, and have towing coverage from a road service, Good Sam or AAA, call the road service provider before you call the tow company. Most providers of road service coverage have tow companies under contract that they call when service is needed; there should not be any additional costs to the person who needs the service. Determine the exact street address or one closest to your location. In Alice's experience, she told the AAA that she was at a particular gas station next to a specific off ramp, but they wanted the actual street address of the gas station.

Obtain necessary information related to the accident.

After the accident, obtain necessary information related to the incident, such as:

- **Location**
- **Milepost markers**
- **Name of police agency handling the investigation**
- **Name of tow company**
- **Other person's information: name address, phone, and insurance company**
- **Witness information (if there are any)**
- **Where you will be staying**
- **Where you can be reached by phone and in person**

WHAT TO DO IN CASE OF FIRE

How to prevent RV fires:

Most fires are preventable. Proper maintenance will prevent most fires from happening in the first place. Again, these emergencies do happen and you must be prepared.

At an RV rally one year, John and Betty's rig caught on fire and he was burned on forty percent of his body. John made an incredible recovery by six months after the accident, and he and Betty are off traveling again. John's experience, as related to us, highlights two key warnings to all RVers:

Proper maintenance will prevent most fires from happening, but be prepared just in case.

1. **Respect the dangers of working with propane.**
2. **Be sure to know how to operate your fire extinguisher.**

Another couple had an electrical problem that destroyed their rig. Luckily they got out, and the fire was caught in time so it didn't spread to the neighboring rigs.

What can we do to prevent these occurrences? Here are suggestions from several excellent sources. Check out their websites listed in the Resources section at the end of this chapter for more information.

Mac McCoy, known as Mac the Fire Guy, served 33 years in the fire service in all capacities. He holds a BS degree in Fire Science and a Masters degree in Fire Administration. He now travels to various RV rallies to teach fire safety workshops. Check out his schedule on his website. He has a number of excellent articles, including "34 Fire Facts That Can Save Your Life." Here are the first three:

1. A pinhole-size leak in a radiator or heater hose can spray antifreeze on hot engine parts. Antifreeze contains ethylene glycol concentrate and water. When the water boils off, the remaining

ethylene glycol can self-ignite at 782 degrees F. During your monthly fire inspection, check all hoses for firmness, clamp tightness, and signs of leaking.

2. Rubber fuel lines are commonly used to connect metal lines to the electronic fuel injection system, or to the carburetor in older coaches. Check all the lines and connections between the fuel tank and the engine on a monthly basis. If there is any sign of a leak, have the lines replaced and the entire system inspected by a qualified mechanic as soon as possible.

Check all hoses for firmness, clamp tighness, and signs of leaking.

3. A hard-working engine manifold can get as hot as 900 degrees F. The heavy insulation in the compartment reflects the heat back to the top of the engine, and a fire can easily break out. Inspect your radiator and have any problems repaired by a qualified person as soon as possible.

Nationwide Insurance has shared some general guidelines with RVers:

1. **Check extinguishers.** Before traveling, be sure your fire extinguisher is functional and contains proper pressurization. You should keep multiple extinguishers on hand throughout the vehicle and understand which extinguisher is effective on different types of fires. Also, be sure to verify that your smoke detectors are in working order.
2. **Avoid transmission fires.** Many fires are caused by fluid leaking from the transmission, which can be ignited if it comes in contact with the exhaust system. Complete a thorough check of the underside of your RV as part of your pre-trip inspection.
3. **Inspect electrical systems.** A common cause of fire is a short in the 12-volt electrical system. Check the engine compartment wiring as another part of your pre-trip inspection. Replace any damaged or frayed wires and make sure the connections are secure.

4. **Have an evacuation plan.** While it may seem simple, a key step to fire safety is ensuring that everyone traveling knows how to operate the latches of doors and windows, allowing for a quick exit in an emergency situation.
5. **Stay kitchen savvy.** Be sure to keep clothes, linens and other combustibles far from the kitchen area. Stay alert while cooking as items such as paper towels and curtains are likely to be close to the stove, creating a fire hazard.

Vehicle fire safety while traveling

Since RVs are on the go so much, NFPA (National Fire Protection Assn.) and AAA teamed up to offer these suggestions in case you have a fire while on the road. According to a report by NFPA, released in 2008 and covering the years 2002-2005, 75 percent of vehicle fires are due to mechanical (50%) or electrical (25%) failure or malfunction. It is essential that you get your vehicle checked out by a trained, professional technician each year. In addition to visual clues, be aware of unusual sounds and smells.

Remember three steps: stop, get out and call for help.

To further reduce the risks associated with vehicle fires, it's important for motorists to know what to do—and not do—should their vehicle catch on fire. AAA advises motorists to remember three steps: stop, get out and call for help.

1. **Stop**– If possible, pull to the side of the road and turn off the ignition. Pulling to the side makes it possible for everyone to get out of the vehicle safely. Turn off the ignition to shut off the electric current and stop the flow of gasoline. Put the vehicle in park or set the emergency brake; you don't want the vehicle to move after your leave it. Keep the hood closed because more oxygen can make the fire larger.

2. **Get Out**– Make sure everyone gets out of the vehicle. Then move at least 100 feet away. Keep traffic in mind and keep everyone together. There is not only danger from the fire, but also from other vehicles moving in the area.
3. **Call For Help**– Call 911 or the emergency number for the local fire department. Firefighters are specially trained to combat vehicle fires. Never return to the vehicle to attempt to fight the fire yourself. Vehicle fires can be tricky, even for firefighters.

WHAT TO DO IN CASE OF A NATURAL DISASTER

What would YOU remember to take if you had to evacuate rapidly in an emergency? **Alice** was at her home park in Southern California a few years ago during one of the fires and discovered how unprepared she was for that disaster.

> "One of the fires came licking up the hillside at the back of our park. We did have to evacuate for one night. Luckily we had no fire damage. A few rigs experienced wind damage. It was a shock to see how unprepared so many of us were after all the 9-11, Katrina, etc. disasters we've had and the lessons we had supposedly learned. Even our park was unprepared. We discovered we did not have a good communication plan in place telling us when to leave and where to go. We do now!

In a disaster you may only have a few minutes to evacuate. Be prepared.

> "I had only a few minutes to evacuate. I knew to take all my medications (but not copies of the prescription numbers) and the laptop computer with all of my writing projects. Luckily I had never put away my classic Martin guitar after

playing it the day before so I remembered to take it after stumbling over it. I took my neck pillow and change of clothes. At the last minute I remembered the charger for the cell phone. That's it. I forgot my file box of important records, the only photomontage I have of my parents, and the zip drives with all my backup files.

"After speaking with others, I discovered many of my fellow RVers had similar experiences. One man didn't even bring his ID. Another forgot his allergy medications. Although one person wished she had brought a radio and a flashlight, she made sure she didn't forget to bring the clothes she had packed for her cruise at the end of the month."

"We don't have to worry about cots in stadiums, hotels and motels, as full-time RVers."

Full-time RVers take everything with them. Full-timers have it easier because their house is always with them. **Dave Baleria**, Personal Safety & RVing Lifestyle Instructor for Life on Wheels RV Conferences, agreed. "We don't have to worry about cots in stadiums, hotels and motels, as full-time RVers," he said. "We are like turtles with our shells on our back, only faster, but only if we pay attention to weather and events going on around us."

However, even for full-timers, an emergency could develop where they have to abandon their RV at a moment's notice. **Dave** offered this advice: "If you keep your valuables in a fire safe and have to abandon your RV, take the fire safe. That's what we do. We actually have three; two are briefcase size. They are small and light enough to take. Even if you are gone and a wildfire burns your RV to the

Take the time NOW to prepare for an emergency.

ground, your important papers are in the fire safe, so you still have not lost them." [Dave has since died of natural causes, but his teachings live on. He is sorely missed by many in the RV community.]

Part-time RVers must plan for an emergency before it happens.

Cindy Quigley, coordinator of Riverside County Emergency Services, offers these reminders of what you should pack into a kit so it is ready to take on a moment's notice:

- **On a flash drive or CD, include your ID numbers** for Social Security, Driver's License, Life, Health and Homeowners Insurance.
- **Assemble copies of important papers.**
- **Compile a list of contact information** for your doctors, family and friends.
- **Prepare a week's worth of your medications.**
- **Put together a personal hygiene kit.**
- **Bring favorite pillow, bedding, change of clothes, flashlight, radio, batteries.**
- **Make a kit for your pet(s).** Include dry food, water dish, plastic bags.
- **Take photos of your belongings and have them on a CD or flash drive.**

The Red Cross is an invaluable asset. They are not only organized to respond immediately to crises, they have compiled excellent guidelines to help you prepare for any disaster. Please take the time NOW to download the abundance of information available at the flick of your cursor. See Resources at the end of this chapter.

Some RVers assemble a "bailout bag" with copies of important papers, meds, key files on a flash drive that they leave by the exit of their RV or carry in their tow vehicle, ready to grab in case of emergency.

SUMMING UP

Now that you've read this chapter, we hope you will take the time to prepare yourself so that if an emergency should happen, you will feel in control because you know what to do. And be assured, people will come to your aid. You too will be "touched by the kindness of strangers." Please do not be overwhelmed by this information. Life on the road is great, and at the same time we do need to take some precautions to keep it that way.

Karin Callander shares her experience of what happens when unexpected emergencies occur even after you think you're "safe."

> "We got off to a good start, leaving our friends' driveway tearful, but excited to begin our new Workamping experience in Branson, MO. Of course, we had to make our rounds of relatives and say goodbye, so we had several hundred miles to cover before our start date.
>
> "Bump-bump-bump we went, for about 100 miles, until we hit the South Carolina line, and finally the road quality was better. But, boy, did it get hot. It was the end of July, after all, and by noon, the outside temperature had climbed to 101. We were heading down a particularly boring stretch of I-95 when all of a sudden, KA-POW! Hubby looked at me and I looked at him, and we both asked, *'What the heck was THAT?'* In the next breath, we both exclaimed, *'FLAT TIRE!'* Somehow, we got off the road and on the shoulder and stopped in about 30 seconds. We got out and looked, and sure enough, flat as flat could be. *'OK,'* we thought, *'We'll just call Good Sam Emergency Road Service and they'll be able to help us in no time.'* And, yep,

Life on the road is great, and at the same time we do need to take some precautions to keep it that way.

they were able to engage a wrecker service that just so happened to be only 10 minutes away from our location.

"While we waited, though, my thoughtful husband insisted I take the dog and a blanket and go sit far from the camper, in that lush, green grass, in the shade of the blackberry brambles. He's always concerned about my safety and health and didn't want me anywhere near the camper in the event of an onlooker smacking into its rear. So, there I sat, on my blanket, in the shade, like the Princess I am. As it turned out, I was not alone. There were about a gazillion chiggers waiting for their next meal, and I was an easy target. For the next six months, I fought those little buggers and their itchy welts. Out of one emergency into another. And I still love RVing."

"Out of one emergency and into another. And I still love RVing."

JJ Dippel describes her emergencies with her pets and the successful outcomes.

"I've had two emergencies with my cat, in two different places, while traveling on the road. I travel in a 31-foot Class C and don't tow a car. Instead, I use an electric bicycle for my local transportation (*EgoVehicles.com* for an example of the electric bicycle I own). Veterinarians are often located in small facilities and don't have room to park an RV. During my travels, I had often wondered what I would do if my cat were to need veterinary service. In the summer of 2008, I found out what I can do. TWICE.

"The first emergency occurred in Sequim, Washington in June 2008. My handsome male Siamese/Tabby cat, ten years old at the time, suffered urinary blockage. For a cat, this is a life-threatening situation. Fortunately, the RV park where I was staying had WiFi and I located a vet online. Also, it was a weekday, and vet offices were open. I packed the cat into its carrier, straddled the carrier across the foot rest area of my bike, held the carrier with my knees, and rode to the vet on my bike. The cat did not appreciate this ride! However, the vet managed to get the cat unblocked and save its life.

"The second emergency occurred two months later (August 2008) in Twisp, Washington. My cat suffered an emergency that was going to ultimately require surgery. This time, it was a Saturday, and no vets were open. However, I called around and found a vet that was already dealing with another pet emergency, so I was told to go ahead and bring the cat in. This vet specialized in horses so the parking facilities were large enough for horse trailers. Plenty of room to park my RV!

"If you need help it will be there for you."

"Since the vet specialized in horses, he was reluctant to do the surgery my cat needed. The vet's wife and co-owner of the vet service could have done the surgery, but she was out of town. The vet kept my cat for two nights and was able to get it stabilized to the point that I could drive back home and take the cat to its regular vet.

"When I got home, my cat got the needed surgery and is now doing fine. My cat is bouncing around like nothing happened. All I can say is if you have an emergency on the road, just rely on blind faith (or the faith of your chosen deity) that if you need help, it will be there for you."

RESOURCES

- **Fire Safety: 34 facts article from Mac McCoy:** ***(MactheFireGuy.com/Articles/34_Fire_Facts_That_Can_Save_Your_Life)***
- **Nationwide Insurance:** ***(Nationwide.com)***
- **NFPA and AAA recommendations for vehicle safety. See Safety Information for Consumers:** ***(NFPA.org)***
- **Mark Polk's article on fire safety:** ***(EzineArticles.com/?Preventing-RV-Fires&id=593764)***
- **Photos of RV fires:** ***(RVAppraisals.com/Fire-Investigations.htm)***
- **Companies Providing Emergency Repair Service:**
  - ★ **Good Sam 800-947-0770:** ***(GoodSamClub.com)***
  - ★ **PoliSeek RV Insurance 800-521-2942:** ***(Poliseek.com/RV)***
  - ★ **Foremost Insurance 800-262-0170:** ***(Foremost.com)***
  - ★ **Progressive Insurance 800-776-4737: (*RV.Progressive.com*)**
- **The Red Cross:** ***(RedCross.org)***
  - ★ **Build a Disaster Supplies Kit:** ***(RedCross.org/www-Files/Documents/pdf/Preparedness/Checklists/Be_Red_Cross_Ready.pdf)***
- **Prepare.Org:** ***(Prepare.org)***
- **Prepare an RV bailout bag:** ***(RVLifestyleExperts.com/Free-RV-Info/Full-Time-RVing/RV-Bailout-Bags)***

"If you always do what interests you, at least one person is pleased."
Katherine Hepburn

Chapter 29

Is the RV lifestyle for me?

Don't let fear of the unknown hold you back from living the full-time RV lifestyle.

We've covered all the bases in these last chapters. Is there anything else that's keeping you from living the RV lifestyle? Are you the type of person who lives full out or do you hesitate, waiting for everything to be just right? Must everything be lined up, all questions and possibilities answered before you step forward? Are you dreaming about living the full-time RV lifestyle yet still wavering?

WHAT'S HOLDING YOU BACK?

If your house hasn't sold or you haven't figured out how to get health insurance coverage, those can be legitimate obstacles. They will probably be resolved in time and you can move forward. However, if you are wondering about the "what if's?"—like what if one of us or someone in the family gets sick or dies or what if our RV has a breakdown—then you could be letting the fear of the unknown hold you back.

Certainly you need to do research, investigate RVs and make sure you get one that meets your needs. You should have an idea of your budget and whether your income will cover that. If not, check into Workamping to make up the difference.

Living full out doesn't mean reckless. It means going for something that is right for you at the time. If your gut or intuition is saying yes, listen. It doesn't mean everything will be smooth, but that is the direction to go for your growth and accomplishing what your heart desires.

Our friend, **Nick Russell**, taught a class at the now defunct Life on Wheels called "Reluctant RVers." In his blog a while back, he said:

> "Everything in life has a certain amount of risk associated with it, whether we are driving to the grocery store, having a Sunday picnic with the family, or watching a baseball game. I don't know what calamities may befall you as you enjoy the full-time RV lifestyle, but you can rest assured that sooner or later something will go wrong. Just as it would if you stayed in your sticks and bricks house."

"What would I do in that situation if I were still in my house?"

Ask yourself, "What would I do in that situation if I were still in my house?" You'd deal with it somehow. Living in an RV is the same—you'll deal with it.

- The wife of a younger RV couple had some serious health issues. She found a job with health benefits and got treatment. They were parked in an RV park for a couple of years and then got back on the road.
- Several RVers we know have had parent issues to deal with. Since they have more flexibility in the RV lifestyle they were actually able to provide more help because they could return to help. One friend hired a geriatric case manager to oversee her mother's care. They now have peace of mind and can visit when more convenient for them.

- RVers can arrange their schedules to visit family. In fact, staying in the RV is an ideal way to visit. You might be able to park in their driveway or on their property yet you have your own space. If that's too close, find an RV park or Workamping assignment close enough to visit but far enough away to reduce babysitting assignments. Since Southwest Airlines has good airfare sales, periodically Jaimie flies to visit her sister and grandkids if their travels don't take them near there.

Choosing the RV lifestyle isn't a one-time decision that you have to get right and then live with forever.

Choosing the RV lifestyle isn't a one-time decision that you have to get right and then have to live with it forever. It is a decision. You can always make another decision.

Janice Lasko looks back at their RV life, one that began in 1985. They now travel part-time, illustrating how the RV lifestyle is a series of decisions.

> "This story may sound familiar because it is simply a variation on a similar theme. It could be your story or very much like your story.
>
> "But it's our story. It's about two people, Gabby and Janice Lasko, who love to travel, who found a way to make traveling a lifelong, almost permanent pursuit and subsequently discovered that the best way to follow that pursuit was in an RV.
>
> "Some people don't even realize traveling in an RV, either full- or part-time is a dream come true until, for one reason or another, the dream ends. However, the dream doesn't need to end on a permanent basis.

"It was 1985, and we hadn't yet heard about the Escapees RV Club; actually, we didn't know anyone who traveled all the time in an RV. All we knew was, once we started traveling in an RV, even though we thought two years would give us enough time to cover the country, we wanted to keep on going.

"Two years turned into four and four turned into more, many more, until after 21 years we felt we needed to find a home base. Where that home base is doesn't matter. The facts are that, after 21 years in one type of rig or another, we learned how to be extremely flexible, both in terms of space and with each other's moods. We figured out how to adjust to changing climates, regional accents and zonal time changes, often several times in one traveling day. When the budget tightened, we found seasonal jobs.

"We hiked, biked, snow-skied, wind-surfed, line danced, overdosed on museums, hit almost all the state capitol buildings and toured governor's mansions. We ate healthy and delicious meals at college campus student unions and sat quietly in their libraries. (Did you know that many colleges and universities have free museums and galleries to tour?) And we ate not-so-healthy-but-delicious meals in as many regional restaurants as possible.

Each RVer chooses based on individual considerations and budget—so will you.

"Still, time and mirrors can play terrible jokes on one's psyche. While time passes, the mind takes its time catching up. And sometimes it is better to walk right on past a mirror.

"Step back in time with me—back to 1985. We didn't know the first thing about RVing, let alone full-time RVing. Consequently, we thought the safest things to do would be to make a pro and con list and a budget.

"The funniest thing I remember about that budget was allowing for $1 per gallon of fuel. Surely it would never go higher than that. (Another one of life's little lessons.)

"The pro list took care of itself. It far outweighed the cons. After all, we were already prejudiced toward and excited about this way of life, so we stacked the deck.

"The finance columns seemed to take care of themselves, too. A simple steno pad divided into columns, with one page equaling one month, was our tool.

"Here are the column headers we followed. A dollar amount was given to each header, and we followed the budget to the penny, listing under the category the amount we spent, the date we spent it and where we were when we spent it:

- Fuel
- Campgrounds
- Groceries
- Medical/Insurance
- Entertainment
- Dining Out
- Clothing
- Family Gifts
- Miscellaneous

"You will note that there is no column for communication. At the time, of course, there were no cell phones, no onboard computers, thus, no spreadsheets to do this kind of budgeting and planning, no emails and no GPS. As a matter of fact, there were no ATMs.

"We stayed in touch the old-fashioned way, pay phones and snail-mail letters. It just occurred to me, the word snail-mail hadn't come into common use yet; we just said, '*I mailed some letters today to family and friends.*'

"Would we do this again? You betcha!"

"Why, we even acquired our money the old-fashioned way, by stopping in a bank before 3:00 p.m., when they used to close to the public. (No, we didn't rob banks.)

"Would we do it this way again? You betcha! As it turned out, those steno pads, one for each year for about 10 years, are a journal, and, when the days, weeks and months run together, they are a terrific memory jogger."

HANGING UP THE KEYS

If you do decide it is time to get off the road, either permanently or temporarily, there are a number of possibilities.

- **Keep the house:** If you like your area, keep your house—perhaps rent it out—while you RV or until you are sure you don't want to go back. At least you'll have a house to go back to.
- **Look for a new location:** There's a good chance you'll want to settle down in a different area. Keep your eyes open as you travel and get some ideas for when the time comes. There are options at all price levels. **Joei Carlton Hossack** now travels part-time.

  "In 2006, after ten years of solo full-time, I purchased a condo in Surrey, British Columbia. I made the mistake of being in a campground during the winter and it was horrible. I asked my nephew (also living in BC) if it was worth buying something to live in and his response was, and I quote, *'You'll never lose money buying a property anywhere close to Vancouver.'* Two weeks later I purchased a one-bedroom, one-bathroom condo in a resort called Chelsea Gardens with RV parking at the rear of the complex. I love it but I'm still on the road at least six or seven months of the year."

➤ **Buy an RV lot:** Buy into an RV or mobile home park/resort with the activities and amenities you like or in an area you like. This is usually a much less expensive option than purchasing another house.

➤ **Join the Escapees:** The Escapees RV Club has a CARE center in Livingston for members who need short or long term assisted living care plus an Alzheimer's unit.

A solo RVer had knee surgery and needed assistance for a couple of months while she recuperated. As an Escapees Club Member, she stayed at the CARE assisted-living unit in Livingston, Texas until she could get back on the road.

➤ **Settle down temporarily:** If you or your partner has a serious illness, you can always stop where you are or travel to a location with good treatment. You might have to get off the road at least temporarily. That could mean renting an apartment or finding an RV park to stay in.

➤ **Get temporary housing:** If you are between RVs, you might find a Workamping job that provides housing such as managing a storage facility. Couples who have lost their RVs have moved in with family temporarily, rented an apartment, or found work where housing was provided. We have friends who sold their RV and now housesit or volunteer where housing is provided. Someday, they may go back to RVing.

You might have to get off the road temporarily.

RVing can keep you young. **Ginny and Bob Odell** lived full-time in their RV until age 82 when they decided it was time to make some changes.

"1988 was the year we enthusiastically purchased our first RV. We knew nothing about RVs or RVing. Good friends encouraged us by saying, *'Come on you'll like it!'* Our friends took us on our first trip through the Southwest and Mexico.

"We were on our way. For the next 15 years we were on the road six to eight months of the year. We helped build Park Sierra (an Escapees co-op RV park) beginning in 1990 during the spring and fall. By 2003 we began traveling less and staying at Park Sierra more.

"In 2006 we began talking about where our next home would be. Were we ready to hang up our keys? We were 82 and felt that we wanted to choose where to move rather than wait and have our kids have to make those decisions when we couldn't.

"Ten months ago the decision was made. We would move to a house in Windsor near one of our daughters and keep our site at Park Sierra until we decided that the move was the right one. We now spend part of the spring and fall at Park Sierra and the rest of the time in Windsor, California. Getting the house livable has been great fun for us.

Changing life situations may prompt a decision to change your RV lifestyle.

"Our time at Park Sierra continues to be a joy. Giving up RV living and traveling little by little is working for us. We will complete the move sometime in the not too distant future."

John and Kay Hasty have been full-time RVers for 20 years and are in their mid-60s. They love the lifestyle but are also looking ahead.

> "My husband of 43 years and I have been full-time RVers for 20 years. We've been on the road for the last 12 of those years. During that time, we've been seasonal Workampers in order to support our lifestyle. We've had many memorable and some exciting experiences, and we don't really know how or when to change back to a more stationary life!
>
> "We are in our mid-60s and still in very good health. The main factor in our concern about our mobile lifestyle has been the cost of fuel. Here's where we are in our plans:
>
> 1. Our first step was to buy a wooded half-acre lot in a sub-division in the Texas hill country. Like many of the other property owners, we developed our lot with full-service RV sites for ourselves and a guest.
> 2. Our next step in this process has been to spend more than just a few months on our property to see how that feels. During that time, we began exploring our options for a house.
>
> "We realize that we aren't ready to give up our RV lifestyle, but we think we'll know when it's time to get a permanent home, and we'll have laid all the groundwork when that time comes.
>
> "Having made these plans, we feel secure in our future."

A step in the wrong direction is better than staying on the spot all of our life.

If you have the dream of RVing, a Maxwell Maltz quote is excellent advice. "A step in the wrong direction is better than staying on the spot all our life. Once you're moving forward you can correct course as you go. Your automatic guidance system cannot guide you when you're standing still."

Doesn't that sound like a GPS? It can't guide us unless we are moving either. So take steps forward. As Jaimie often says, "If not now, when?"

ACTION PLAN

The next step is to create an action plan. In a notebook or on your computer, create a chart where you can map out your plan.

It may be a challenge to incorporate all the ideas in this guide to make a decision right now. Seeing all these suggestions at once can be overwhelming. One effective way to make changes in your life is to create a plan and start small. Use this Action Plan Form as a place to begin. Buy an inexpensive spiral notebook to write down the results of your research. Go back through this book and pick out four or five topics you would like to research. After you finish, pick four or five more.

Here are some suggested headings and sample answers to get you started. As a sample of further investigation into the topic, "Become familiar with different types of RVs," here are some steps you might follow to find the answers you need.

MY PERSONAL ACTION PLAN

Topic	What will I do and when?	What Internet resources will I use?	What other resources do I have?	Have I made notes in my notebook?	Have I discussed the results with my traveling partner?
Become familiar with different types of RVs.	Read about them. Go to RV mall next weekend.	Start with sites from Chapter 12 *RVBG.com* *NadaGuides.com* *RVDA.org* *RVIA.org*	Telephone directory Newspapers RV Traders magazine in markets.	Make separate pages for notes on trailers and motorhomes.	We'll go together.

FINAL WORDS

RVing is not for everyone, but for those who venture into the unknown, it can bring experiences with beautiful places and a variety of people you might never have had otherwise. Having this special experience as an RVer is bonding with other travelers who share your enthusiasm. Family members may be fascinated, but only other RVers can really understand the freedom and what this lifestyle is like.

Alice has made music and played bridge in many different places, attended festivals she would not have known about. Jaimie has kayaked in Glacier Bay, Alaska, and climbed Long's Peak. RVing led both of them to writing and publishing. Others pursue the nation's history or their own family's history. There is no end to the possibilities on the road.

Are you ready to take a chance on RVing? The RVers we have met have nearly all said, "I wish I'd started sooner." Give it a try. And, you can always make another decision. Our guess is you'll have no regrets and much gratitude for what the RV lifestyle brings you.

Section VI.

55 Ways to Save Money Living the RV Lifestyle

SAVE ON THE AMOUNT OF YOUR INVESTMENT

1. Buy a second-hand rig. If you're not sure you will like the RV lifestyle or are unsure of what RV you want, give it a try in an inexpensive rig. That will give you time to see other rigs and get feedback from others. Or, if you get off the road, you won't be out as much money. New rigs depreciate 20% or more as soon as you drive them off the lot.

SAVE ON MAINTENANCE

2. Weigh your RV once a year to make sure it isn't overloaded and that the load is balanced evenly. Save your transmission and tires.
3. Check the water level in your battery regularly and add more as needed.
4. Cover your tires when parked in one spot for several days. This protects tires from UV damage. Most RV tires get more wear and damage from sun than driving.
5. Do preventative maintenance on vehicles. Save in the long run.
6. Replace or clean your air filter as directed.
7. Take a class in repair so you are more knowledgeable and you can do some of your own repairs. You'll also be better able to deal with service people.

8. Use a checklist when unhitching and hitching up. Many are available and you can customize one to suit your own routine. Avoid damage to your rig and possessions and unnecessary repairs.
9. Use a surge protector for your computer and appliances. Replacing appliances or critical parts is expensive.
10. Use an AC voltage monitor that checks polarity. Check the outlet at the utility pole and then keep the monitor in view inside your RV, particularly when running the AC or microwave. Avoid damage from low or high voltage.

SAVE MONEY ON PROPANE

11. Turn your gas water heater on first thing in the morning and shut it off when the water is hot. Your water should stay hot for the rest of the day unless you need to shower.
12. Turn off the propane at the tank when traveling. Your refrigerator will be fine for at least four hours. At lunch, either turn it back on while you eat to cool things back down, or run your generator as an alternative. You not only save propane, but it's safer too.
13. Install a catalytic or ceramic heater. It is much more efficient and will use less propane plus it doesn't run down your battery. Be sure crack a window or vent slightly when you are operating your small heater.
14. When you are plugged into shore power, use a small electric heater rather than your furnace.
15. Close off the bedroom during the day and use your electric or catalytic heater to heat only the area you are in instead of the whole RV.

SAVE FUEL

16. For motorhome owners: save fuel by disconnecting your toad and have your spouse drive it when ascending long, very steep grades.
17. Drive at 55 mph. You get more miles per gallon at a lower speed.

18. Stay in one place longer.
19. Use a tow or toad vehicle that gets better fuel mileage to sightsee.
20. *The Mountain Directories– East and West* can help you plan your route to avoid high passes, steep grades and thus use less fuel.

SAVE MONEY ON MAINTENANCE AND FUEL BY KEEPING YOUR RV'S WEIGHT DOWN:

21. Every six months or so, go through all your storage areas. If you haven't used something in six months, consider whether or not you really need it.
22. When you purchase something new like a shirt, get rid of an old one. Donate it to a charity or recycle it.
23. Look for book exchanges at RV parks where you stay. Trade an old book for one you haven't read.
24. Libraries often have shelves of books they no longer want priced very reasonably. Also, look for a box or shelf with older magazines. Some may still be interesting reading or have useful articles.
25. Go to the library for a morning or afternoon to read the latest issues of your favorite magazines.
26. If you are in an area for a while, see if you can get a library card. You can check out recent books. Many libraries have a movie/ DVD section as well.
27. Carry dried foods instead of cans.
28. Tools are heavy. Carry a minimum of basic tools and borrow the others.

SAVE ON CAMPING FEES

29. Boondock or camp without hookups now and then—more if you are comfortable.
30. Work or volunteer. Often you receive a free or reduced-rate RV site when you work in an RV park. You might also be able to do an exchange with an employer: so many hours for a site.

31. Buy reduced rate camping through a half-price camping club or a membership campground.
32. Outfit your rig with solar panels, batteries and inverter to boondock. After your initial investment, you can camp free on many public lands, particularly in the West.
33. Stay in Walmart parking lots and other blacktop sites for overnight travel (not camping!)
34. Rely on less power– Use a top-of-the-stove toaster and coffee percolator. (Purchase at an RV or Camping store.) Extend your boondocking stay.
35. Cook in a solar oven. Take advantage of solar power and use no propane or electricity at all.

SAVE MONEY ON PURCHASES

36. Obtain an "America the Beautiful—National Parks and Federal Recreation Areas Pass" for $80 if you'll be visiting more than four or five parks. You'll save on admission fees. *(NPS.gov/Fees_Passes.htm)*
37. Seniors 62 and over pay a one-time fee of $10 for an "America the Beautiful—National Parks and Federal Recreation Areas Pass - Senior Pass." The Access Pass for those with a disability is free. *(NPS.gov/Fees_Passes.htm)*
38. Volunteer at least 500 hours for the National Park Service and receive a Volunteer Pass good for the next year that gives you free admission to federal recreation sites.
39. The RV lifestyle is casual. One dress-up outfit is more than enough. Jeans and t-shirts are the basic uniform. If you need something a little fancier, check at a thrift store for a bargain.
40. Eat lunch out instead of dinner. Often restaurants have the same menu but the prices go up at dinnertime. Prices for buffets in casinos go up sometime in late afternoon but the menu is the same.
41. Trade books and DVDs with friends.

42. Buy clothing and household goods at second hand stores. If you need an outfit for one event, you could find just the thing at a low price. Donate it back when you are finished with it.
43. Make your own entertainment. Play cards, read, watch videos.
44. Use your stove and oven in your RV to cook with instead of eating out as often.
45. Shop on sale days at the market.
46. Buy fewer processed foods. They cost more. Cook a double batch of your main dish to have a ready-made dinner another day.
47. Vacuum seal your food (fruits, veggies, meat) to keep longer without spoiling. The machine is sold at RV and home shows.
48. Slow cook in crock pots if you have a hook-up.
49. Grow your own herbs in a small pot rather than pay the high prices for them in the market.
50. Combine and eat leftovers in a stir-fry or a stew.
51. Stick to your shopping list.
52. Look for discount coupons in local papers offered by grocery stores, restaurants and attractions. Tourist brochures often have discounts. Also look on the Web at the attraction's site plus search for "Discounts at (name of attraction.)"

SAVE ON CELL PHONES AND INTERNET ACCESS

53. Choose a cell phone plan that allows free weekends and evening phone calls and make family and friend calls then.
54. Purchase a WiFi detector to locate unsecured WiFi hotspots. The least expensive way to access the Internet is to use RV Park WiFi and find other WiFi hotspots at coffee shops, libraries and other places. If you don't need regular access, then this could work for you.
55. A prepaid cell phone can help you budget and save money too. Check Groupon *(Groupon.com/* for the area you are in for special deals.

NOTES

Section VII. RESOURCES

Resources by topic

RV LIFESTYLE

RV clubs and organizations:

- Escapees RV Club, 100 Rainbow Drive, Livingston, TX 77351, 888-757-2582: *(Escapees.com)*
- Family Motor Coach– FMCA, 8291 Clough Pike, Cincinnati, OH 45244, 800-543-3622: *(FMCA.com)*
- Good Sam Club PO Box 6888, Englewood, CO 80155-6888: *(GoodSamClub.com)*
- RVing Women: *(RVingWomen.org)*
- See Choosing an RV– Types of RVs on page 303 for brand name clubs.

Clubs for solo travelers:

- Loners on Wheels– LOW: *(LonersOnWheels.com)*
- Wandering Individual Network– WIN: *(RVSingles.org)*
- Escapees has a Birds of Feather– BOF for solos. Check with other clubs too.
- See Solo Travel– Clubs on page 311 for additional clubs and organizations for solos.

Newsletters and magazines:

- *RV Lifestyle Ezine* published by: *(RVLifestyleExperts.com)*
- *Coast to Coast*– for members: *(CoastResorts.com)*
- *Escapees*– for members: *(Escapees.com)*
- *Family Motor Coaching*– for members: *(FMCA.com)*
- *Gypsy Journal*: *(GypsyJournal.net)*
- *Highways*– for members of the Good Sam Club: *(GoodSamClub.com/Highways)*
- *MotorHome*: *(MotorhomeMagazine.com)*
- *Trailer Life*: *(TrailerLife.com)*
- *Workamper News*: *(Workamper.com)*

Regional publications:

- *RV Life*– western states: *(RVLife.com)*
- *RV West*: *(RVWest.com)*
- *RV Journal*– western states: *(RVJournal.com)*
- *RV Lifestyle*– Canada: *(RVLifeMag.com)*
- See Go RVing Canada for additional Canadian RV magazines: *(GoRVing.ca/RVMagazines_Forums.asp)*
- Additional magazines listed at RVUSA: *(RVUSA.com/RV-Guide/RV-Magazines)*

Books:

- *Complete Guide to Full-Time RVing: Life on the Open Road.* Bill and Jan Moeller, Trailer Life Books.
- *The Complete RV Handbook* by Jayne Freeman.
- *Live Your Road Trip Dream* by Carol and Phil White.
- *The Woman's Guide to Solo RVing* by Jaimie Hall Bruzenak and Alice Zyetz, Pine Country Publishing: *(RVLifestyleExperts.com)*
- *RV Traveling Tales: Women's Journeys on the Open Road.* Jaimie Hall Bruzenak and Alice Zyetz, Pine Country Publishing: *(RVLifestyleExperts.com)*
- *Support Your RV Lifestyle! An Insider's Guide to Working On the Road* 3rd ed. Jaimie Hall Bruzenak, Pine Country Publishing: *(RVLifestyleExperts.com)*
- *RVers: How do they live like that?* Judy Farrow and Lou Stoetzer: *(RVLifestyleExperts.com/RV-Books/Life-On-The-Road)*
- There are any number of directories for RVers and other useful e-books and DVDs. Check at: *(RVLifestyleExperts.com)* and other RV bookstores.

RV forums:

- RV.net: *(RV.net)*
- Workamper: *(Forums. Workamper.com)*
- Escapees: *(RVNetwork.com)*

Websites:

- Great site for the new RVer: *(NewRVer.com)*
- Checklists you can use: *(RVNetlinx.com/HTCklists.php3)*
- Free campgrounds site: *(FreeCampgrounds.com)*
- *Woodalls* is chock full of information: *(Woodalls.com)*
- Recreational Vehicle Industry Association: *(RVIA.org)*

Even more info from the following sites:

- *(RVEducation101.com)*
- *(AmericanJourneys.com/Links—Lifestyle.html)*
- *(RVKnowhow.com/Discoveries.html)*
- *(LoveTheOutdoors.com/Camping/RV_Resources.htm)*
- *(RVTraveler.com)*
- *(OutdoorPlaces.com/Links/RV_Info.htm)*
- *(Everything-About-RVing.com)*
- *(RVBasics.com)*

CHOOSING AN RV

Basic information:

- Better Business Bureau– Buying a Recreational Vehicle DVD with Chuck Woodbury: *(RVBookstore.com)*
- Information about RVs: *(RVIA.org)*
- *Insider's Guide to Buying an RV* e-book: *(RVLifestyleExperts.com/RV-Books/RV-Education-101)*

Ratings:

- RV Consumer Group publishes *RV Rating Book*, also available in some libraries: *(RV.org)*
- Excellent for comparing RVs, includes free articles: *(JRConsumer.com)*
- Safety issues: *(RVSafety.com)*

Safety-related issues:

- RVSEF– Recreation Vehicle Safety Education Foundation, for more information on RV weight and safety issues: *(RVSafety.org)*
- Excellent article on RV construction at RV Buyers Guide: *(RVBG.com/Articles/?id=2007793)*
- To find out special driver licensing requirements (for larger vehicles) in all 50 states: *(ChanginGears.com/RV-Sec-State-RV-License.shtml)*
- Canadians purchasing an RV in the U.S. should check with the Registrar of Imported Vehicles: *(RIV.ca)*

Types of RVs:

- Do an Internet search on types of RVs.
- Links to clubs by RV brand name: *(RV-Clubs.US/RV-Clubs.html)*
- Comparison of a medium duty truck and a heavy duty truck as a tow vehicle for a large fifth wheel: *(RVLifestyleExperts.com/Free-RV-Info/Getting-Started/MDT-Or-HDT-Tow-Vehicle)*

Pricing:

- RV Finder– Will give comparative prices: *(RV-Finder.com)*
- RV Buyers Guide: *(RVBG.com)*
- NADA RV Pricing: *(NadaGuides.com)*

RV INSURANCE COMPANIES

- PoliSeek: *(Poliseek.com)*
- Foremost Insurance Group: *(Foremost.com)*
- Progressive Insurance: *(RV.Progressive.com)*
- GMAC Insurance: *(RVInsurance.com)*

RV SAFETY

- See Safety-related issues under Choosing an RV on page 303.
- PoliSeek offers excellent free articles about Safety and other issues: *(Poliseek.com/RV-Insurance-Articles)*
- More free articles on travel, vehicle safety, etc.: *(FunRoads.com)*
- RV Safety Features, Tips and Tricks– DVD: *(RVLifestyleExperts.com/RV-Books/RV-Education-101)*

RV driving schools:

- RVing Women: *(RVingWomen.org)*
- RV Driving School: *(RVSchool.com)*
- RV Trainers (Northern California): *(RVTrainers.com)*
- "Drive Your Motorhome Like a Pro"– DVD: *(RVLifestyleExperts.com/RV-Books/RV-Education-101)*

RV REPAIRS

- Find RV repair facilities in the U.S. or Canada: *(MotorhomeDirectory.com/RV-Services)*
- Technical information DVDs by Mark Polk. See: *(RVLifestyleexperts.com/RV-Books/RV-Education-101)*
- Check out service facilities before you make an appointment: *(RVServiceReviews.com)*
- Maintenance– home study courses on RV maintenance, including one for ladies: *(MobileRVAcademy.com)*

FRUGAL RVING

- Detailed budget worksheet, see: *(RVLifestyleExperts.com/pdfs/Budget_Worksheet.pdf)*
- Trip Fuel Calculator: *(FuelCostCalculator.com/TripGasPrice.aspx)*
- Adventurous and affordable RV travel: *(Frugal-RV-Travel.com/Index.html)*

CHOOSING A DOMICILE

- Federation of Tax Administrators website– Compare state taxes in several categories at: *(TaxAdmin.org/FTA/Rate/Tax_stru.html)*
- RetirementLiving.com– gives the overall tax burden for each state, broken down by tax. Excellent resource for choosing a domicile: *(RetirementLiving.com/RLTaxes.html)*
- "How to Be a Real Texan." Free download for members at Escapees RV Club's website. Or purchase booklet at their store for $2.95: *(Escapees.com)*
- Choosing Your RV Home Base. See Recommended Books at: *(RVLifestyleExperts.com/RVBooks/Recommended-Books)*

KEEPING IN TOUCH

Mail-forwarding services:

- RV Clubs: Do an Internet search for "RV clubs mail-forwarding service"
- Texas– Escapees RV Club: *(Escapees.com)*
- Ohio– Family Motor Coaching Association (FMCA): *(FMCA.org)*
- Florida– Good Sam Club: *(GoodSamClub.com)*

Other:

- South Dakota– Alternative Resources (Sioux Falls): *(AlternativeResources.com)*
- South Dakota– Americas Mailbox (Rapid City): *(Americas-Mailbox.com)*
- Check RV magazine ads for additional mail-forwarding services.

Major cell phone companies:

- Verizon Wireless: *(VerizonWireless.com)*
- AT&T: *(ATT.com)*
- Sprint: *(Sprint.com)*
- Find the best cell phone rates: *(BillShrink.com)*

Connecting via Internet:

- List of free blogging platforms: *(NewestOnTheNet.com/Ultimate-List-Of-Free-Blogging-Platforms)*
- Virgin Mobile, offering pay-as-you-go mobile broadband: *(VirginMobileUSA.com/Mobile-Broadband)*
- Skype: *(Skype.com)*
- MagicJack: *(Magicjack.com)*
- Vonage– VOIP plans: *(Vonage.com).* Do an Internet search on VOIP for additional services.
- Find free WiFi hotspots, including RV parks and campgrounds at: (*WiFiFreeSpot.com)*

Free blogging sites:

- Google's Blogger: (*Blogger.com/Start*)
- WordPress: (*WordPress.com*)

RV forums:

- RVNet: *(RV.net)*
- Workamper: *(Forums.Workamper.com)*
- Escapees: *(RVNetwork.com)*

PLACES TO CAMP

Government agencies:

- Bureau of Land Management– BLM: *(BLM.gov/NHP/Index.htm)*
- National Forest Service– USDAFS: *(FS.Fed.us)*
- National Park Service– NPS: *(NPS.gov)*
- National Wildlife Refuges– NWR: *(FWS.gov/Refuges)*
- US Army Corps of Engineers– COE: *(SPN.USACE.Army.mil)*
- Each state park system has a website. Search the Internet for state parks or for lists by state: *(TouristInformationDirectory.com/Parks/State_Park.htm)*

Membership parks:

- Western Horizons: *(WHResorts.com/aor)*
- Coast to Coast: *(CoastResorts.com)*
- Resort Parks: *(ResortParks.com)*
- Thousand Trails: *(ThousandTrails.com)*

Half-price clubs:

- Passport America (half-price club): *(Passport-America.com)*
- Happy Campers (half-price club): *(CampHalfPrice.com)*

Boondocking:

- Don Wright's *Free Campgrounds– West* with campgrounds that are free or with fees of $12 or less.
- Find free campgrounds at: *(FreeCampgrounds.com)*
- Links for boondocking: *(RVNetlinx.com/DBA/DBA.php?ID=6626&Cat=Genl)*
- The Frugal Shunpiker Guides to RV Boondocking (6) by Marianne Edwards: *(RVLifestyleExperts.com/RV-Books/Other-ebooks)*
- Boondockers welcome– Membership site with boondocking spots all over the world: *(BoondockersWelcome.com)*
- For more articles on camping and boondocking see articles at: *(RVLifestyleExperts.com)*

PLACES TO VISIT

- RV Net Linx Tourism Guides: *(RVNetlinx.com/WPTourism.php)*
- RV Net Linx Shows and Events: *(RVNetlinx.com/WPShows.php)*
- National Scenic Byways Program: *(Byways.org/Explore)*
- United States Adventure Travel: *(iExplore.com/Travel-Guides/North-America/United-States/Overview)*
- Road Trip America: *(RoadTripAmerica.com)*
- National Monuments by state: *(Gorp.Away.com/Resource/US_NM/Main.htm)*
- Factory Tours: *(FactoryToursUSA.com)*

WORKING ON THE ROAD

- *Support Your RV Lifestyle! An Insider's Guide to Working on the Road* 3rd ed. by Jaimie Hall Bruzenak: *(RVLifestyleExperts.com/RV-Books/Books-for-Working-on-the-Road/Support-Your-RV-Lifestyle)*
- *Workamper News*– Find links to Workamper Store and forums: *(Workamper.com)*
- Coolworks: *(Coolworks.com)*
- *Caretaker Gazette*: *(Caretaker.org)*
- See articles on working at: *(RVLifestyleExperts.com)*

VOLUNTEERING

- Comprehensive site for volunteer opportunities with public agencies: *(Volunteer.gov/gov)*
- Habitat for Humanity Care-A-Vanner: *(Habitat.org/RV)*
- US Fish and Wildlife Service: *(Volunteers.FWS.gov)*
- National Park Service VIP program: *(NPS.gov/Volunteer)*
- National Park Service IVIP program for international volunteers: *(NPS.gov/oia/Topics/IVIP/Application Process.htm)*
- American Red Cross Disaster Services– Contact your local chapter to find out about training and opportunities to help: *(RedCross.org)*
- DVD: RV Volunteers Make a Difference: *RVLifestyleExperts.com/RV-Books/Audio-Visual-Courses)*

HEALTH INSURANCE/HEALTHCARE

- *The New Health Insurance Solution: How to Get Cheaper, Better Coverage Without a Traditional Employer Plan* by Paul Zane Pilzer.
- *Drugs for Less: The Complete Guide to Free and Discounted Prescription Drugs* by Michael P. Cecil, M.D.
- Additional articles on this topic can be found at: *(RVLifestyleExperts.com)*

Reduce medical costs:

- Find clinical trials at Centerwatch.com: *(Centerwatch.com)*
- More clinical trials: Free treatment for certain conditions if you participate in a study:
  - ★(ClinicalTrials.gov)
  - ★*(TrialCheck.org/Services)*
  - ★*(BreastCancerTrials.org/BCT_Nation/Home.Seam)*
- Some hospitals may have an obligation to provide free services to low-income patients under the federal Hill-Burton Free Care Program: 800-638-0742 or *(HRSA.Gov/HillBurton)*
- Check with Medicaid for your state. Find information and links at: *(64.82.65.67/Medicaid/States.html)*

Medical emergency services:

- Medical Air Services: *(MedAirServices.com)*
- SkyMed: 800-475-9633 *(SkyMed.com)*

Find healthcare on the road:

- DocFinder– Physician Profiles provides information about physicians including education, training, specialty, malpractice and disciplinary proceedings: *(DocBoard.org/DocFinder.html)*
- Vitals.com– Free site with physician ratings: *(Vitals.com)*
- HealthGrades.com– Rates both physicians and hospitals. Find the best hospital for your condition: *(HealthGrades.com)*

Storing personal medical information:

- Care Memory Wristband: *(CareMemoryBand.com)*
- Medical Identification Online: *(MedIDs.com/Free-ID.php)*
- Vial of Life: *(VialOfLife.com)*
- ICE in FL: Store emergency contact information with your driver's license information so it is available to police and emergency personnel: *(Services.FLHSMV.Gov/ECI)*

EMERGENCY PREPAREDNESS

- Fire Safety– 34 facts article from Mac McCoy: *(MacTheFireGuy.com/34_Fire_Facts_That_Can_Save_Your.htm)*
- NFPA and AAA recommendations for vehicle safety. See SafetyInformation, For Consumers, Vehicles: *(nfpa.org)*
- Mark Polk's article on fire safety: *(EzineArticles.com/?Preventing-RV-Fires&ID=593764)*
- Photos of RV fires: *(RVAppraisals.com/Fire-Investigations.htm)*
- The Red Cross: *(RedCross.org)*
- Build a Disaster Supplies Kit: *(RedCross.org/www-Files/Documents/pdf/Preparedness/Checklists/Be_Red_Cross_Ready.pdf)*
- Pepare.Org: *(Prepare.org)*
- Prepare an RV bailout bag: *(RVLifestyleExperts.com/Free-RV-Info/Full-Time-RVing/RV-Bailout-Bags)*

Roadside service:

- Good Sam: 800-947-0770 *(GoodSamClub.com)*
- PoliSeek RV Insurance: 800-521-2942 *(Poliseek.com/RV)*
- Foremost Insurance: 800-262-0170 *(Foremost.com)*
- Progressive Insurance: 800-776-4737 *(RV.Progressive.com)*

HOMESCHOOLING AND RESOURCES FOR FAMILY TRAVEL

- National Home Education Network: *(HomeSchool-Curriculum-And-Support.com/National-Home-Education-Network.html)*
- Families on the Road: *(FamiliesOnTheRoad.com)*
- Judith Waite Allee: *(DreamsOnAShoestring.com)*
- Homeschooling: *(Home-Ed-Magazine.com)*
- Pit Stops for Kids– fun places, adventures and road trips that will interest children: *(PitStopsForKids.com)*
- Find a play area as you travel– if you are traveling with kids, check out this resource for finding a great play area in your travels: *(PlaySpaceFinder.Kaboom.org)*

SANDWICH GENERATION

- Online resource for caregivers– information for navigating through Medicare, lists of caregiver organizations, and support from other caregivers:
  - ★Medicare resources: *(Medicare.Gov/Caregivers)*
  - ★How to find caregivers nationwide– the motto is "Don't give up your parents for adoption. Keep them at home." Here's a directory of caregivers: *(ChoiceEldercare.org)*
  - ★Free information on all aspects of elderly issues like living will, etc.: *(Caring.com)*

SOLO TRAVEL

Clubs:

- Loners on Wheels: *(LonersOnWheels.com)*
- RVing Women: *(RVingWomen.org)*
- Wandering Individuals' Network– WIN: *(RVSingles.org)*
- RV Singles Discussion Forum: *(Groups.Yahoo.com/Group/RV-Singles)*
- Solo-Net: *(Skally.Net/Solo-Net)*
- Thousand Trails– several singles groups: *(ThousandTrails.com)*
- Escapees RV Club singles group: *(Escapees.com)*
- Loners of America: *(LonersOfAmerica.net)*
- Maintenance– home study course on RV maintenance for ladies and other courses: *(MobileRVAcademy.com)*

Other:

- *RVers: How Do They Live Like That?* Judy Farrow and Lou Stoetzer: *(RVLifestyleExperts.com/RV-Books/Life-on-the-Road)*
- *The Woman's Guide to Solo RVing* by Jaimie Hall Bruzenak and Alice Zyetz: *(RVLifestyleExperts.com)*

RELATIONSHIPS

- *RVers: How Do They Live Like That?* by Judy Farrow and Lou Stoetzer: *(RVLifestyleExperts.com/RV-Books/Life-on-the-Road)*

TRAVELING WITH PETS

- U.S. and Canada Dog-friendly Campground and RV Park Guide: *(DogFriendly.com/Server/Travel/Guides/Camp/Camp.shtml)*
- PetFriendlyTravel.com: *(PetFriendlyTravel.com)*
- Documentaton for pets traveling into Canada: *(CanadaWelcomesYou.net/TravelReminders.html)*
- Documentation for pets traveling into Mexico: (*MexOnline.com/Mexpets.htm*)
- Documentation for pets traveling into or returning to the U.S. *(CBP.gov/LinkHandler/cgov/Newsroom/Publications/Travel/Pets_Wild.CTT/Pets.pdf)*

TRAVELING WITH DISABILITIES

- The Handicapped Travel Club: *(HandicappedTravelClub.com)*
- Customize RVs: *(RV-Info.net/RVSpecialty.html)*
- Vehicles for the disabled. Search: "By RV Type" click on "RVs for Disabled:" *(GoRVing.com/Where-to-Find/Manufacturers)*
- Travelin'Talk Network: *(TravelinTalk.net)*
- Access-Able Travel Source– information on accessible attractions and HTC-identified accessible RV parks: *(Access-Able.com)*
- For hearing and vision impaired– The Sidekick II Signature Series, by Silent Call: *(SilentCall.com/Catalog/Index.php?Intro=1)*
- Links to access travel guides throughout the country: *(DisabledTravelers.com/Access_Guides.htm)*

Index

V

W

AUTHOR BIOS

CO-AUTHORS BIOS:

JAIMIE HALL BRUZENAK is an RV lifestyle and Workamping expert, writing and speaking about RV lifestyle topics and working on the road. She has been on the road in an RV, full- and part-time, since 1992. She loves to share the possibilities found in the RV lifestyle and help others achieve their RV dreams. She has been interviewed on radio, TV, online and in print.

Needing to earn an income, Jaimie and her late husband, Bill, worked in a number of national parks, volunteered, did temporary work, sold Christmas trees and worked in tourist businesses. Her book, *Support Your RV Lifestyle! An Insider's Guide to Working on the Road*, was the result of those experiences and is considered by many to be the bible of Workamping.

Jaimie writes for and teaches classes on the Web for Workamper.com, plus writes for other RV websites and publications. With Alice, she co-authored three other books on RVing: *RV Traveling Tales: Women's Journeys on the Open Road*, *The Woman's Guide to Solo RVing*, and *Taking the Mystery Out of RV Writing*. She produces a bimonthly newsletter *RV Lifestyle Ezine* and blogs regularly at RV Home Yet? *(Blog.RVLifestyleExperts.com)*

Jaimie traveled solo after Bill passed away. She now travels with George, her husband. Her website *(RVLifestyleExperts.com)* is full of resources for RVers. Reach her: *(CalamityJaimie@gmail.com)*

ALICE ZYETZ passed away May, 2012 before seeing this book in print. She had been on the road since 1994 and was an RV lifestyle expert who wrote and spoke about a variety of RV topics, specializing in women travelers, Boomers ready to retire, and handicapped travelers. She authored two books: *You Shoulda Listened to Your Mother*, based on her pre-RV experience as a business consultant, and *Taking the Mystery Out Of Retiring to an RV*, a compact, resource-filled introduction to RV retirement.

Prior to this book, Alice, with Jaimie, co-authored several books on RVing: *RV Traveling Tales: Women's Journeys on the Open Road*, *The Woman's Guide to Solo RVing*, and *Taking the Mystery Out of RV Writing*.

For several years Alice contributed to Jaimie's website *(RVLifestyleExperts.com)* and the accompanying twice-monthly electronic newsletter, *RV Lifestyle Ezine*, showcasing their RV books and providing information to those interested in the RV lifestyle. With Jaimie, Alice founded the RV Authors' Co-operative.

Alice wrote many articles and blog entries about the RV lifestyle and was interviewed a number of times on radio, cable TV, and in print. She was a seminar leader at RV conventions.

Alice traveled alone and with her late husband. She loved the lifestyle and the people she met along the way. Alice was compelled to share her knowledge and enthusiasm with the rest of the world.

BIOS OF OUR CONTRIBUTORS:

Thank you to all of our contributors, who have added their voices of experience to our book. Many have offered their email, blog or website addresses so that you may contact them for more insight into their own lifestyles. After the address, you'll find the chapter numbers in which their contributions are located.

Joanne Alexakis and husband, Nick, started full-time RVing in April 1994 and wholeheartedly enjoy this gypsy lifestyle. They have worked seasonally in many state parks and have been parked on construction sites acting as 24-hour security. Now they both have full-time jobs and have been parked in one spot at an RV park in Southern California for almost three years. Nick claims he hasn't quit full-timing at all. He is just parked at this site longer than others. Joanne is an active member of the Escapees writing group, Penwheels. *(JAlexakis@earthlink.net)* 3, 5, 6, 12, 15, 21, 26

Verna Baker and her husband, Wally, are full-time RVers with a home base in Coarsegold, California. They have three married sons and five grandchildren. The entire family has become reconciled to, and even appreciative of, their nomadic lifestyle. A retired elementary schoolteacher and author of numerous skits and plays, Verna enjoys the freedom of RV living. 8

Lynne Benjamin, author of *Jacob's Tails*, travels in a Class C motorhome with her husband, Fred. They have been in three countries, eight provinces and over 33 states. Lynne has conducted workshops at the Okanogan RV Lifestyle Seminars in BC. Lynne is editor of Penwheels and has written many RV articles. *(FirstepandLifeGoesOn.Blogspot.com)* 1, 4, 18

Barbara A. Bowers and her husband are lifetime members of the Escapees RV Club, having joined in August 2002. She has had pieces published in a wellness book, chapter newsletters, and the *Escapees Magazine*. She also contributed an essay for *Looking Back: Boomers Remember History from the 40's to the Present* by Kay Kennedy. She is a member of Penwheels, a sub-group of Escapees for traveling writers. *(Blessed-B.Blogspot.com)* 15

Larry and Adrienne Brauer planned to become full-time RVers when they were married in 1993. In 2001, they both retired, sold their house, and fulfilled their dream of becoming full-time Rvers. When people ask when they will settle down, their answer has always been, "When we get tired of this lifestyle!" website: *(BrauersRVTravels.com)* 1, 4, 9, 11, 14, 18, 21

Karin Callander and husband, Dick, after a particularly stressful Tuesday workday, sat down in front of their computer at 9 pm to compose their resume. At 11 pm, it was published, and by 10 am the next day, they had their first "job." They find it more exciting to travel without keeping meticulous records or sticking to a rigid timetable. You can keep up with them and their travels on their personal website: *(TheCallanders.name)* 28

Arline Chandler, author of *Road Work II, The RVer's Ultimate Income Resource Guide*, travels and workamps from her home base in Heber Springs, Arkansas. Contact: *(ArlineChandler@sbcglobal.net)* *(ArlineChandler.com)* 2, 3

Bill Chatham has been writing in one form or another since he was sixteen, starting in the newsroom of a major metropolitan newspaper as a copyboy. He had a 30-year career in the computer industry where the writing was largely business and technical. He is now retired and has been writing novels and screenplays and just finished his bio/memoir. Contact him: *(WJCIII@ptd.net)*10

Myrna Courtney and her late husband, Gerry, traveled part-time for more than 30 years, publishing magazine articles as they went, enjoying the U.S., Canada, Mexico and Europe in RVs of various styles and sizes. Myrna now lives at their home in California and hops in her Class C motorhome now and then, with her dog, Cosy, as companion. 8, 9, 25, 26

JJ Dippel, a retired federal auditor, currently substitute teaches just for fun. RVing since 2004, JJ travels with a cat and is currently working on a blog of tips on RV travel without a tow car. Read her blog at: *(RVingToadless.Blogspot.com)* 9, 12, 21, 25, 28

Samantha Eppes traveled with her parents in an RV from three months of age until she left for college a few years ago. Her parents worked at Disney World several winters. Samantha insisted they return the year she turned 16 and was eligible to work there too. 19

Authors **Jill and Jose Ferrer** are full-time RVers who were featured on The Oprah Winfrey Show. They publish the Your RV Lifestyle website where you can find advice for choosing, affording and enjoying your RV lifestyle. Contact them: *(Your-RV-Lifestyle.com)* 3

Bernie Fuller is a retired Regular Army Lt. Col. A freelance writer for over 40 years, his work has appeared in most national magazines dealing with the outdoors. One of the early members of Escapees (member #32), he is a frequent contributor to Escapees magazine. Author of the e-books: *Amateur Radio for RVers* and *Cooking Your Flying Feathers*, available at his website: *(WriteOutdoors32.com)*. He currently has two books in various stages of completion dealing with assorted aspects of RVing. 1, 9

Kay Hasty and her husband, John, were Workampers on the road for twelve years. They have recently "retired" from their retirement and live in the Texas Hill Country. Kay is the author of a piece about Workamping for ARVC (Association of RV Campground Owners) and a guest blogger for Evanne Schmarder's RV Cooking Show. 15, 29

Barbara L Heller and her husband, Alan Steinberg, spent their one-year sabbatical traveling the U.S. in a 210 Roadtrek. Back at home in upstate New York, she is a psychotherapist in private practice. Barbara is also a writer who has authored *365 Ways to Relax Mind, Body, and Soul* and *How to Sleep Soundly Tonight*. The blog of their traveling year is posted at: *(TheDreamYear.Blogspot.com)* Barbara can be contacted at: *(BHPurple@aol.com)* 11

Joei Carlton Hossack is the author of seven RV adventure-travel books, including *Everybody's Dream, Everybody's Nightmare* and *Kiss this Florida, I'm Outta Here*. She is an entertaining and inspirational speaker and a memoir and travel-writing instructor. Reach Joei at: email *(JoeiCarlton@hotmail.com)* her website *(JoeiCarlton.com)* 9, 11, 20, 23, 29

Ted Kasper has been RVing for 18 years. Now that his children are grown, Ted and his wife, Jayne, and their dog, Jasper enjoy the freedom of the RV lifestyle by camping and traveling in their class C motorhome. Ted has been a regular contributor to publications of the Michigan Association of RVs and Campgrounds, including its annual RV & Campsite: *(TedKasper@comcast.net)* 19

Jane Kenny and her husband, Jack, took to the open road as full-time RVers for the first nine years of their retirement. Jane's two RV guide books: *Casino Camping*, a guide to RV-friendly casinos and *Corps Camping*, a guide to Corps of Engineers campgrounds, are available from *(TravelBooksUSA.com)* 1

Terry King and her husband, Ken, traveled for many years in their fifth wheel. They recently settled down again to be near their children and grandchildren. A degree in criminology gave Terry her great jobs: social worker, drug halfway house counselor, and for the 18 years before she went on the road, she was a human resource director. Our guess is that the lace tablecloth adorns her table again. 3

Adrienne Kristine has been RVing for 40(!) years starting with a modified 1970 VW camper van, and along the way sampling a class B van conversion, a 35-foot fifth wheel, a classic 18-foot 1972 Travco Custom 2000, and now living in a 27-foot Fleetwood Southwind. Currently a volunteer camp host at a California state park, she has been full-timing solo for 10 years. She is the author of *Frugal RVing or Pinching Pennies without Getting Bruised and Other Advice from the Road* and *I've Got a Convection Oven in My RV: Now What?* Adrienne is a contributing editor and forum administrator for *(RVTravel.com)*, *(FreeCampgrounds.com)*, *(FreeRVStays.com)* and the RV Travel Women RVers blog. Contact her at: *(Aadrienne.Kristine@gmail.com)* 3, 20

Janice Lasko and her husband, Gabby, began full-time RVing in 1985. Their love of skiing led to seasonal jobs in several ski areas. (Yes, camping in the snow in an RV is not only doable—it's cozy.) In late 1997 Janice was offered and took the position of editor for *Escapees* magazine, a job she's now doing from either the road, Escapees headquarters in Livingston, Texas, or from a home they bought in 2006. 29

Patty Lonsbary and husband, Ed, began a two-year Grand Tour in September 2007 that took over 28,000 miles through the U. S and Canada in "Dolly's Pride," their Prevost bus-conversion motorhome. Her blog called, "Did Someone Say RV Road Trip?" *(Glotours.Blogspot.com)*, chronicled this trip with 405 stories and hundreds of photos. In November 2008, B*udget Travel* magazine recognized this blog for its travel writing content. Patty has also published articles about the full-time RV lifestyle and travels in *Escapees* magazine, *Family Motor Coaching Association* magazine, CNN iReport, and *(IGoYouGo.com).* Patty and Ed are now back in a stick house. 1, 3, 4

Bess McBride made her first serious writing attempt when she was 14. She shut herself up in her bedroom one summer while obsessively working on a time travel/pirate novel set in the beloved Caribbean of her youth. Although that book was never finished, she did go on to write a series of what she calls "Romances for Armchair Travelers." Seven have been published. Bess can be contacted through her: email *(BessMcBride@gmail.com)* or website *(BessMcBride.com)* 1

Peggi and John McDonald are RV Lifestyle Consultants with 23 years of full-timing experience and still counting. Peggi's comprehensive how-to print book, *RV Living in the 21st Century; The Essential Reference Guide for ALL RVers*, continues to gain a long list of supporters. In the words of one reviewer, "Peggi provides the answer long before you thought of the question." Follow their travels in P&J's Weekly Diary with an upfront and personal report of "Life On The Move." *(RVLiving.Net/Home.htm)* 14

Annise Miller has been RVing both part-time and full-time for the last couple of decades. She first traveled with her late husband and now travels solo. Annise has had a variety of rigs and experiences during these years, including a trip to China to teach English to graduate students. *(Rovers3@hotmail.com)* 20

Darlene Miller and husband, Terry, have RVed full-time for twelve years. Darlene has written numerous articles and two RV books: *RV Chuckles and Chuckholes- The Confessions of Happy Campers* and *More RV Chuckles and Chuckholes- More Confessions of Happy Campers.* Please email or use her website to order: *(RovingPen@hughes.net)* or *RovingPen.com*) 14

Ginny Odell and husband, Bob, have been on the road for many years. They currently live part of the year in the Escapees resort near Yosemite National Park, Park Sierra. They have been active in many areas of the RV lifestyle. 13, 29

Juanita Ruth One has traveled all of her life beginning with a 48-state, five-province, three-country tour of North America before she even began school when she traveled with her journalist parents. Her RV history has included pulling an Airstream from one end of the country to the other, driving a Class A 3,500 miles while towing a car, and retiring into a Class C in 2007. She currently resides in Ecuador. 3, 12, 14

Jerry and Kimberly Peterson, no relation to Joe and Kay Peterson, founders of the Escapees RV Club, are freelance writers, photographers, entrepreneurs and jacks-of-all-trades. They are living their dream on "A Wing and a Prayer." Visit their website: *(HitTheRoadJackEnterprises.com)* 1, 3, 5, 6, 7, 12, 14, 25, 26

Joan Pomeroy and her husband, Jerry, became RVers in 1977. In 2002 they retired from Los Alamos National Lab in New Mexico and traveled full-time until May of 2009 when they bought a house in Texas. Joan is the author of "Pomeroy's Travelogues" on the Web and has been published in magazines, a book—*More RV Chuckles and Chuckholes* by Darlene Miller, as well as several newspapers. 1

Betty Prange has been a full-time RVer since 1993, the first six years with her husband Lin Strout, and now as a widow. She is a photographer, writer and interpreter of the human and natural history of the land, working in places like the ghost town of Bodie, California and Yellowstone National Park where she drives a mid-thirties vintage yellow tour bus. See her Nomad's Notes blog at *(PrangeDePlume.Blogspot.com)* 1, 5, 6, 7, 9, 12, 13, 15, 20, 28

Beth Ramos writes from the road and Celebration, Florida. A lover of the Word, she served as a Religious Educator for several denominations before starting the "Adventure Stage of Life" with her husband Art and their dog Zak. She is a member of the "Penwheels" BOF. *(BethRamos@earthlink.net)* 12

Brooks Rimes and his lovely wife, Brenda, retired when he was 50 and spent five years full-timing. They have gone back to the suburbs of Buffalo, New York, to work a few more years in IT jobs and then plan to return to RVing. Email: *(Brooks@RimesRV.net)* Website where Brenda has all their full-timing pictures: *(PicasaWeb.Google.com/BSRimes)* 15

Sharon E. Runyon is a solo RVer and former president of Wandering Individuals' Network (WIN). She contributed to our previous book, *The Woman's Guide to Solo RVing.* 13

Doug and Rhonda Salerno have been full-timing since August 2005 in a fifth wheel. They enjoy traveling and working on the road. 11, 15, 16

George Stoltz and his wife, Sandra, began their full-time RV life in September of 2009. They travel in a 2000 U320 Foretravel and tow a Honda CR-V. They sold or gave away everything that did not fit into their motorhome. They endured a disastrous real estate market, but are free of debt and doubt. George is known as FoxRiverGuy on many forums. Reach him: *(FoxRiverGuy@hotmail.com)* 1, 2

Diana and Allen Storm had been camp hosting for five years when they wrote their book, *The Adventures of Campground Hosting.* They have traveled extensively throughout North America and are currently establishing a home base in New Mexico. They can be reached: *(ADStorm04@yahoo.com)* Their book is available: *(Amazon.com)* 16

Sharon Vander Zyl and her husband, Rollie, retired to RV living in 2006. They volunteer at National Wildlife Refuges. Sharon has written one book *Taking Care of You: Stress Management for Nurses,* two monthly newspaper columns and numerous magazine articles. She is currently trying her hand at fiction. Sharon is a member of the Penwheels BOF of Escapees. *(Sharon.VanderZyl@gmail.com)* 2, 7, 26

Fran Vogt, after moving from one stix-and-brix house to another all her adult life, discovered RVing and found that this solved relocation problems. Now retired for almost ten years, she enjoys the full-time lifestyle every single day. 15

Carol Weishampel is a solo RVer, writer, speaker, and mother of twelve. She has just published her first novel, *A Venture in Faith, Texas to Alaska.* Prior to this book, Carol has written several non-fiction books describing her travels with her large family from Texas as far as Alaska. Read *Grandma's on the Go* and *Adopting Darrell.* Contact Carol through her blog *(Carol-Weishampel.Blogspot.com)* 9, 12, 26

Sharon Whitaker and her husband, Bill, have been full-timers since May 2003. In that time they have been to all but two of the lower 48 states, Alaska and six Canadian provinces. They spend the winter in the San Diego area where they reconnect with friends and family. Sharon and Bill's dream RV trip would be to Australia and New Zealand. At this point, they have no plans to get off the road soon. It is just too much fun seeing new places and meeting new people. (*SharsWhitaker@aol.com*) 1, 2

* * *

We also gratefully acknowledge the help of George Bruzenak for review of the chapter on RV Systems. We were fortunate to have the experience of writers Myrna Courtney, Adrienne Kristine, Lynne Benjamin and Betty Prange who read the manuscript offering additions and corrections. Betty Prange also took our cover photograph and Robert Aulicino designed the cover. We believe it captures the call of the road. In addition, we'd like to thank Sue Bizek who was instrumental in editing and formatting this book.

There is no one "right" way to
live the RV lifestyle.

NOTES

Retire To an RV: The Roadmap to Affordable Retirement

by Jaimie Hall Bruzenak and Alice Zyetz

Pine Country Publishing
127 Rainbow Dr., #2780
Livingston, TX 77399-1027

For additional books and e-books from Pine Country Publishing, see our website:

(RVLifestyleExperts.com)

Other information:

Subscribe to our free bimonthly ezine, *RV Lifestyle Ezine* at our website
Blog: *(Blog.RVLifestyleExperts.com)*
Facebook: *(Facebook.com/RVLifestyleExperts)*
Contact Jaimie: *(CalamityJaimie@gmail.com)*

Pine Country Publishing
(RVLifestyleExperts.com)

Also available:

RV Traveling Tales: Women's Journeys on the Open Road

Support Your RV Lifestyle! An Insider's Guide to Working on the Road

"Support Your RV Lifestyle" CD

Includes:

- **Complete Resource section and appendices from the book with active Web links**
- **Printable forms from the book**
- **Workamper experiences and advice; Jaimie's articles**

Purchase with book for only $10 more; $14.95 if purchased separately.

In e-book and CD format:
The Woman's Guide to Solo RVing

Taking the Mystery out of RV Writing

and other e-books

RV Lifestyle Electronic Newsletter
Subscribe at *(RVLifestyleExperts.com)*

Order form

For fax orders: 866/500-5251. Send a copy of this form.
Email orders: *(CalamityJaimie@gmail.com)*
Postal orders: Pine Country Publishing, 127 Rainbow Dr., #2780, Livingston, TX 77399-1027
Telephone: 928/607-3181
Credit card orders: *(RVLifestyleExperts.com)*

Retire to an RV

The Roadmap to Affordable Retirement

at $19.95 (U.S. funds) per copy

Name: ______________________________
Address: ______________________________
City: ______________________________
State and zip code: ______________________________
Number of books: _____ @ $19.95 U.S. $______
Media rate shipping & handling: $4.95 $______
Priority mail shipping & handling: $5.95 $______
Shipping & handling for additional copies: @ $2.00 $______
Texas residents add sales tax 6.25% $______
(Polk Cty- 6.75%) $______
Total enclosed: $______

Payment information:

Make checks payable to Pine Country Publishing
For Visa or Mastercard orders, complete the following:
Name as it appears on your card: ______________________
Card number: ______________________ Exp. date: ________
Check digit: (last 3 digits on back in reverse italics) __________
Telephone number or email: ______________________
Signature: ______________________________